Footprints in the Wilderness

A Quest to Day-Hike the
Appalachian Trail
both ways in One Year.

by

P. J. Wetzel

Copyright © 2024 by P.J. Wetzel
All rights reserved

No part of this book may be reproduced, or stored in a retrieval system, or transmitted in any form or by any means, electronic, mechanical, photocopying, recording, or otherwise, without express written permission of the author.

Published by
P.J. Wetzel
411 Walnut St, PMB 10345
Green Cove Springs, FL 32043

ISBN 9798303387881 (black and white paperback)

Interior Design: Kim Emerson
Cover design: P.J. Wetzel

Second edition

One of three copies of the George Noble plaque set along the Appalachian Trail in Georgia. The 1930's hiker used as model was the Georgia AT Club's second president, Warner Hall, who had these plaques made to help promote the new and still unfinished 2000-mile trail.

P. J. Wetzel

INTRODUCTION

The Appalachian Trail is not just a path through the woods; it is, in many ways, a miracle. Long-distance hikers who venture onto this winding woodland way soon realize that it is not only a first-class natural wonder—a showcase and haven for everything wild—but also a monument to human achievement. Its route was hard-won against the onslaught of 'progress' in a busy, crowded part of the United States that did not gladly yield to nature's rhythms.

Even a hundred years ago, when Benton MacKaye single-handedly dreamed the trail into existence, private owners and special interest groups had already made deep inroads into the mountains of the eastern United States. It was tough finding an unspoiled continuous corridor for the trail to follow.

But those early trail pioneers, notably led by Myron Avery, got it done. By 1937 the American people had been gifted a continuous 2100-mile walking path that followed the spine of the Appalachian Mountains from North Georgia to central Maine.

Despite the human inroads, that natural setting—the Appalachian Mountain chain—arguably remains closer to its pristine wilderness state than any other temperate ecosystem in the world. That's because it was only fifteen thousand years ago that the landscape first felt human influence, when America's first peoples arrived across the land bridge from Asia. Their spread across the continent happened every bit as quickly as the second wave—the arrival of the European colonists.

Humans did inevitably begin to degrade the continent's wilderness; but the point is not to place blame or wallow in regret over what has been lost. What matters (what we can do something about) is our future choices. All of us, from fifteen thousand years ago right through to today, understand, deep in our bones, one simple moral principle: It is right and good that we tread lightly, that we strive to respect and sustain that which nature spent four billion years preparing for us. This is the Golden Rule applied equally to all species, to all elements of a natural system.

The Great Law of Iroquois Confederacy, recorded in wampum symbols sometime between 1142 and 1492 C.E., well before there was any European-style written language, speaks of '*Ongwehonweka*,' the way of life of the Original People, the ancestors. It includes a 'Duty owed to Creation' and 'The Seventh Generation Principle' regarding decisions about natural resources. "People are to live in harmony with nature."

F.I.T. Wilderness

Aldo Leopold, a contemporary of Benton MacKaye and co-founder of the Wilderness Society, was among the first European arrivals to actively and persistently advocate for treating all natural systems as an interdependent whole. In his *Sand County Almanac* of 1949, he wrote that our inner sense of connectedness "changes the role of *Homo sapiens* from conqueror of the land-community [ecosystem] to plain member and citizen of it. It implies respect for his fellow-members and also respect for the community as such."

After just fifteen thousand years of human influence, the Appalachian Mountain ecosystems have managed to retain more of their inherent nature than, say, the Alps. That Americans have come together to stop further decline at this relatively early stage is a powerful accomplishment, of which we can be proud.

It was truly a collective achievement. The Appalachian Trail enjoys greater member and volunteer support than perhaps any other trail in the world. Three million people walk a portion of this famous trail every year. Here they find a haven of tranquility within an easy drive—an escape from the urban sprawl, commercialism, pollution, stress, and noise that plague their daily lives.

It is a place we need. It is a place that preserves our roots, that grounds us, that reminds us who we really are. We have set aside and protected a corridor, about as long and continuous as any hiker could want, to which the victims of modern civilization can come, reconnect with their true nature, and lay down some footprints in the wilderness.

There is an ancient and revered Hindu tradition that says that when one's hair turns gray, when the first grandchildren are born, we begin to withdraw from our responsibilities to society and go to dwell in the forest. The *Vanaprastha*, the forest dweller, seeks solitude and spiritual insight. It can be a permanent withdrawal, a pilgrimage, or merely a state of mind. Ideally it is a path to *Sannyasa*, the final stage of life, and is ascetic, spiritually focused, detached, nomadic, with few material possessions and no emotional attachments. One walks into the woods and sets aside their individual identity.

That's exactly where I was as I stepped onto the Appalachian Trail in January 2012 to begin this epic adventure. I was sixty-three, retired from an Earth Science position with NASA, and an empty nester seeking to down-size and simplify—seeking, as Thoreau did, to go live in the woods for a while.

PART ONE

Alone and Frostbitten:
Central Virginia Southbound
into the heart of the Hiker Bubble

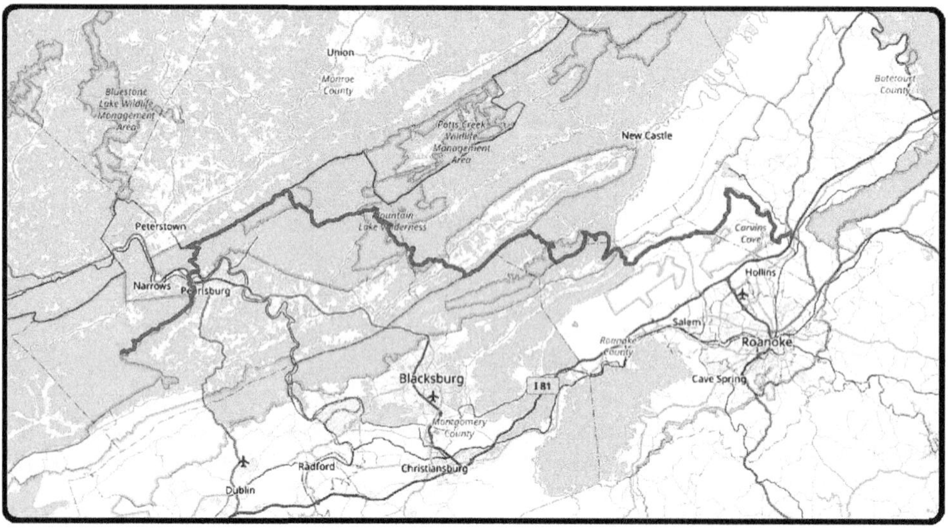
Union
Monroe County
Bluestone Lake Wildlife Management Area
Potts Creek Wildlife Management Area
New Castle
Botetourt County
Peterstown
Mountain Lake Wilderness
Carvins Cove
Narrows
Pearisburg
Hollins
Salem
Roanoke
Roanoke County
Blacksburg
I 81
Cave Spring
Montgomery County
Radford
Christiansburg
Dublin

CHAPTER 1

Daleville, VA to Woods Hole Hostel, Pearisburg, VA
January 1 - 19; 134.5 trail miles one way

Is this crazy?

It was getting real way too fast. I had officially been on the trail for only three days and already I had frostbite on both cheeks and felt so weak that I didn't think I could make it to the top of the next hill.

And I thought I was prepared. I had been doing long training hikes on the Appalachian Trail (AT for short) in Maryland and northern Virginia for most of the last three months. I was in good physical shape, ready to put in the miles. I had all the cold weather gear I needed. I was wearing a big hooded puffy down coat—the kind people use to climb Everest.

What I didn't have was cold weather savvy. Winds were easily 20mph with temperatures around 12 degrees F. I had a balaclava and ski goggles in my pack but didn't think I needed them this day. As I came up over the exposed rocky ridge at McAfee Knob in central Virginia, the wind chills neared zero. I had the place to myself; there was no one to help me take a portrait at the ledge, probably the most iconic photo op on the entire AT. So I did it all myself, I hung around in the bitter wind, fiddling with my camera's self-timer, running back and forth between the camera and the ledge, trying to set a pose. I'm sure that's where the frostbite set in. I finally got a shot then continued hiking north. By noon, I had gone seven miles from the parking lot on Rt. 311 and had turned around

McAfee Knob, January 3rd. Temperature 10°F, wind chill well below zero – moon overhead, snow showers passing over the distant hills.

F.I.T. Wilderness

at Brickey's Gap, where I had ended the previous day's out-and-back segment. Every day my plan was to hike another small piece of Appalachian Trail in both directions.

But by the time I began the 700-foot climb back up to McAfee Knob, I was flagging. I could barely put one foot in front of the other. Nobody else was crazy enough to be out hiking on this bitter day, so I was alone and still six miles from safety.

I had to stop. With crude, clumsy arm motions, I pushed the snow off a rounded rock beside the trail and sat down with a groan. Why was I so weak? I knew it wasn't the miles or the slope—both were well within the range of my recent training hikes. It had to be something else. My body was totally out of whack.

Was it the cold? By then my cheeks had a sickly white area in the middle that had no feeling but were stinging around the edges. For the next three weeks, those cheeks would fester and ooze before they finally healed. But this was something deeper, more internal. As I pulled out my water bottle, it dawned on me. I hadn't taken a sip of water all day, and had drunk very little yesterday. When it's that cold, you just don't get thirsty. Yet the cold dry air sucks moisture out of you as surely as if you're in a desert.

I sat right there and forced down a full liter of water. I drank another liter over the next mile. Wow, it felt like I had taken a wonder drug. Suddenly, I was bounding up the slope, taking big gluttonous strides. I was not going to die alone and cold in the middle of nowhere. That bitter, cloudy winter afternoon ended up being one of the most joyful and memorable experiences of my entire Appalachian Trail adventure.

Nietzsche was right: what doesn't kill you makes you stronger. Over the course of the next 267 day hikes, never again did I let myself get dehydrated; not even close.

I had started on January 1st, heading south from US 220 near Roanoke, Virginia. I planned to hike right through the teeth of winter into spring. I was no athlete, so I figured I might need every one of the 365 days to hike the AT my own way—a way nobody else had ever done—hiking the entire trail twice, by out-and-back day hikes. I expected weather delays. I knew there might be weeks when I couldn't hike because of big snowstorms, especially in the high mountains of southern Virginia and in the Smokies. But a couple inches here and there and some cold winds were not going to stop me. So that day, January 3rd, I was hiking through some of the prettiest and best-known parts of the Appalachian Trail.

The trail runs 2,190 miles from central Maine to North Georgia, but I chose to start my hike in the middle, in central Virginia, because the elevations are much lower than farther south and the average climate is warmer than farther north. It made sense in theory, but the weather can still get pretty brutal in the middle of winter.

There were three parts to my overall plan:

1. I hoped to become the first person to hike the Appalachian Trail both ways end-to-end in one calendar year without spending a single night on the trail. To be 'home' every night before midnight (home being my 'two-ton motorized steel tent'—a Chevy Express Cargo Van with a mattress thrown in the back (my dear daughter called it the 'pedophile van')—or some other accommodation such as a motel or hostel).

2. I would visit and photograph every official AT shelter, all 260 of them, and make the side trip to most scenic attractions, such as waterfalls and views, as long as they were located within a half mile of the AT on blue-blazed trails. I'd take plenty of photos to document these attractions as well as side trail junctions, road crossings (and associated parking areas), and some notable camp sites, oddities, monuments, trees, wildlife, flowers, footbridges, streams, ponds, and lakes, etc. In other words, a big part of the mission was to 'smell the roses', not just log the miles.

3. As I hiked, I was going to report what I experienced, particularly the nature of the trail, by publishing a daily blog entry with the best of the photographs included, and with a complete GPS track to 'prove' that I did what I say I did.

I would attack that first goal in a unique way, by walking from a parking/access point back and forth along a small piece of the trail each day. The conventional method of hiking the Appalachian Trail twice in one year is to backpack from Georgia's Springer Mountain, the southern terminus of the trail, north to Katahdin, Maine, at the northern terminus, then turn around and hike all the way back. It's called a yo-yo. Nobody keeps official records on this, but from what former AT Information Services Manager Laurie Potteiger told me, only about a dozen people had reported completing the "AT double" in a calendar year, and none of them were over 50. And certainly, none of them had done it utilizing only day hikes.

Our family Christmas gathering in southeast Pennsylvania was my send off. Mom, Dad, my two grown kids, my brother, sister-in-law, nephews and niece and their spouses took turns offering that one last farewell hug before I headed south to Daleville, VA with my jaw set, ready to press grimly into the dead of January, the coldest month of the year.

F.I.T. Wilderness

View of the Catawba Valley from Tinker Cliffs, looking southwest.

There was no snow on the ground when I started. New Year's Day was pleasantly mild for the season, in the 50's; and plenty of people came out to hike the pretty ridge line overlooking the watershed of Carvin Cove Reservoir, Roanoke's city water supply. Kids were scrambling on rocks in shirt sleeves. I had my jacket tied around my waist. But late in the afternoon, dark clouds rolled in, bringing some squally showers, and by the next morning, it was 20 degrees. I hiked the gorgeous ridgeline along Tinker Cliffs that day, coming up to Scorched Earth Gap via the 3.1-mile, side trail called the Andy Lane Trail. Then I experienced that close call on Day 3. Fortunately, the weather never got any worse than that. The cold spell moderated so that when I made the tough rock scramble up to Dragon's Tooth a couple days later, it was sunny and in the 50's again.

The climb of Dragon's Tooth is another popular destination for local day hikers. And here I faced another steep learning curve. Literally. This is one of the few places along the AT, south of New Hampshire's White Mountains, where you face Class Three climbing, meaning nearly vertical rock scrambling where hand holds are needed and a fall could be fatal (based on the Yosemite Decimal System, formerly known as the Sierra Club grading system).

I had planned my distance for the day as if I could just stroll along at my usual easy 2½ mph pace. But there were two miles of rugged, rocky up and down trail beyond the spire of the tooth proper. My trusty GPS told me I had done just four miles in 3½ hours. Yikes. Still, I decided to go ahead with the plan (down the trail 7¼ miles then back over the same rugged terrain). I expected to finish in the dark, because I also had a side-trip of nearly half a mile to the Pickle Branch shelter. These shelters that are far off the trail don't get used much, especially in winter. I was the first person in more than a month to sign the shelter's register book.

Then came another rookie problem. My Asics trail runners were not well broken in; and I had to stop to perform surgery, cutting through a seam in order to relieve pressure on the bony knob at the base of my left big toe. And although I always have to keep my pace slow, (so as not to inflame my chronically bad left knee—more on that later), I still managed to finish by 5:25, just ten minutes after sunset. It was a long tough day with a couple more important lessons learned.

Now seems a good time to talk about my hiking gear. Those Asics trail runners never gave me any more trouble for as long as I wore them; and I wore them until they practically fell off my feet. Most people get about 500 miles out of a pair of shoes on the AT; they took me 1,500 miles.

My pack was another seasoned veteran—a venerable old forest green nylon, leather bottomed day pack that I'd bought at the REI store in Fort Collins, Colorado in 1971. It was in perfect working condition, and at 50 years old, still is.

The advantage of doing the trail by day hikes is that you can carry a lot less weight. My average pack weighed just five or six pounds. Each day I chose clothing for the expected weather, and left the rest in the van. I packed all the water I would need. I did not filter water from streams, although I did carry a Sawyer filter in case of emergencies. I took only the food I would need to sustain my energy during the day. I hiked with two Leki collapsible titanium walking sticks, and carried a fancy Ultra-sil nylon tarp/tent/poncho as my emergency shelter and rainwear.

I always carried some basic emergency gear—first aid kit including an antihistamine for bee stings, a length of paracord, matches and a little tea-candle, and a dry pair of socks—packed in a zip-lock bag. One of the things I was fastidious about, perhaps even obsessed about, was keeping my feet dry. Dry feet do not get blisters. Wet feet get loads of them. Keeping feet dry will be a recurring theme through this adventure.

Other things I carried with me every day were a small tube of sunscreen, a pen and note paper, a Swiss Army Knife, my Canon Elph point-and-shoot camera, my cheap 3G flip phone, and my expensive Garmin Hiker's GPS with spare batteries.

Finally, the most versatile piece of gear I carried was a simple $1 cotton bandana. I tied it to my shoulder strap so it was right there if I needed it. It served as a handkerchief, sweat band, sun and bug-shield for my neck, towel for drying off my feet after fording a stream, and as an emergency layer of clothing when stuffed inside the front of my t-shirt on chilly mornings or evenings. I also used it as a cheap balaclava and wore it as a band over my cheeks. Ever since the frostbite damage, my cheeks were much more sensitive to cold, and would get frostbite again much more easily. Ounce for ounce, a bandana is hands-down the most valuable piece of gear I carry. It even comes in handy in dust storms and pandemics, and, of course, if you need to rob a bank.

On Day 6, the day after climbing Dragon's Tooth, I found the trail mercifully smooth, or at least free of rocks. I made good time. I had a 1,500-foot climb and descent up over Brush Mountain, but the only real landmark of the day was the rock monument and flagpole along the mountain ridge where Audie Murphy crashed his airplane at age 46 on May 28, 1971. Murphy was a well-loved actor and highly decorated WWII veteran who came back from the war with PTSD at a time when that term didn't exist. Back then we called it 'battle fatigue' or 'shell shock.' He was a strong early advocate for better treatment of war veterans with this affliction.

Day 7 took me over Sinking Creek Mountain to Sarver Cabin and back to the parking area in Craig Creek Valley. The walkway was treacherous, requiring you to traverse side-sloping bedrock that, when wet or icy, would be impossibly slippery. When I reached my turn-around point at Sarver Cabin at noon. I found two ladies there. They told me they were hunting for the old Sarver family cemetery, which was supposed to be somewhere in the woods nearby. One of them was a member of the Roanoke AT club, and she said nobody in the club remembered for sure where the cemetery was, though older members claimed to have been there. I never heard whether they found it or not. The old family log cabin used to be the AT hiker shelter there, but in recent years the club had built a fancier new shelter with a great big porch farther up the hill closer to the trail. The trail along the ridge near the cabin had been farmed once, and the trail passed dozens of big round stone cairns made from the rocks cleared from the fields. The old homesteaders here, and in many other rocky areas around the country, certainly knew the meaning of a hard day's work.

Now it was Day 8, and I got to pass by one of the largest, most venerable old trees on the trail: the white oak called the Keffer Oak, which sits in a grassy field near the edge of a woods and could hardly be missed. One of my greatest loves is trees with history and character. I

The venerable old Keffer Oak.

P. J. Wetzel

lingered there, took lots of photos, and enjoyed a wonderfully mild day. The warm weather preceded a storm. Late in the day, the sky was darkening as I climbed up to Kelly's Knob. Four girls from Virginia Tech were there enjoying the view, all veterinary med students. It was a Sunday and classes would resume the next day following the winter break. I asked them what would be a fun outing in Blacksburg, since I was expecting my daughter to come down for a visit soon. The girls could not think of a single thing to recommend. It reminded me of my college days at Penn State in the beautiful Nittany Valley back in the '60's. It has wonderful mountain scenery, but the town is built around the university and was about as dead as they get.

So, the expected storm hit the next day, with plenty of rain and more valuable lessons. Gladly, these were all positive ones. My day started off rainy and just barely above freezing. But I was dressed for it. I chose not to use my poncho since it doesn't breathe well. I just layered lots of non-down clothing, including my poly-filled mountaineering pants. I met a hiker I had seen going to Laurel Creek Shelter late in the afternoon the day before and so we walked together and had a great chat. He was the first long distance hiker I had come across. Peter (no trail name yet) started in Harper's Ferry on Dec. 10th and was hiking to Springer Mountain. He said how much he loved winter hiking and that he hoped for snow. He was even carrying snow shoes. After reaching my turn around point, Peter went on and I never saw him again. But later, when I read his comments in the Rice Field Shelter log book, I learned that his rain gear had failed him that day and that he was headed into Pearisburg to re-tool. I had better luck. It rained like hell all afternoon but I was delighted to find that my clothes, particularly the insulated mountaineering pants, remained warm even when soaking wet. Better yet, when the rain finally stopped, everything dried out really fast. The secret is lightweight layers of artificial fabric. I would later experiment with the poncho, and in future years I purchased a Go-Lite umbrella, which I now swear by.

Now I have to note other big advantages of my Two-Ton Steel Tent. First of all, of course, it's waterproof. Second of all, it has all the heat you want, so that you can turn your shelter into the inside of a clothes-dryer. Everything I had worn was bone dry before midnight.

The one thing you can't just dry out and expect to be immediately as good as new are your feet. The next day I saw how much wear and tear my feet had taken as a result of spending twelve hours hiking in wet shoes. Even though I wore smooth nylon liner socks under my wool socks, and even though my feet were well callused from months of hiking, I had several very sensitive spots that seemed close to erupting into blisters. I babied the worst of those—the fleshy pad in the middle of the bottom of my left big toe—by avoiding putting too much pressure on it. It eventually stabilized and no blister developed there or anywhere else that day. But this just sealed my determination to avoid wet feet.

There's a popular saying among AT long distance hikers: "No pain, no rain, no Maine." Sometimes, the popular wisdom declares, you just have to hike in the rain. But there's another highly revered saying on the trail: "Hike your own hike." I was determined my feet were going to stay dry. I would experiment with several different ways of accomplishing that, including taking what they call a 'zero' day when it rained.

The very next day, Day 11, would present that challenge. It was going to rain most of the day, and my feet weren't yet fully healed. Logistics of parking places, something a typical backpacker cares nothing about, helped me make up my mind to attempt only a short day. I waited until there was a break in the rain then donned the waterproof but non-breathable poncho and headed out. Immediately I knew I didn't like the poncho. It had flimsy snaps on the sides that came undone when it caught on a snag. Because it didn't breathe, it caused me to sweat, so soon I was as wet as if I hadn't worn it at all. And it was totally unwieldy in any sort of wind. My relationship with that poncho remained rocky for the rest of the adventure.

Day 12 was spent in Peters Mountain Wilderness. It was a mild, misty day and the trail wasn't too challenging. I did not meet a single person all day. Amazingly, just 20 minutes after I got back 'home' at the end of the day, the heavens opened up and we had a serious deluge of rain. Later that night the rain changed to snow, but we got no more than a quarter inch.

Now it was Friday the 13th, and it was a nasty windy and cold day. I was hiking Rice Fields—a wonderfully open high mountain ridge with hundred-mile views, but of course that meant constant skin-freezing winds. But this time I was ready. I had brought along enough clothing to survive a summer in Antarctica, including those ski goggles. I used it all. I also traversed the 2.8 miles of civilization

The AT crosses the Rice Fields along the ridge of Peters Mountain.

10 **P. J. Wetzel**

down in the New River Valley, crossing that major river and passing through the town of Pearisburg. There's a fair amount of road walking there, and with the lower elevation, it was a lot less windy and a lot more comfortable.

It was tough to get lost on that road walk. There was one place where some overzealous trail maintainer had painted ten consecutive white blazes like footprints, two feet apart, on the pavement to direct the hiker out of an underpass and up to the concrete staircase where you walk over the bridge you've just walked under.

The entire AT is marked with those white blazes—two inches wide and six inches high normally. They are usually on trees at eye level, or on posts in open areas—sometimes on rocks, less often on the ground. Theoretically, when you're standing beside a white blaze you are supposed to be able to spot the next one. Reality, however, is not quite that simple. In some remote areas there were places where I feared I might have missed a turn. And there were places where I did miss turns and had to backtrack. Turns are marked with two white blazes, one above the other with the upper one sometimes offset in the direction in which you're supposed to turn. Sometimes the blazes become blocked by new growth; some get weathered away, or fall when the tree they're on dies and the bark peels off. Maintainers have a constant challenge keeping the trail marked, and for the most part, they do a super job. Whenever I meet a maintainer along the trail, I make a point to thank them for their dedication, hard work, and for their freely offered time and energy.

That set me up for a great Day 14. There was snow on the ground but barely an inch, and the temperature had warmed up a lot. I completed the 1,700-foot climb from Pearisburg up to Angel's Rest, a spot with a spectacular panoramic view of the New River Valley. I took a full panorama with my camera and later stitched it together into one big wide shot. Beyond that viewpoint, the trail leveled off along the ridge and I hit a couple miles of 'Green Tunnel' hiking on an ancient road lined with dense, overhanging Catawba Rhododendron bushes. I'm 6' 2" and winter snows had pushed the roof of the 'rhodo-tunnel' down to about 5' 6". By the time I emerged, my back was aching from constantly bending over and ducking.

On the way back, as I came to the Wilburn Valley overlook, I met a couple out for a day hike. They had a young Manx cat trailing behind them, barely older than a kitten. They said it was not theirs but it had followed them all the way from the Morris Avenue parking area, 2½ miles away. I came back down faster than them, but before I left that parking area, the couple arrived with the poor cat still tagging along. They were, of course, just going to leave it there. There are houses in the area, and it's likely that the tenacious little thing would find somebody to adopt it.

I was finding that hiking the trail both ways each day gave me two very different looks at the same trail. Things that catch your eye hiking northbound, you might miss completely going southbound, and vice-versa. Weather changes, sun angle changes, even changes in your mood make a difference. The view from Angel's Rest in the afternoon was entirely different from what I had photographed earlier that morning.

F.I.T. Wilderness

That evening in Pearisburg, I went to the Lucky Star Chinese all-you-can-eat buffet and had a huge dinner. I stocked up on supplies at the Food Lion next door, and then fell fast asleep in the van; the food had gone to my head. When I woke up a few hours later, it was snowing. I stayed put to do my usual two to three hours of post-hike journaling, photo uploading, GPS track processing, and blog writing—both on my own blog (pjwetzel.com) and on Trail Journals. I was using my Wi-Fi jet pack so I had good internet access. Finally, after midnight I headed up Sugar Run Road past Woods Hole Hostel (where I had made a reservation for a few days later) to the trailhead where I would start hiking in the morning. With half an inch of new snow on the road, it was slippery going up the hill, but by keeping my speed up and the wheels spinning, I got there without a problem, other than some frayed nerves.

The problem came the next morning when I stepped out of my van. There were two additional inches of new snow, and my very first step onto the trail was on a slick patch of ice hidden under the snow. My feet slipped out from under me and I slammed down hard on my back and right elbow, giving me a sore butt and a deep bone bruise in my elbow (which has been sensitive to the touch ever since).

Great. I didn't need another war injury to add to my list; it was already long enough. There's the Chondromalacia I developed in my left knee in my 20's and early 30's as a result of years of hard bicycle racing and training doing almost daily 100-mile training rides. (Eventually I had to give up biking altogether, cold turkey, and the knee problem flares up if I run at all, even a few steps, and even if I walk too fast.) Then there's the broken left ankle I got when a tree I was cutting down fell on me in 1986 (don't ask). The doctor chose not to repair the floating bone chip, saying the joint was stable enough that surgery wasn't indicated. While he said it was stable, I would probably develop arthritis as I got older. Finally, there's that bony knob at the base of my left big toe, the one that I had to do shoe surgery on my trail runners to accommodate. It's like a bunion and is permanently swollen and arthritic from persistently bending my toes back too far while working on my knees in my garden—a hobby that had become an obsession of mine in the '80's.

You might have noticed that all of these 'war wounds' are on my left side. I have another one to add to that list—my left wrist was permanently damaged during an auto assembly line job when I was 20 years old. So that day's damage to my right elbow was an anomaly, but most likely occurred because of my dependence on my right side. My stride is not balanced; in essence, I'm hiking on one leg. I wear down the right heel of my shoes first, and wear out the toe of the left shoe.

Despite that inauspicious first step, I thoroughly enjoyed the rest of the day, meandering through Big Horse Gap and along the ridge line of Sugar Run Mountain in a fairytale-like setting. Every twig and branch carried its own delicate glazing of frost and ice. The 'Green Tunnel' had been transformed into the grand nave of an ice cathedral fit for the gods.

Today's snow cover, and my vow not to hike in wet feet, gave me the inspiration to try an experiment. No, I didn't yield to the logic of wearing my heavy

Fresh snow and rime ice along the trail above Woods Hole Hostel

mountaineering snow boots and gaiters; I was still going to wear my trail runners. But to keep my feet dry, I would try using plastic bags as outer 'socks'. I had bought a box of drawstring kitchen garbage bags, intending to use them as cheap waterproof stuff bags to keep things dry in my backpack, but today I placed two of them on my feet, outside my wool socks, inside my shoes. They worked great. My light trail running shoes still got wet, but my feet were kept warm and my socks kept reasonably dry (except for sweat). Then I reached a ford of Dismal Creek about a third of a mile above the Wapiti Shelter, which was my turn-around point. There were stepping stones, but one was loose, and it toppled over under my weight, plunging me into the icy water up to my ankles–but thanks to the garbage bags my feet stayed dry.

Day 16 was, to use a word, dismal. I hiked along Dismal Creek in dismal cloudy weather and made the dreary half mile side trip to Dismal Falls, which was barely five feet high—in other words, a dismal disappointment. The only plus was that the hiking was easy and nearly level. The following day was just as easy, but gladly there was nothing dismal about it. It was windy and mild and got up to a snow-eating 60 degrees F. I passed through quaintly named Lickskillet Hollow, and continued my mission to visit every trail shelter. Since Pearisburg, I had seen no entries from Peter. *Did he quit the trail after his frustration with his rain gear?* I wondered. Later on, I began to see trail register entries signed with the trail name 'Lasher'. Turns out, that was Peter; he had just acquired a trail name. The handwriting was the same, and there was the same WV→GA tag after the name. For the second time, but far from the last, I got back to my van at the end of the day just before a monstrous downpour.

The dismal theme returned for Day 18. It was cloudy and cold and snowed lightly all day. Worse, there was nothing to see. I hiked along Brushy Mountain's meandering ridge toward Bland, but turned around at Helvey's Mill shelter. This was the only shelter I'd seen with an outdoor privy—nothing but a toilet seat in the woods, sitting there in plain view. Maybe the structure was being replaced? In any event, that was the highlight of the day, which is pretty sad when you think about it. I got back to my van early because I was meeting my daughter Ellen in Blacksburg this evening.

We met for dinner at Fatz. Our waitress was interested in Appalachian Trail hiking, friendly, and easy to talk to. Their menu lived up to their name. Despite my hiker's appetite, I ordered nothing but a cheese fries appetizer. It was so gargantuan that it was all I could eat. Ellen ordered three vegetable side dishes. We then headed up the highway and arrived at the Woods Hole Hostel about 9:15 pm. Michael, the host, and his three dogs and three cats were there to meet us. His wife, Neville, granddaughter of the originator of the hostel, was away in Georgia for a couple of weeks, so we missed the chance to meet her. Michael showed us our room, the Garden Room, which has windows on three sides and three twin beds. I took my first shower of the New Year (Ellen said I was 'really stinky') and soon we both settled into our warm comfortable beds.

We were the only guests at this iconic and well-loved AT hostel that night, an experience that few hikers who stop there ever enjoy. We had Michael all to ourselves. We helped with breakfast and clean-up the next morning while I picked his brain. Breakfast included an omelet, homemade bread, and a porridge of mixed grains, all served with home-made preserves and grape juice. It was not only wholesome and filling, but also totally delicious. Ten years into their proprietorship, Neville and Michael's commitment to an earth-friendly lifestyle, and their welcoming atmosphere, have only improved. Woods Hole is so close to the trail—much less than the 2.7 mile walk down to Bland, for example—that in my opinion it would be crazy to miss the experience.

After breakfast we headed out, and Ellen and I hiked a short out-and-back leg on the AT from the road crossing at Bland to Helvey's Mill shelter. Then we headed into Blacksburg and caught a movie. It was *War Horse*, one of Stephen Spielberg's lesser efforts, and I missed the first half of it because I managed to lock my keys in the van while leaving the engine running. I had to wait around until a service truck from AAA arrived, which took an hour. But we had a great dinner at Red Lobster and then headed back to our warm beds at Woods Hole.

Woods Hole Hostel in January 2012

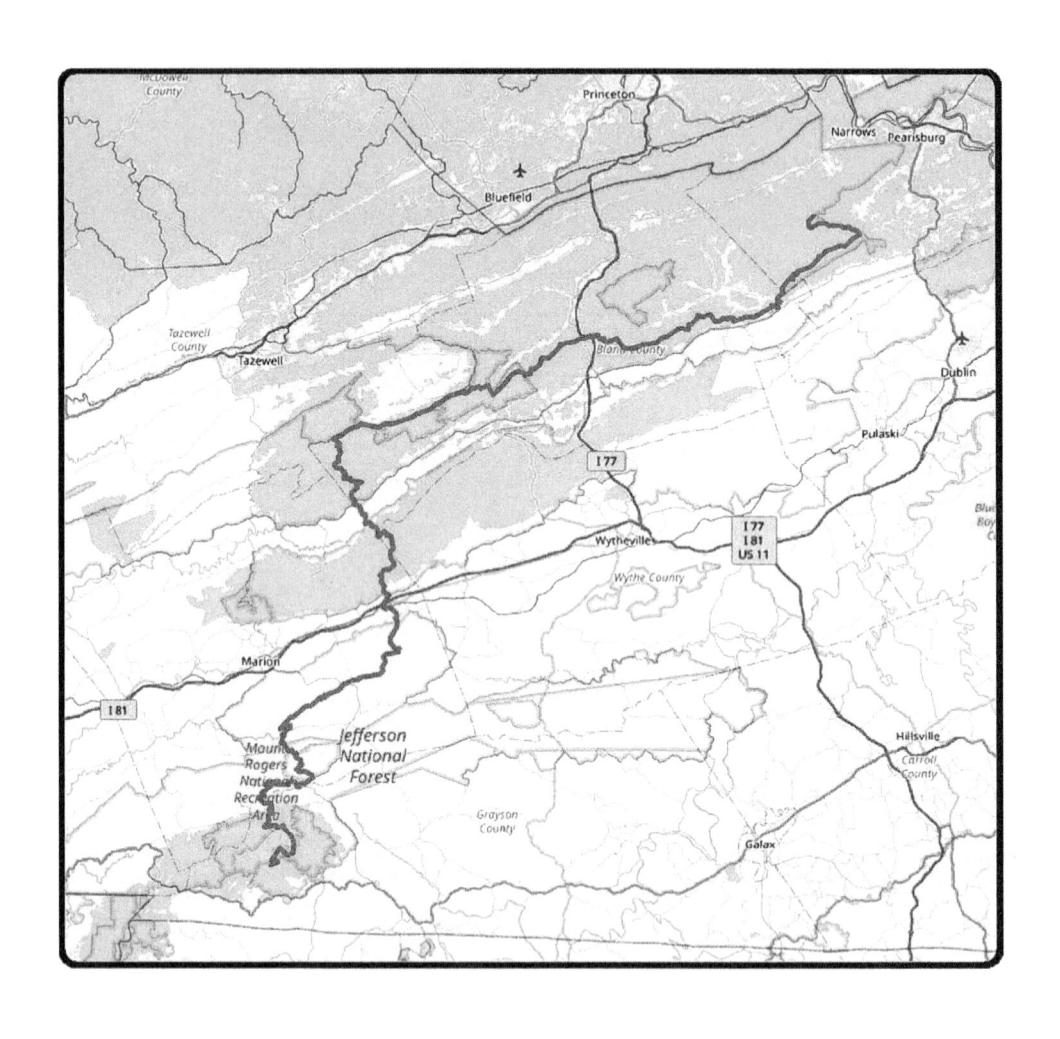

16   **P. J. Wetzel**

CHAPTER 2

Woods Hole Hostel, VA to Grayson Highlands, VA
January 20 - February 2; 100.4 trail miles one way

Let me stick my neck out and make some outrageous claims: the Appalachian Trail is the most famous long distance foot path in the world; nothing else comes close. Doing a "thru-hike"—hiker slang for walking the entire 2,190 miles in a single year—is on more people's bucket list than any other long-term activity, with the possible exception of writing a book. Both of these are inherently solitary activities and yet the AT is the only trail I've ever hiked that I would call a social experience. If you leave Springer around April 1st and head north, you're likely to be in a 'bubble' with between 100 and 250 other hikers. Shelters will be packed to overflowing. At nearly every road crossing you'll find some form of 'trail magic'—food and/or drink left by 'trail angels,' which is free for the taking. Often the trail angels are there in person, eager to share your experience. Most of them have hiked the trail themselves. It's almost like a long, linear university campus, complete with frat houses (the hostels and shelters), fiercely loyal alumni whose lives were forever changed by the trail, and of course a world-class sports team, of which you are a member.

As with any good sport, a thru-hike requires physical conditioning, a lot of solid preparation, die-hard determination, and the flexibility to adjust to changing conditions. The old saying 'expect the unexpected' applies here in spades. To return to my outrageous claims, I guarantee you that, if you decide to tackle the AT, the experience will not be anything like what you expect. The highs will be higher, the lows lower. If you're not a deep-down nature lover who is comfortable 'in your own skin,' the long periods of monotony will be your biggest challenge. Basically, you'll be bored out of your mind. You'll be physically taxed beyond what you thought you could bear, and just plain suffering much of the time. And yet, the human mind has an amazing capacity to filter out the pain. When you reflect upon them, your AT memories will be some of the most cherished of your life; and you'll practically remember it all. You'll make friendships that will stick with you for your whole life. And, for many of you, the trail will change your life in ways you might never have imagined.

That's what happened to Michael Lasecki. In the summer of 2005, while thru-hiking the AT, he stopped at Woods Hole Hostel. There he met Neville, who happened to be helping her grandmother that day, who still ran the day-to-day operation.

The rest is history. Basically, Michael came back after his thru-hike, and became co-host of Woods Hostel.

Ellen and I enjoyed our second night in the Garden Room, which was upstairs in the attached building west of the original log cabin. It was a frosty night, and when we got up early and came down for breakfast, Michael was outside loading more wood into the HeatMaster SS outdoor wood furnace. He served us another hearty, hot breakfast. We helped with clean up, and then it was time for Ellen to start her long drive back home. We exchanged a good-bye hug and I felt my heart sink as her car disappeared down Sugar Run Road. The loneliness of the long-distance hiker came crowding back in. Before leaving Woods Hole, I snapped a few photos of the place, and of Michael in his kitchen. I gave my regrets for missing Neville, and was on the road heading to the Day 20 parking area before 8:30. It was a nice, calm day that warmed up quickly, and I spent it easily hiking along Brushy Mountain where a forest road called Wyrick Trail parallels the AT but remains just out of sight. The next day started out rainy and I waited out the rain before starting the day's hiking about 10:00. I still got pretty wet before the rain let up for good around noon. I crossed the picturesque footbridge over Laurel Creek and dropped down off Brushy Mountain to turn around at Jenkins Shelter. The scenery was pleasant, but hardly spectacular. This is what I mean about monotony. The vast majority of the past two days was just walking in the woods, which were damp and gray and deep in winter's hibernation. Nobody else was on the trail; I had seen not a single soul out there in the last week.

Day 22 brought me a new, interesting challenge. I was handed the full playbook on what fog can do. I was hiking Garden Mountain, which separates the real world from an idyllic, broad oval-shaped valley called "God's Thumbprint". Its more proper name is Burke's Garden, and it was the first choice of George W. Vanderbilt II as a location for his "little mountain escape". But the residents wouldn't sell their land; not at any price. They loved their ultra-secluded little valley too much to part with it. Eventually Vanderbilt settled for his second choice near Asheville, NC, and forever changed the character of the area. He bought up nearly 700 parcels of land, including 50 farms, and constructed the Gilded Age's grandest monument: the 178,926 square-foot Biltmore Estate.

Meanwhile, Burke's Garden retains its to-die-for peaceful, pastoral isolation. The day I was there, up on the 4,000-foot ridge of Garden Mountain, the fog was so thick you couldn't see fifty feet ahead of you. There was no rain falling, but a steady moaning wind carried through the winter forest. Branches were swaying and clacking together and sopping up so much moisture from the fog that it was just like rain. I made the descent to Jenkins Shelter, at 2,500 feet elevation, wearing my poncho and needing it, and then, on the climb back up, the temperature began to drop. The fog continued just as thick, but the trees stopped dripping and began accumulating rime ice. Before long, it was an inch thick on the windward side of every twig, needle, and blade of grass.

As I passed the parking area on 623—the narrow mountain road that switches back and forth over Garden Mountain and is the only way into Burke's Garden from the south—I saw a vehicle parked and there were prints from one person and one dog. It was the first sign of anyone besides me on the trail in a week. Visibility remained obscured and, with all the ice, footing was getting hazardous. I thought it a strange day to pick to drive all the way up here for a day hike. I headed west to Walker Gap where I hoped to turn around, but the footing was rocky and I was going much slower than planned thanks to the fog and ice.

All of a sudden, out of the fog comes the hiker and his dog. He was a big guy with a cropped but still bushy black beard. He had a good quality hiker's GPS strapped to his pack's shoulder strap over a bright yellow rain jacket. His dog looked like a gun dog—a lean wiry German shorthair. He greeted me and we stopped to talk.

"Do you know how far it is to Walker Gap?" I was thinking I'd have to turn around before I got there. I sure didn't want to hike in the dark in these conditions. He checked his GPS.

"That's where I turned around. It's 1.2 miles," he said.

"Hmm, I guess I can make it then." I had 45 minutes left on the clock before I had to turn around to get back by dark.

"You a thru-hiker?"

"Well, I hope to be. I won't call myself one until I've done it."

I explained my goal of using out-and-back day hikes to hike the whole trail both ways this year.

"My motto is 4,368.4 miles or bust."

I borrowed the 'or bust' part from the early migration to the west. Pioneers on the Overland Trail heading to Colorado during the 1859 gold rush used the motto 'Pike's Peak or Bust.' I'm not really sure I can be called a genuine thru-hiker, even if I finish, since I'm not doing one continuous walk 'through', from point A to point B. But then almost everybody who hikes this trail accepts rides or gets off the trail for a break, making their walk technically not continuous either.

"I've been following a guy named 'Seeks It' on Trail Journals," he said. "You wouldn't be him, would you?"

"Whoa. That's me all right."

"Wow. No kidding." His eyes lit up. He almost looked star struck. "I live near here, come up here a lot. I want to hike the whole trail someday."

If I had a nickel for every person who has said that to me, I'd be rich. It's hard for most trail dreamers to find the time, and to get away from life's commitments. I sympathized. We chatted about the weather a little and then headed our respective ways. I had to get going in order to get back in time. I contemplated our meeting as I headed toward Walker Gap. Somebody was actually reading my journals online; my first 'fan.' Suddenly I felt a new sense of purpose that I had not even considered. I had picked up some followers on Facebook too, but here was one in the flesh and blood. Real people I had never met were following my adventure. Welcome to the age of social media, you old fuddy-duddy.

By the time I got to Walker Gap, the fog had lifted and I got some clear glimpses of Burke's Garden 1000 feet below. I had been through the area way back in

1976 on one of my meandering road trips from Colorado—where I was going to grad school—back east to visit family vacationing in Nag's Head, NC. It was a magical drive back then, passing by all too quickly. I was longing to revisit the place and spend some time there, but I knew the lure of distractions was the biggest obstacle to completing my mission. I was already heading back home for a three-day break in just a few days, and didn't have time to do the tourist thing.

The next morning, Day 23, started out rainy, so I got a late start. The 2,100-foot ascent to Chestnut Knob had several sections of varying terrain, including one with 120 log steps that covered a quarter mile. The last 500 feet of ascent were in open meadows that had recently been bush-hogged. The rain had stopped but fog lingered on the mountain top, blocking the panoramic views. One major advantage to hiking every section twice: on my return leg, the fog had lifted and I was able to see and photograph all the scenery. I thought the windy open space atop Chestnut Knob was a weird place for a hiker shelter, but this was a different kind of shelter. Instead of an open-faced lean-to like most shelters, it was a high-mountain stone structure, closed off from the weather. At one time, it even had a fireplace inside, but that had been mortared over. The 900-foot descent to Walker Gap was steep and direct—mostly right on the windy ridge—and provided some good winter views of Burke's Garden.

The next day I had great weather—a little breezy but nearly 100% sunshine, and it warmed up from a morning low in the 40's. I started right at sunrise and hiked north over Brushy Mountain, along its ridge briefly, then down to a babbling stream near Knot Maul Shelter.

What's a Knot Maul? Well, I think I actually found one not far from the shelter. It's a piece of pine heartwood, nearly indestructible, consisting of a sturdy branch that serves as the handle and a big clump of heartwood where the branch emerged from the main trunk of the tree—the knot. With a little shaping, it could serve as an excellent short-handled sledge-hammer—a maul—and you'd never have to worry about the handle coming loose.

The terrain that day was endlessly variable, which kept me interested all day. I crossed Lynn Camp Creek, climbed Lynn Camp Mountain, and then descended to the Lick Creek footbridge where I ended my hike yesterday. There was some open low pasture land and finally a serious ascent up to the ridge of Walker Mountain. I gave up using two trekking poles and almost threw them down in a sudden fit of disgust five miles into the hike. They were nothing but a problem, and were just one more thing I had to babysit, tying up my hands, adding weight, and rarely doing anything useful. I buried them under leaves beside the trail and picked them up on the way back. The ultimate reason to reject them was because I had developed a muscle pain on the right side of my back just below the shoulder blade. It spasmed almost every time I tripped on something or took a wrong step. Tripping, and even falling at least once every couple days is normal on the AT. More than once, I had actually tripped over one of those damn hiking poles. The shoulder blade muscle in question seemed to be one that I used to control the pole, and I found that, without it, the muscle got a chance to relax. This was the last I would ever hike with two trekking poles, though I would later return to using one of them and, when needed, I would pick up a stick to help me balance as I crossed a stream.

Day 25 started out frosty and in the 20's. It was the day I crossed I-81, so there was some lowland hiking in pasture. I came upon Davis Path Camping area where there had been a shelter until 2008. It had been deliberately demolished because of 'misuse.' Because it was located too close to the freeway, and wasn't a difficult hike, it had probably become a party venue for locals.

Davis Fancy is the original 1750's settlement in this area. Associated with this history is the Settler's Museum, a couple miles south of US 11 and featured on Day 26's AT walk. I drove there and settled into their nice huge AT hikers and museum parking lot for the night. That day's hike had been full of variety, and the weather was unseasonably warm—in the 60's and humid; my first sweaty day. Even the cold rocks embedded in the trail were sweating.

"Say 'ahhhh'" – cherry tree putting its 'hand' in the mouth of an old dead oak on the ridgetop, Glade Mountain. Detail of the 'hand' in the inset.

I loved all the variety. This stretch of trail included grassy areas, young woods in abandoned fields, vistas of the valley, and even a railroad track crossing. A train came by with its rumbling clackity-clack racket. The trail takes 2.7 miles to cover what the (far from straight) drive covers in just over a mile. Next came a basically straight-up ascent to 4,100-foot Glade Mountain. The trail quickly picks up Vaught Branch, a tributary to the Middle Fork of the Holston River, and follows it up to 3,500 feet in elevation where there is a perky little spring coming out of the ground right beside the trail. All along that route, the walk follows the briskly tumbling stream among big rocks and features interesting 'secret' settings of rhododendron thickets and overhanging trees.

The ambiance of Chatfield Memorial Shelter is perhaps the most welcoming I had found so far. It overlooks the stream with its soothing babble bathing the

F.I.T. Wilderness   21

area. Just above the shelter is a section of rock and log steps that is right out of a dream garden setting (at least, according to my taste)—all mossy and over-draped with tropical-like rhododendrons.

Then on top of Glade Mountain, I passed and photographed some surprisingly contorted and strange behaving trees. There was a cherry tree that seemed to have its 'hand' in the 'mouth' of a big old oak—a root that reached out horizontally at eye level from the trunk of the cherry and delved into a big gaping knothole in the oak, six feet off the ground. There the root forked into five distinct fingers that curled around the lower 'lip' and into the interior of the oak. I never saw anything like it before or since. Many of the trees in this area had been badly contorted, likely by heavy accumulations of freezing rain or snow. I continued down the other side to Forest Road FR86 where there is a 'party' parking area (marked by a fair amount of litter and trash), then hiked another 15 minutes to the top of Locust Mountain before turning around for the day.

That evening I treated myself to a buffet dinner at the KFC in Marion. Their speakers were blaring country music from WMEV, 93.9 FM. The big hit song of the moment was Toby Keith's "Red Solo Cup," an ode to the ubiquitous throwaway plastic cups. The tune got stuck in my head; I was singing or humming that song on the trail for the next two weeks.

What it replaced in my head was "Jingle Bell Rock," which had been rattling about in my brain like a bad dream ever since Christmas. I was glad to exchange that present.

The next three days I left the trail to take care of some personal business. First thing I did was stop in at the ATC Headquarters in Harper's Ferry. The main reason I visited was to buy a life membership, and thereby qualify for their life member patch and sticker. I talked with a volunteer at the desk, and with another guy who was planning a NoBo thru-hike starting April 7th. I tried to memorize his face, but as far as I know I never did see him on the trail. Lastly, I sat down with the long-time ATC information officer, Laurie Potteiger, who sort of interviewed me about my hike, and who did some scouting for information on other hikers who were planning to use a similar format. That's when I learned that my hike would be the first of its kind, if I succeeded.

I got an oil change for my good ol' Steel Tent, picked up mail in Maryland, paid some bills, and watered house plants at my beach condo in North Carolina, and was back at the KFC in Marion on the evening of the third day. I had planned to take one of these business-breaks every so often and expected them to be during snowstorms or other lousy weather stretches. As the adventure went on, I found myself doing these less and less. Turns out, I was getting hooked on the trail life.

On Day Hike number 27, I had company on the trail. Seeing anybody out there in January was rare, yet here were three other hikers. They weren't together but were close enough to have possibly been with each other: a woman who seemed to be semi-running, a man in shorts and a short-sleeved shirt (I didn't envy his clothing choices) who seemed older than me, and a slightly younger man who asked whether there was water up ahead. I told him there was none until the fantastic spring that feeds Vaught Branch on the north side of Glade Mountain.

I stopped in at the Mt. Rogers Visitor Center to ask about snow cover there. With an elevation over 5,000 feet for a number of trail miles, this time of year there would normally be several feet of snow in the area. But there had been none that year, and, best of all, the long-range forecast called for mild dry weather. I was fully expecting to have to slog through deep snow but it turned out that it had been one of the strongest 'La Niña' years on record. I'll spare you the details (I'm a research meteorologist by trade), but what it meant was that most of North America had January-March temperatures as much as 7 degrees Fahrenheit above average, while Siberia and Alaska were a similar amount below average.

Right on cue, Day 28 proved to be really mild. The highlights of the day were encounters with two very different kinds of people. First, I ran into the older man who I met yesterday near the visitor's center wearing shorts with a white broad-brimmed Aussie Breezer hat. This time I had shorts on too. We stopped and had a friendly chat. He was from Knoxville and was hiking day hikes as well, working northward from Damascus. He said he planned to do a big chunk of the trail this summer. I found the other person I met, whose name was Ted, holed up in Trimpi Shelter. He had a bicycle behind the shelter, piles of food beside him, and a German Shepherd named Jack nearby. He had tarps draped over the opening of the shelter. I found him sitting up in the back corner of the shelter with his legs in his sleeping bag, munching on chocolate chip cookies. Without being prompted, he quickly launched into his story. He was chilling here, waiting for a court date on a DUI charge. He seemed an intelligent guy and was very curious about my adventure, but I sensed that it was a deflection. I took my obligatory photos of the shelter and made only a very brief entry in the log book, noting that Ted had not signed it. The previous entry was from Christmas.

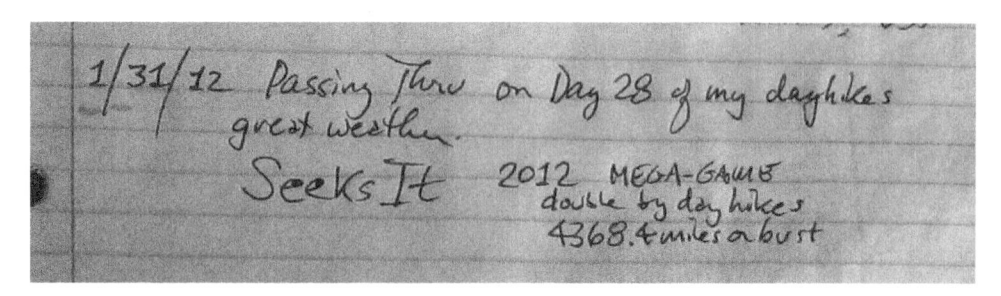

Example of my Shelter Register entries – Trimpi Shelter, VA

I always put little 'seeking' eyeballs inside the 'e's'. MEGA = Maine to Georgia, i.e., southbound. GAME = Georgia to Maine, i.e., northbound.

I got an early start on Day 29, hoping to beat some forecasted rain. But by the time I got to Old Orchard Shelter, it was steadily misting and getting harder. My poncho kept me comfortably dry from the knees up, and I was warm in these mild conditions. Hiking through the upper forests of Pine Mountain in the rain reminded me distinctly of the rain forests on the west slopes of the Olympic Peninsula of Washington State—very mossy with hemlock as the dominant species. I turned around there, at a stile where the trail emerged into a high meadow at nearly 5,000 feet elevation. This was the start of the AT's meandering tour of Grayson Highlands, which I would start tackling the following day.

Day 30 was Groundhog Day. Rain and fog had continued overnight, but by 8:00 there were patches of blue sky. The fact that it had just rained instead of snowed at over 5,000 feet elevation in the middle of winter was not lost on me. I hiked past the Wise Shelter and then reached the expansive open pastures and semi-alpine savannahs around The Scales, a former cattle round-up and loading station. It was windy and the bases of the clouds were toying with my elevation, so the vistas were somewhat limited, but I had hopes of better weather on the return trip, which was indeed the case. So I got my fill of vistas with unlimited visibility in the afternoon—and it made for one of the more pleasurable hiking days I had. In the afternoon, I hiked up to Wilburn Ridge where the trail goes through a tunnel under the rocks called Fat Man's Squeeze. There was lots of rocky and marshy footing along the way, so the going was slow, but again, the vistas and unexpected cave-walk were more than enough reward for the inconvenience.

Judging from the viewpoint at 5,461 feet when I turned around on Wilburn Ridge, I would have a lot more semi-alpine grassland to walk the following day. This is the kind of hiking I love most: under the open sky on top of a mountain. I guess I was spoiled by my high-country hiking during the ten years I lived in Colorado between 1970 and 1980. And, as a meteorologist, I love being tuned in to the weather around me. I was seriously looking forward to the next few days, and they turned out to even exceed my expectations.

The AT meanders toward Whitetop Mountain, as viewed from Buzzard Rocks, Mount Rogers vicinity

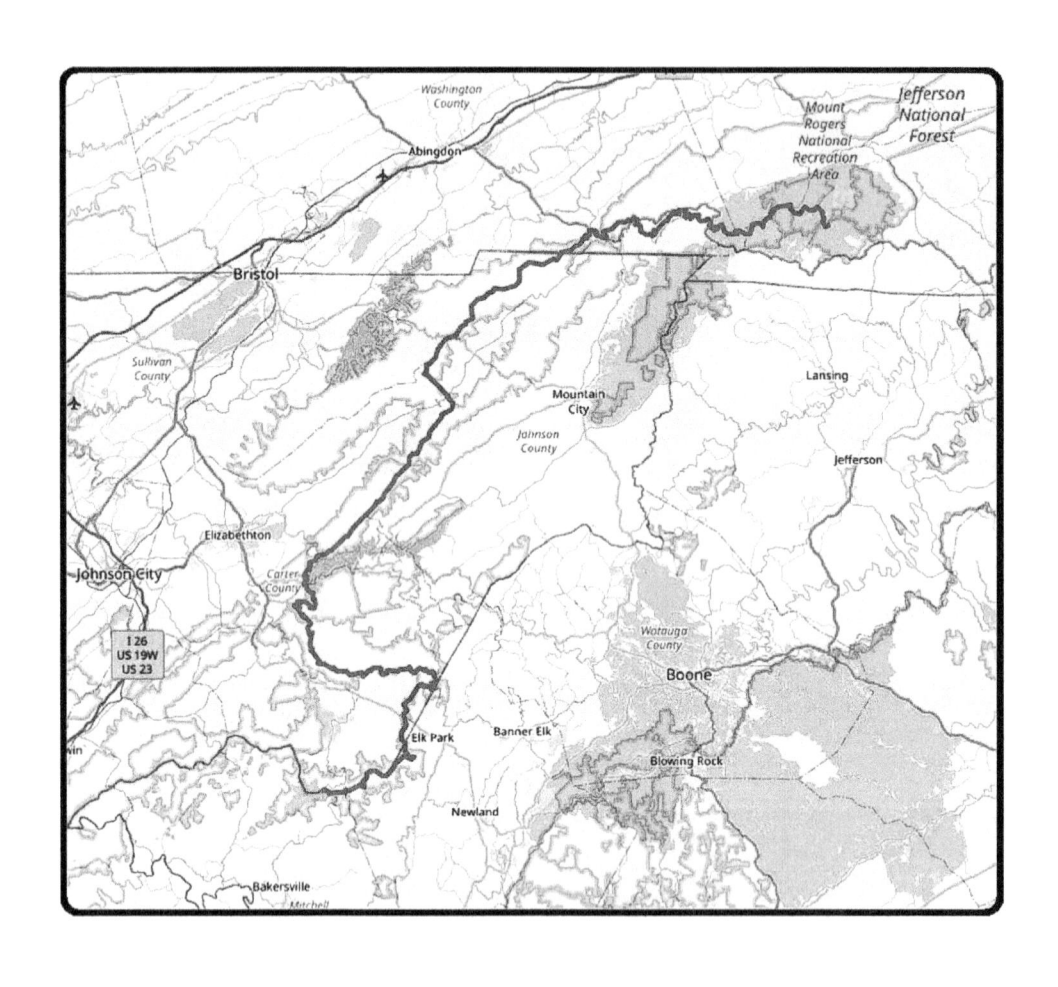

P. J. Wetzel

CHAPTER 3

Grayson Highlands, VA to Carver's Gap NC/TN
February 3 - 17; 118.4 trail miles one way

"It may have been in 1891, while I was listening to bearded, one-armed Maj. John Wesley Powell recount to an enthralled audience in Washington City his historic trip through the Grand Canyon. ...

"It may have been in 1897, in the White Mountains of New Hampshire, as Sturgis Pray and I struggled through a tangled blowdown. ...

"Or it may have been in 1900 when I stood with another friend, Horace Hildreth, viewing the heights of the Green Mountains. ...

"Somewhere, sometime back there near the end of the old century, the notion of an Appalachian Trail occurred to me. But it wasn't until 1921 that the idea had crystallized. On Sunday, July 10, at Hudson Guild Farm in New Jersey, I sat down with Charles H. Whitaker, editor of the *Journal* of the American Institute of Architects, and Clarence S. Stein, chairman of AIA's Committee on Community Planning. I explained my idea for a trail that would run in a wilderness belt from one of the highest mountains in New England to one of the highest mountains in the South.

"Both friends encouraged me to write an article setting forth the idea. I did, and in October 1921 the *Journal* of the AIA published 'An Appalachian Trail, A Project in Regional Planning.'"

Those were the words of 93-year-old Benton MacKaye, written for the Foreword to a National Geographic Society book entitled *The Appalachian Trail*, published in 1972.

I consider that little known specific date and place—July 10, 1921, just nineteen miles SE of the Culver's Gap Trailhead on the current AT—to mark the true birth of the Appalachian Trail. The year I did my hike, on the other hand, everybody was celebrating the 75th anniversary of another landmark moment. On August 14, 1937 the full length of the Appalachian Trail was officially declared completed, largely through the tireless work of another trail legend, Myron Avery. For me, that date marks the trail's 'coming of age,' literally her 'Sweet Sixteen.'

Avery was the very first person to hike the entire AT, though he did not do it in one calendar year. The first to do that was WWII veteran Earl Shaffer, who completed his thru-hike on August 5, 1948 at 1:30 pm.

F.I.T. Wilderness

Portrait of a Grayson Highlands 'wild' pony.

That was the year I was born. By the time I graduated from college, only 59 people had reported completing the trail. Then the explosion in popularity began the year of the first Earth Day in 1970. A new generation was looking to nature for both escape and inspiration. Hiker numbers have roughly doubled every decade since. In the most recent decade, the 2010s, more than 1,000 hikers reported completing the full trail every year, which is about 20% of those who try it.

Why do 80% of the people that make the attempt fail? Interestingly, the 20% success rate seems to be built in to human nature for projects that anybody can attempt and that require a good deal of preparation and sustained effort. According to the Bureau of Labor Statistics, 80% of all small business start-ups fail within the first year. In both cases, most of the failures result from too little planning and preparation, unrealistic expectations, or lack of sufficient motivation.

I'm not going to attempt to motivate those of you who may aspire to do a thru-hike. Nor am I going to pontificate about what to expect or what it will take to succeed. Everybody's different, and there are plenty of resources available. What I'll do here is just share my example.

My preparation actually began five years before the hike began. At the time, I was a real couch potato, overweight and totally out of shape. When I had the chance to retire early from my Civil Service research meteorologist position at NASA's Goddard Space Flight Center, I decided to revive a long-time bucket list goal of climbing a 20,000-foot mountain in South America.

As I've mentioned, I had developed Chondromalacia, degradation and thinning of the cartilage on the underside of the left kneecap, from excessive bike riding back in the late 70's. It got so bad that, in addition to giving up bike riding, I had not been physically active since then because the doctors told me there was no cure for Chondromalacia and that the knee would be a problem for the rest of my life.

So, I started my preparations for mountain climbing modestly, and with the attitude that if my knee couldn't handle it, I would give up the attempt and move on to some other bucket list goal. I lost 25 pounds and started hiking a local trail in Maryland with a good 1,000-foot elevation gain in about a mile and a half. The knee was not bothering me too much, as long as I didn't run or walk really fast. I found some newly developed information on the internet about Chondromalacia. It seems that it's the only cartilage damage that would, in fact, heal over time. Buoyed by that, I started hiking with a backpack full of five-gallon containers of water and putting on heavy ankle weights. I joined a gym and used its tread mill regularly, doing interval training with the incline turned up to the max and with 50 pounds of water in my backpack.

Still the knee wasn't bothering me. So I signed up for a mountaineering expedition, and on 25 January 2010, I achieved my 20,000-foot summit in the high Atacama Desert of NW Argentina.

Once I got back home, I didn't want to lose the conditioning I had worked so hard to build, so I started hiking the AT—first in Maryland, where I was only an hour's drive away, and then extending south into central Virginia. During the six months leading up to the start of my MEGA-GAME Double attempt, I had already hiked all of the AT between Caledonia State Park in southern PA and the parking lot off US 220 in Daleville, VA where I began this sojourn.

So, I felt I had adequately prepared. As far as expectations are concerned, the 'Or Bust' tag line on my Trail Register entries tells the tale. I did not *expect* to finish, I only expected to give it my best. As I got deeper into the hike, I realized that giving my best was going to require some serious focus and dogged persistence.

This speaks to the motivation. A successful thru-hike requires putting a lot of other goals and desires on the back burner. Ellen's visit at Woods Hole had shown me that I could get derailed too easily by putting social and even family connections ahead of my goal. The three days I spent off-trail to take care of business at home further reinforced that. If I was going to be successful, I would have to have laser focus on one thing and one thing only until that thing was done: getting up every single morning and putting one foot in front of the other. That had to be the one and only important thing; less important than being entertained, comfortable, clean, warm, or even well fed—all of it.

Fortunately for me, the trail itself, and the wild untamed beauty that surrounded me, were more than adequate entertainment. I was now in one of the grand high mountain venues on the trail—Grayson Highlands, the centerpiece of which is Mount Rogers, the highest natural point in Virginia. And I was loving it.

Day 31's hike picked up at Wilburn Ridge, went past Mount Rogers and Whitetop Mountain, with a stop at Thomas Knob shelter. I met no people on the trail all day, but was far from lonely. I had several close encounters with the gentle, sturdy wild ponies that keep the grass mowed on these high mountain prairies. They're just heartachingly cute, no more than five feet tall at the head, with shaggy fur and super-long manes and tails. Their manes are so long, they hang over their eyes. In this location, the majority of the trail runs through the open grasslands that the ponies maintain. On top of that, the weather was sunny, starting out with frost but turning wonderfully mild. Really, it could not have been a more perfect day.

The AT does not go over the summits of either Mount Rogers or Whitetop, the two highest peaks in the state, and I didn't take the side trips to visit them. The summit of Mount Rogers is wooded and has no view, and the dirt road that goes to the top of Whitetop didn't look particularly inviting.

On Day 32, I did just 7¼ miles because of lots of heavy rain. The next day turned out to be just as rainy, but I did nearly twenty miles. For the first time ever in my hiking history, I used an AT shelter for ... shelter. I hunkered down in Lost Mountain Shelter for half an hour while a heavy downpour rolled through. I was hiking a section where the AT runs parallel to the Virginia Creeper Trail, a paved bike trail that follows an old railroad grade along Whitetop Laurel Creek. South of Saunders Shelter, the AT does merge with the Virginia Creeper for a little under a mile and also crosses it at Creek Junction Trailhead eight miles farther east. If I wasn't being a strict purist about hiking past every white blaze both ways, today would have been the perfect opportunity to do one trail out and the other back. The two trails are even within sight of one another during a good deal of that stretch. It hurt not to have the chance to explore the other trail, especially since it was the prettier alternative, following the rambling noisy creek among lush forest and rhododendrons. The AT, on the other hand, gets relegated to rocky side slopes, with 1,000 feet of elevation change,

Detail of the rime ice on a white pine frond, northern Tennessee.

sixteen switch backs, and three short but intense climbs of rugged rocky knobs. I had to cross half a dozen rain-swollen creeks along this section, many of which presented me with tough footing decisions. Then I had to turn around and do that all again. Somehow, I managed to keep my feet dry.

Day 34 was the day I arrived in Damascus, one of the AT's premier trail towns. It is the site of the annual "Trail Days" gathering that happens in mid-May each year around the time that the northbound 'hiker bubble' passes through the area. I spent time shopping for gear in Mount Rogers Outfitters and talking extensively with one of the sales people, who I think may have been one of the three owners (Tom Davenport, Jeff Patrick, or Steve Webb). We had some fun discussions about gear and about the trail. It was so great to be able to "talk trail" after a lonely month out there in the wilderness. That never could have happened during their busy season, but when I was there, the store had more employees than customers.

Out on the trail, I passed through an unfinished trail relocation at Feathercamp Branch. There used to be a footbridge, and I think a new one was in the planning, but meanwhile, here in the dead of winter, I had to ford that 20 foot-wide, knee-deep, fast-flowing stream—twice. It was pure ice water. Meanwhile, I'm no Bear Grylls. He would have dived right in and swam across naked, dried himself off with snow, and then dressed while doing push-ups to keep his core warm. Me, I just yelled my brains out to distract my senses from the pain.

On Day 35, I crossed into Tennessee. That meant I had now hiked the AT through the whole states of Virginia, West Virginia, and Maryland (if I counted the hikes completed the previous year). I was counting on those to fall back on if I ran out of time or energy. The last thing I was going to attempt was repeating those parts I had already done; doing them both ways by day hikes if it turned out to be possible. On Day 35, I did 21 miles between Damascus and Abingdon Gap Shelter—the first of Tennessee's uninspiring concrete block shelters without privies—and back. This is a pretty easy piece of trail, which some call the 'Damas-

An island in Watauga Lake during a snow squall.

F.I.T. Wilderness

cus Freeway'. The slope is gentle, and the trail is wide, smooth, and lacking rocks. Unfortunately, it's also lacking scenery. My best photo was one of a long section of straight, smooth, nearly level trail in a pretty woods.

The next day the weather began to turn on me. It started snowing at 6:30 am, but I headed out anyway. The next problem? I forgot my backpack. The old 1971 REI pack is so comfortable that I rarely notice it. I was half a mile down the trail before I realized I'd forgotten it, so I decided to do without it for this ten mile out-and-back leg to Abingdon Gap Shelter. As it turned out, I didn't miss it. I did need toilet paper, but I used a couple of empty journal pages from the shelter, and the half liter of water in my jacket pocket was enough. On this northbound leg, I passed a tent about two miles into my hike, then on the way back I passed its owner hiking north. It was my first NoBo (north-bound thru-hiker)!!! His trail name is Mickey D and he said he doesn't stay at shelters. He said he left Springer on January 2nd and had taken no zero days (i.e., days when he didn't hike at all), but planned to take two at Damascus. He was the first of what I expected would be hundreds.

I got kind of miserable as the snowfall continued. By the time the ten miles was over, my shoes and socks and the lower cuffs of my pants were wet, as was the (poorly chosen) down jacket I used for an outer layer. Down just turns into soggy mush when wet and loses all its insulation power. By afternoon, thick fog had rolled in but the snowfall had diminished to just a light pelleting of little grains. The wind was increasing and it was getting chilly, but I now had on two fleece layers under my rain/wind shell and felt comfortable. This leg was a little shorter, about nine miles, and I met another serious hiker just south of Double Springs Shelter, where he was headed for the night. He didn't specify how long he'd been hiking or his destination, but that didn't matter to him. His trail name is Winter Hiker and he had a job lined up, scheduled to start in April, where he lives in Vermont, and he just loved hiking. I think he said he'd done the entire trail already. The most interesting thing about him was that he was 'wearing' an umbrella. It was somehow propped up by one strap of his backpack, and seemed very secure. Hiking with an umbrella was something I had casually thought about, but to see it so well executed was interesting. After my AT adventure, I got one and now swear by it, and I can thank Winter Hiker for the inspiration. He seemed otherwise very well geared, with gaiters, some sort of little clock and meter on his belt, nice trekking poles, etc. He looked outlandish with that 'hands-free' umbrella, but he was no weirdo. We talked for a few minutes and then I continued for another half mile to my turn-around point at a spring. When I passed the shelter again, his gear was there, but he was apparently down at the spring. The fog began to lift as I approached the end of the day, and so I got one photo in at a vista. But the prettiest photo was of the delicate rime ice in an otherwise typical trail scene.

Light on-and-off snow continued the next day as I made the 600-foot climb up to the Nick Grindstaff Memorial. Not far from that 1923 monument, I met a young kid sitting on a log with his pack off, smoking a cigarette. He was not the talkative kind, but I got his trail name from the register: Cody Coyote. He had stayed at Iron Mountain Shelter the night before and was hiking north on a multi-day hike. I never met him again, but I would see his entries in shelter registers far and wide—and in ways that didn't make sense. He appeared to be a drifter or perennial hiker with no real destination. I've met a few others like that. There was a guy named 'Thor' who was taking the day off at Pine Swamp shelter the rainy day I passed through there. He was working his way north but was taking his good old sweet time. Most notably was a guy named 'City Slicka' who I ran into in several places along the trail later in the year. I recently learned that he had been on the trail for at least ten years before passing away in 2019.

The story of Nick Grindstaff fits this same pattern in a way. The gravestone simply says, "he lived alone, suffered alone, and died alone." Records show he was orphaned at age three, that he drifted around a lot as a young man, and that he lived as a hermit on Iron Mountain for the last forty years of his life. But there's more legend than fact surrounding many details of his life. Some say he had a series of setbacks as a young man—possibly losing his young wife, or getting beaten and robbed while traveling out west. But soon he was so disillusioned with the world that he left it behind. The few that knew him in those later years considered him a kind man. This must have been true, or who would have bothered to erect and maintain such a monument? How many of us have our lives memorialized in a published 693-line epic poem by a county poet laureate? His tale was written in 1926 by Johnson County poet, A. M. Daugherty:

> "He roamed up there for forty years
> Under the heaven's chandeliers ...
> And thus he slept within his rights,
> Fourteen Thousand four hundred nights ..."

I did 23 hard miles on Day 38, most of which was along the ridge of Iron Mountain at 4,000 feet. It included passing the Vandeventer Shelter, which has a killer view of Watauga Lake below, but also a killer hike to the nearest water supply. Near the end of the day, I checked in at Watauga Lake Shelter where I met 'Lone Wolf.' He had thru-hiked twice but was just out for a week this time. I couldn't spend time chatting because it was getting dark. In fact, I had to use my headlamp for the last hour, getting me back to my van a bit after 7:00 pm.

The next day was bitter cold to start so I had arranged to meet a high school classmate and her husband who live in Mountain City, TN. We were going to have lunch at the Cracker Barrel in Abingdon, right at the interstate exit. But it started snowing hard, and before the arranged time she called and canceled, saying that, when they had headed out, they began skidding around and had understandably given up and returned home. I hung around the Food City parking lot in Damascus, but when the snow began to let up, I plotted a lowland driving route to Watauga Lake, which was also at low elevation, and headed out there via an 80-mile circuitous route on main highways. It turned out that, beyond the vicinity of Iron Mountain, there was almost no snow, so when I got to the AT parking area on US 321 at the west end of Watauga Lake, I found only a quarter inch on the ground. Squally showers were still falling, but I managed to hike almost nine miles, climbing 1,800 feet to Pond Flats where there was a lot more snow, maybe five inches. The AT follows Shook Branch Road for the first quarter mile off the highway, and where the trail leaves that road, there was a big fenced yard with a horse and a goat inside. The two animals came up to me begging for a hand out. The horse was the most outgoing horse I've ever met—almost like a puppy. And the goat was just as friendly, raising its front legs up on the fence to compete with the horse for attention. Both were reaching for my hand, letting me pet them, and the horse literally started nibbling on my hand. I had nothing to offer them though and felt a little guilty.

The cold weather continued overnight. And the next day I had one of my most serious driving scares of my life. I was trying to drive up steep, switch-backed

Ice-crusted Laurel Fork Falls in the dead of winter.

Dennis Cove Road to get to the trailhead at the top, near a popular hostel. Not too far up, it was becoming obvious that the road was too icy to continue. I saw a set of tire tracks from somebody who had turned around, then in the next slippery spot, there were tracks from somebody who had been seriously spinning. My wheels spun at that spot too but never lost their forward momentum. But I had plenty more switchbacks to negotiate, and a long way up.

I should have known better than to go on. The road was paved, and the lower half of the tough part had guard rails, but suddenly those ended. Then I finally lost all forward momentum. It was obviously time to give up. I had noted a good roomy spot to turn around at the last switchback I'd passed. So I backed down almost inch by inch, staying on the uphill side and making sure not to slip. That worked fine. At the sharp turn, I backed up into the little, unused side road with complete success and plenty of room to turn and head back down. But what I hadn't counted on was that on that switchback, the road was banked steeply toward the downhill side—toward a fifty-foot drop with no guard rail.

Yep.

I pulled out of the side road, turned the wheels to the right, and they immediately lost all traction. Suddenly I was sliding helplessly toward the cliff, heart in my throat, accepting fate, already picturing the van flipping over and rolling, landing upside down smashed against the trees at the bottom of the drop, praying that I'd not be too injured to call 911.

Then came a miracle. Where the pavement ended, right before the cliff, there was a dirt shoulder just a foot or two wide. And that dirt was soft. It stopped my van safely enough with maybe a foot to spare before the drop.

OMG. I mean OMG. My heart was racing like an Indy car on Nitro.

My van had stopped, and I was not going to die, but it was now cross-ways, blocking the road with no possible way of backing up unless I spent hours scraping the ice down to the pavement.

I got out, took several deep breaths, assessed the situation, started calming down, and called the state police to report the problem. It was 7:30 am and none of the non-emergency services were available because it was off hours. I got a message to someone who then transferred me to someone who then transferred me to a recording. I then tried calling the county police and just got another recording. Well, I decided to wait until 8:00 am and try again.

In the meantime, I used my jar of table salt on the track under the right front wheel and a sturdy stick to make a good safe bit of ice-free ground under the left front wheel. I began to carefully inch the van forward, wheels turned at max, just a few inches at a time before clearing the next little patch. When fully turned, the angle of the front wheels soon came to a trajectory parallel to the edge of the road, not facing down to the cliff, so I was sure there was hope of getting turned back onto the road.

I was patiently working this angle when a county sheriff drove up. He had received the message from the state police. We talked and he said he'd stand by to see if I could get the van back onto the road safely. About that time, a local in a 4x4 came by, offering help, but there was nothing to do but keep inching my van around. By then, the back end of it had moved far enough around that the road was no longer blocked, so he was able to get by and go on his way. By 8:30, I had successfully freed my van on my own.

I thanked the officer for his time and then crept slowly back down to the flat land with him following behind. Fortunately, I had an alternative in mind that would allow me to attempt the same hike I had planned to do from Dennis Cove Road: the big Laurel Fork trailhead parking area right on US 321, which has a one-mile side trail to the AT. Longer day, helluva lot safer.

F.I.T. Wilderness

I headed there, parked, and spent an hour regrouping mentally, unwinding, and then preparing for the hike. So it was 9:45 before I finally hit the trail. Fortunately, the planned hike was short enough that I could still accomplish all of it, including the extra mile out and back to the AT.

It turned out to be a very interesting day of hiking. The trail to the AT was a bit less than a mile and had one narrow bedrock section right above the big noisy stream called Laurel Branch. It intersects the AT at a switchback. In one direction, the trail continues along the stream toward a huge and popular waterfall; the other way, which I took first, turns and heads immediately up the side of Pond Mountain. Yesterday's hike up Pond Mountain was on a wonderfully graded trail with switchbacks and smooth footing. The trail on this side of the mountain was much tougher, with narrow side slopes and little level footing, some rocky sections, and, perhaps worst of all, some sections where the trail just powers straight up a ridge line on what seemed like more than a 45-degree slope.

These sections of trail I would call 'cardiac ascents' and 'suicide descents', the latter particularly true today with all the snow on the trail. They're old, and very bad trail design, prone to serious erosion, and risky for the hiker.

After reaching my turn-around point on top of Pond Mountain, I negotiated those 'suicide descents' carefully and still slipped a few times. And I began to notice a reroute full of switchbacks that had been flagged with red plastic and wire flags. There were already sections of the 'wham, crash, bam, straight up the ridge, and the slope be damned' trail that had been abandoned and replaced by switch-

Hump Mountain, my favorite place on the AT, as viewed from Little Hump Mountain in February, with rime ice frosting the tree tops.

backs. I had hiked those switchbacks without noticing the old trail on the way up. The entire way down I was able to identify when I was on old trail and was able to spot the abandoned old trail when I was on new trail. It made for an interesting first-person lesson in modern trail construction. It is these sorts of reroutes that improve the trail experience but at a cost—the AT gets a little longer every year.

Back at the bottom, I took the other direction along the river toward Laurel Fork Falls. There were two impressive foot bridges then a tough rocky climb to the junction of the 'high water trail' and the Laurel Fork Shelter. Then the trail came back down to the water and finally took a precarious route on a narrow rock ledge right next to the stream (the reason for the need of a high-water trail). Finally I reached the payoff: the really big waterfall, dropping 50 feet and chock full of water and streaming with icicles.

From the waterfall, the AT ascends steeply, with more trail builders' craft on full display—265 well-set rock steps. At the top, the AT merges with the high-water trail at a very old railroad grade, which the high-water trail follows from Laurel Fork Shelter. The AT then follows that amazingly ambitious old railroad route all the way to Dennis Cove Road, passing through narrow, deep cuts in the rock, and descending to cross Laurel Fork where there was once a high trestle. There were other people on the trail by now, out for a stroll to the waterfall as the afternoon got sunny, and I talked with two guys who were trail running and had done 34 miles in the time I managed about twelve.

The start of Day 41 found me driving right back up Dennis Cove Road past the site of my near tragedy. It was now completely free of ice. I parked at the trailhead and marched off the other way, making sure, as I always did, to place my feet on the same spot where I'd left off the day before. The hike was arduous. There was more of that tough, steep, eroded old-style trail and a lot of ups and downs, so the 19 miles took 10.5 hours. I didn't have time to knock on Bob Peoples' door at Kincora Hostel, which is in sight of the trail.

The hike the following day took me to the NC border at Elk River. The trail was nice enough and I got to visit the new Mountaineer Shelter, built just a couple years earlier near Mountaineer Falls, which had almost no water. It looks like it would be dry in the summertime. On the way back, I reached the shelter just as a heavy shower rolled through, so I took shelter there for fifteen minutes. It was a short day, less than 14 miles, much like the next day, but for very different reasons.

On the morning of Day 43, I noticed more than usual pain in my left Achilles tendon. It had been sore for unknown reasons since the day I hiked into Damascus from the north. I don't focus on my aches and pains normally, but this issue had reached the level that got my attention. That day heading into Damascus, the pain came fresh with every step. I attributed it to having twisted my bad, formerly broken left ankle at some unrecognized misstep. Whatever the cause, the result was that every step caused a fresh stab of pain. In the succeeding days, I treated that foot with extra care—trying to avoid twisting it or stepping crooked, but not compromising the distance I covered—and the injury responded. Each

F.I.T. Wilderness

day the pain was less. It seemed to be fading into the background more recently, and was no longer a significant issue. Until this morning.

What seemed to be happening was that the tendon was seriously swelling. I didn't know what caused the swelling; the only thing I could point to was a slip and near fall while I was picking my way through the ice off the trail at the base of Mountaineer Falls the day before, trying to get a photograph. In any case, the tendon was throbbing similar to a toothache. It couldn't be ignored, wouldn't go away, and wasn't going to let me sleep. Well, I'd been entirely free of the need to take any medication on this hiking adventure so far, but before going to bed, I took an aspirin, and I continued to take one every two hours throughout the early afternoon. The pain was so strong that the aspirin didn't have much effect, but I was still going to try to hike. It was a mild morning. I parked at the Mountain Harbour Hostel—the first place I chose to pay for parking, because the area was notorious for vandalism of unattended hiker vehicles at trail crossings, even during the day.

I headed out walking really slowly and with a serious limp, babying that left foot. Very gradually the ankle loosened up. By the time I got to the turn-around point at the Elk River, the pain had virtually gone away, though I remained cautious and kept a 1.5mph pace the rest of the day. The weather had become spectacular—very spring-like with bright sunshine and calm winds and temperatures well into the 60's. I stopped at the amazing and spectacular Jones Falls on the way back, taking lots of photos, and then passed back through the most notoriously hated (by locals) section of trail around Buck Mountain Road. ATVs use much of this trail section, there's litter, and at a confusing crossing with a well-used local trail, I encountered one deliberate overpainting of a white blaze with a crude blue blaze. The hate is rooted in the fact that the Feds used eminent domain to 'steal' land from local owners here to create a corridor for the trail. Children and grandchildren of the original owners, or perhaps just friends and acquaintances, have held the grudge ever since.

My ankle didn't bother me anymore, at least not to that extent, and hasn't to this day. The problem on Day 44 was the weather. I started at Mountain Harbour Hostel again and began the 2,500 foot climb up to Hump Mountain, the first of the Roan Highlands balds—mountain tops that have not had forest on them at any time since the last ice age, even though they are low enough in elevation to support trees. The climb up was tough enough, but when I crossed the stile into the open ground on top of the mountain, it was foggy and raining hard and the wind was whipping. The 0.8 miles of open ridge to the actual summit of the mountain was the toughest walk I had done, maybe ever. I could barely stand, had nothing to look at through the grass but the trail in a cocoon of fog accompanied by the howl of wind and the merciless battering of the rain.

Despite this first experience, Hump Mountain has come to be one of my very favorite places on the entire Appalachian Trail. My return visit there the next day from Carver's Gap, crossing all the other magical Balds of the Roan Highlands, was life changing. I was high in the mountains, under the open sky all day, bask-ing in the glory of 100-mile views in every direction—sometimes with miles of the trail itself spread out before me—and enjoying a magical morning coating of rime ice on every leaf, twig, and blade of grass. And I had the trail all to myself. The ridges were lined with heath—a profusion of clumps of Catawba rhododendrons and flame azaleas that I had the pleasure of witnessing in full bloom on a June day several years later. If I could do only one day hike on the Appalachian Trail, this hike from Carver's Gap to Hump Mountain would be my choice. There isn't even a close second.

Flame Azaleas at Round Bald, taken 11 June 2014. Note Clingman's Dome in the background at right.

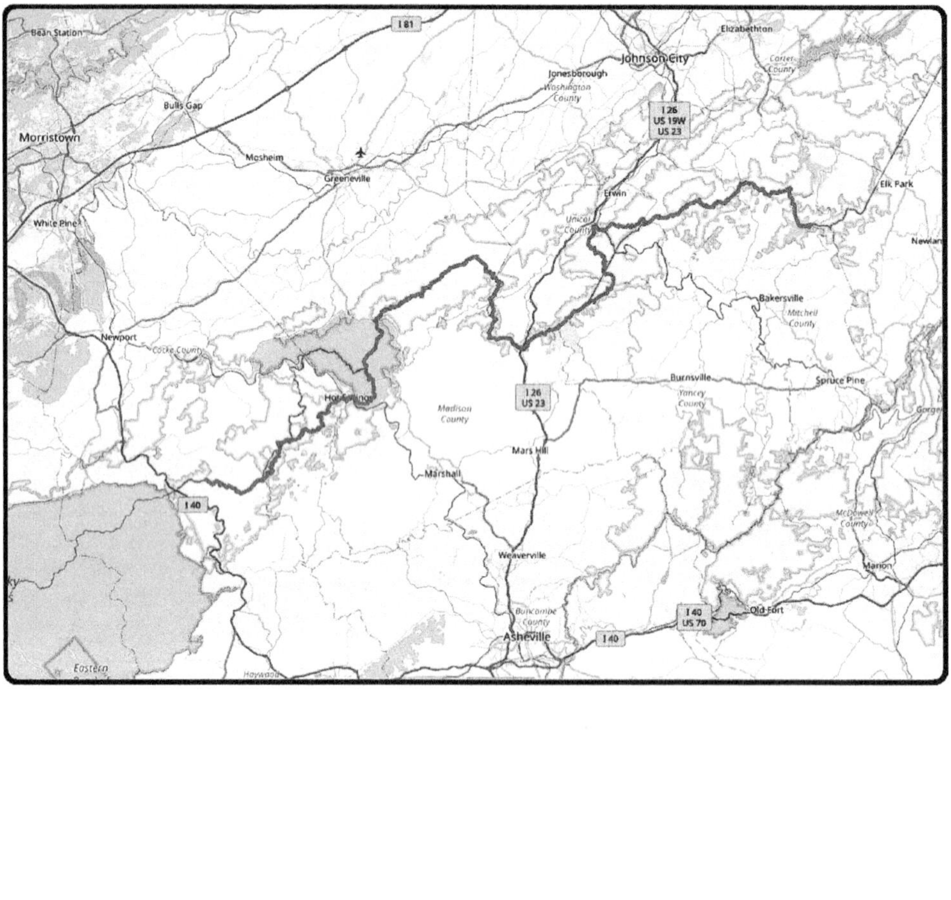
Bean Station
I 81
Elizabethton
Johnson City
Carter County
Jonesborough
Washington County
Bulls Gap
I 26
US 19W
US 23
Morristown
Mosheim
Greeneville
Elk Park
Erwin
White Pine
Unicoi County
Newland
Bakersville
Mitchell County
Newport
Cocke County
Burnsville
Spruce Pine
Yancey County
Madison County
I 26
US 23
Mars Hill
Marshall
I 40
McDowell County
Weaverville
Marion
Buncombe County
I 40
US 70
Old Fort
Asheville
I 40
Eastern
Haywood

CHAPTER 4

*Carver's Gap NC/TN to Snowbird Mountain, NC/TN
February 21 - March 6; 131.5 trail miles one way*

This chapter covers the bulk of what turned out to be my favorite 150-mile section of the AT. It actually started back at Hump Mountain, and ended at Davenport Gap at the edge of Great Smoky Mountain National Park. I do not include the park itself as part of my favorite section just because of the crowds. Of course, everybody's tastes are different. It is because of my love of the high mountain, open tundra-like balds, which this section has a monopoly on, and its two premier trail towns—Hot Springs and Erwin that this is the place I most want to return to and hike over and over.

The journey resumed at the highest point of this special section, and fourth highest peak overall on the Appalachian Trail. At 6,285 feet, Roan High Knob is just three feet below the highest point in New England, Mount Washington (the summit of which the AT no longer crosses). But it has the distinction of being home to the AT's highest shelter. Roan High Knob Shelter is a cozy little log cabin, not a lean-to, which sits in a thick wooded area not far from the summit. I stopped in to sign the register on Day 46 of my AT adventure (though I actually wrote that it was Day 45. These shelter registers get saved, I'm told, so if somebody happens to check, I just thought I'd set the record straight).

There were just three inches of snow on the ground, when, at this time of year, there should normally be three feet, and the climb was gentle, following an old road. The whole summit had once crawled with summer tourists seeking clean air and escape from the heat in the era before air conditioning. The posh 166-room Cloudland Hotel stood on this location between 1885 and 1910. Now all that's left are a couple of interpretive signs and the killer views.

Day 47 could be called the Jekyll-Hyde hike. I hiked northbound from Iron Mountain Gap to my turn around point at Little Rock Knob in beautiful weather. It was an enjoyable 'ridge ramble' over a rolling, loosely defined ridge on trail that was generally pretty smooth. But as I ascended the steep rocky cliff-side trail to the three good vistas at Little Rock Knob, I was hit with snow squalls, wind, and a serious drop in temperature. Fortunately, it settled down to a steady rain that stuck with me all the way back.

The highlights the following day were the bald aptly named "Beauty Spot" and the much higher Unaka Mountain which is inexplicably heavily wooded right to

Roan High Knob shelter – highest elevation shelter on the AT.

the summit. Nobody knows for sure what processes have preserved the balds that exist on some mountains and not others. There is evidence that some of the balds were tundra ecosystems during the ice age 20,000 years ago and were artificially preserved by the megafauna that depended on them. It was a survival strategy. Excavations have found fossils of up to 20 large mammals that occupied the ecosystem, including mammoth, mastodon, bison, horse, tapir, musk ox, and ground sloth, up until 10,000 years ago. After that the paleo first-peoples appear to have used fire to maintain these balds as hunting grounds for bison, elk, and deer. A few of the balds were cleared by European settlers as grazing lands for their cattle; Max Patch is one example of that. Other former balds have become overgrown since cattle grazing was ended by the forest service.

For me, all the balds are 'Beauty Spots.' It would be just two more days before I reached the next one. Meanwhile, on Day 49, I got to hike the Nolichucky River gorge and pass through the outskirts of Erwin, Tennessee. Indian Grave Gap, which had been yesterday's lowest point, was today's highest. On the way back from that turn-around point, I met a talkative NoBo thru-hiker named 'Fire Pit', who said that Uncle Johnny at the Nolichucky Inn had told him he was the seventh NoBo of the season to stop in at that hostel. Fire Pit had started at Springer in November and was taking his time, apparently earning his keep at some hostels by building or improving their … you guessed it, fire pits. When I met him, his pack weighed 75 pounds; I think I saw the handle of a cast iron frying pan sticking out of it. He said he was headed for the fresh, new Curley Maple Shelter for the night.

Day 50 was a chilly winter day. It even snowed for a while in the early afternoon. The hike presented interesting terrain but not a lot of scenery. Starting at Spivey Gap and going northbound first, the trail very steadily descends while meandering the small ridges and dry gullies along the slope of No Business Ridge. Then it continuously snakes out to the ridges and into the little valleys, all the while maintaining the gradual, steady incline to reach Temple Hill Gap. From there, the trail adopts an old woods road that smoothly transfers the hiker around the main summit of Temple Hill to a saddle that marks the end of six small knobs that compose Temple Ridge. The last of those knobs, the one closest to Erwin, was my turn-around point.

On my way back, I got increasingly obsessed with the AT trail logo and all its many manifestations—from formal signs to quick marks carved in tree bark. There are hundreds of them to be found along the trail, and I'd been photographing most of them. The obsession probably started when I passed a huge new blow-down with the logo freshly emblazoned on it with a chain saw. Today I took the time to make a little logo of my own out of sticks in a see-through round hole in a hollow tree. Later I found a 'natural' logo in roots on the trail. Soon I was seriously distracted by this little obsession, and it seemed to act as a release from fifty days of trail 'sameness.' You could call it boredom, or perhaps just too much singular focus on covering distance for too long. But this afternoon I kind of 'lost it', pausing to leave a couple more logo-art examples for the potential entertainment (or annoyance) of other hikers. Finally, as the return climb along No Business Ridge got serious, I snapped out of it and returned to my main focus. I would endanger my 'mission' if I started being the 'AT logo phantom', though it seemed a strangely tempting

First sign of the 'AT Logo Phantom' near No Business Ridge. Leave-no-trace purists are no doubt (rightfully) displeased. This could be considered 'graffiti'.

F.I.T. Wilderness

enterprise. I finished the day at 4:30, having been consumed by creating trail art for perhaps 45 minutes. That hike of 16 miles was enough for the day.

I met nobody on the trail all day, but this was the site of an amazing story. It's the section of trail where, in 2007, NoBo hiker 'Popeye' suffered a major heart attack and lived to tell the tale.

I met Popeye on the trail exactly 50 days later at the 501 Shelter in Pennsylvania, where he was its caretaker. I talked to him, actually sort of interviewed him, for more than an hour on two consecutive days. Here is what I learned: his real name is Bob Pyhel. He worked as a self-employed carpenter, free to hit the trail whenever the urge struck. He had completed a thru-hike in 2001, reaching Katahdin on August 13th.

Then in March 2007, Bob decided to do a second one.

Maybe he was a little out of shape this time. No problem. He'd hike himself back into shape.

Bob 'Popeye' Pyhel, photo taken on April 19th at the 501 Shelter in Pennsylvania, where he was caretaker.

And it seemed he had done just that. Things were going well. Bob had hiked 320 miles of trail. Now he was making the climb up to the memorable vistas on Big Bald (which I would do the next day) when suddenly his chest tightened up.

"It felt like an elephant was sitting on it," he told me.

He sat down, rested, and the discomfort went away. No big deal. He finished the climb over Big Bald, then Little Bald, and down to Whistling Gap. Normal service resumed.

Well, not exactly. The next day Bob was climbing up from Spivey Gap, hiking alone. The elephant returned; it sat down on Bob's chest and this time it wouldn't go away. This time rest didn't help.

Bob's family has a history of heart problems, high blood pressure, and high cholesterol. So he had a pretty good idea that this was a heart attack.

"What did you do?" I asked, thinking the logical move would be to return to the Spivey Gap parking area, (on busy US 19W) and flag down the next passing vehicle.

Nope, Bob would do it the hard way. He had a reservation at the Holiday Inn in Erwin, still eleven miles the other way. It's not a tough hike, except for those pesky knobs on Temple Ridge. But still … eleven frickin' miles after having a heart attack?

When he got to the Nolichucky River, he bypassed Uncle Johnny's Hostel, which is right there as you come out of the woods. He continued up the road to the motel next to the interstate.

He collapsed in the lobby. The clerk called 911. The paramedics measured his blood pressure at 70 over 30. He should've been dead. The cardiologists later said it was a miracle that he could have made it that far with so much heart damage.

Thru-hikers are a tough bunch.

Erwin didn't have the facilities to treat him, so they rushed Bob to Johnson City and into the operating room where the cardiologist found a plaque-blocked artery and installed a stent.

Three months of sitting followed—doing nothing—while Bob's heart healed.

"That was the worst part. I couldn't stand it."

Then Bob started working himself back into shape. He was determined to do a thru-hike come next March.

"The trail beat me in 2007. I was not going to let it beat me again."

I checked the ATC's 2000 miler records and found Bob's 2001 hike recorded there, but I found no reported thru-hike in 2008 or any other later year. Nevertheless, there's plenty of evidence that Bob did indeed complete a thru-hike in 2008, as he said. There are daily Trail Journal entries from his partner/girlfriend 'Lil'Mak' who hiked with him, and there's a picture of Bob with her at the summit sign on Katahdin on the day they completed their hike, Sept. 5, 2008. Lil'Mak (Martha) remained his partner and was with him at 501 Shelter when I met him in PA.

Bob told me at the time that when he finished his caretaker gig at 501 Shelter, he was going to do a SoBo for his third thru-hike. He stayed at 501 for three more years, and Trail Journal records show that he attempted a section hike in 2015, first hiking north from PA, starting April 21st and ending May 10th, then heading south from Monson after climbing Katahdin on June 20th. Lil'Mak entered the daily info for him, but the entries end after 468.6 miles at Trapper John Shelter.

Why didn't Bob tell ATC about his 2008 thru-hike completion when Lil'Mak

F.I.T. Wilderness

did? Who knows? But I'm confident he did actually do it, less than a year after suffering that heart attack.

Day 51 dawned a calm and frosty morning with bright clear skies. I climbed the steady ascent to High Rocks and took the short side trail to the top of the rock with pretty good views, then it was down a few hundred feet to Whistling Gap. From there it was a steady 1,300-foot climb to Little Bald, which was now all wooded. I met a couple guys there at the one small vista point, and we chatted for quite a while. They were out for a six-day hike from Sam's Gap over Big Bald and were finishing up after crossing the Roan Highlands. I descended from Little Bald and followed the ridge, stopping in at the nice Bald Mountain Shelter with its elaborate food suspension cable system. While nearly all the Tennessee shelters don't have privies, this one did. But like most Tennessee shelters, it didn't have a log book. From there I climbed past amazing specimens of twisted and tortured old birch trees to the edge of the woods and emerged into the magnificent area of open mountaintop vistas leading to the summit of Big Bald. But first there is a descent to Big Stamp (stomp, really, named for cattle over-grazing) and then the climb to the 5,516-foot summit of Big Bald proper.

The 360-degree panoramic view took my breath away. I have stood atop three-mile-high peaks in Bolivia and seen the Pacific Ocean. I've stood atop fourteeners in Colorado on days when you can nearly see to Kansas. But east of the Mississippi, I'd never experienced better visibility than I did this morning. I could

View west toward the Smokies from the survey marker post at the summit of Big Bald on a day of near-unlimited visibility.

clearly see Mount Rogers 70.2 air miles to the NE and Clingman's Dome 63.8 miles as the crow flies to the SE. And there were plenty of ridges visible beyond those peaks. I might have been able to see 500 miles if the curvature of the earth allowed anything that far to show up.

Best of all, the wind had remained nearly calm. I couldn't have asked for more ideal conditions to cross this iconic summit. I took lots of photos, of course, and didn't want to leave. The descent down the south side takes you quickly back into the woods and then along a ridge with the Wolf Laurel ski and golf resort development just a few feet to the east. Finally I descended to Low Gap, where I had to turn around if I wanted to get back 'home' before dark. On the hike back, I met several day hikers. One guy had hiked up to Big Bald from Sam's Gap (I-26), and there were four people on the summit who had come the short way up the gravel road from the resort.

I made Day 52 a relatively short day because of the spacing of access points I had ahead of me. I based my hiking out of the roomy Sam's Gap parking area. Almost all day was spent hiking old barbed wire fence line along ridges that mark the boundary of Tennessee and North Carolina. The AT logo phantom was back, despite my vows to keep him suppressed. I couldn't resist making a huge 14-foot AT logo out of an A-shaped broken tree, and manufactured a few other lesser logos as well. I hiked a nice open meadow section as I approached Street Gap from the south. Otherwise the trail either followed the ridge on old-style trail and old roads, or went side-hill on nicely graded new-style trail.

Day 53 was celebrity day. I also dubbed it Opposite Day. It was Opposite Day for two reasons. The first is a numbers thing. When I hike less than about seven AT trail miles (one way) on a given day, I'm actually going backwards. My projected date for finishing gets later, so it feels like I'm further from my goal. I started Day 53 with a projected finish date of November 6th, hiked 13.2 miles out-and-back, and found that, as a result, I was now on pace to finish the trail on November 7th. See? I had hiked backwards. Second, as I hiked along the NC/TN border, I was hiking south when I was going trail-north, and Tennessee was to my east and NC to the west. Yes, geography fans, Tennessee is east of North Carolina. What's more, it is also west of Missouri (and west of the Mississippi River). Look it up.

So now here's the celebrity part. As I hiked over the summit of Lick Rock, I met three hikers from the Carolina Mountain Club. It turned out that they are the current and future maintainers of that trail section. The current ones were Danny and her husband Lenny Bernstein. Danny is a famous blogger and author of hiking books. She wasn't with them; it was Lenny who was handing off this portion of trail to Bob H. and his wife. Some readers may recognize the name Lenny Bernstein. No, not the classical music composer, conductor, and pianist. No, not the *Washington Post* reporter. This was Lenny Bernstein, PhD, of the Appalachian Trail Conservancy, and one of the fourteen current members of their board – wow! We talked for a few minutes and would meet again as I made my return trip. I went on past Rice Gap, where the three were apparently parked, and up to Hogback Ridge Shelter. The weather was gorgeous, sunny, nearly calm, and in the

60's, so I stripped down to just my shirt and shorts. On the way back over Lick Rock, I hiked with Lenny for a while and we chatted again. Lenny passed away on Sept. 25, 2016. It was an honor to have met him.

The next day I hiked Big Butt. Trail guide books are silent as to how this mountain got its name, and I'll work hard here to avoid any bad jokes. It threatened rain all day, but rarely did any fall. Low hanging clouds were constant, but they had the courtesy to remain above mountain top level, except for a brief period of fog as I passed the Civil War grave site of the Shelton Brothers of western North Carolina, Union enlistees. Otherwise, Big Butt and its environs granted me many nice vistas.

AT Conservancy board member Lenny Bernstein near Sam's Gap.

To get to the rocky summit of Big Butt, the AT leaves an abandoned road and scrambles through big slippery boulders—a difficult stretch—to reach the short side-trail to the actual summit.

From there, I went down the other side, past the quaint little shelter called Jerry's Cabin. It looks like a shack, but with an interior fireplace, it's a palace to a high mountain hiker on a cold night.

South of Big Butt, the trail passes a number of marked side trails—plenty of variety for day hikes in this area. It passes Andrew Johnson Mountain (he was a local Greenville boy, and is apparently still a bit controversial), and drops down to a campsite at Lick Log Gap. I finally turned around where the trail forks and the AT goes up over the exposed Firescald Knob while a 'bad weather' trail stays low and in the woods.

The brutal trail and epic scenery of Firescald Knob was the highlight of Day 55. Before reaching the 'money' section of trail over the knob, I stopped in at Little Laurel Shelter, a stone structure that its log book announced as 'The Friendliest Shelter on the Trail'. Appropriately, I met a guy there who was as open and friendly as anybody I'd met to date. He was packing up and getting ready to head out. He had been with a group but lagged behind them so he was now on his own. I apparently just missed this group, who was going northbound. Our conversation flowed easily so we kept talking for longer than either of us planned. He had not settled on a trail name, but was leaning toward Gadget Man since he was carrying a GPS, netbook, charger, cell phone, etc. I said I'd post about him on my blog (and did) and that would sort of lock this in as his trail name. We met again as I passed him climbing up to Camp Creek Bald and then again on my way back on top of Firescald Knob.

The payoff part of the day's 19 miles was the rugged hike over the exposed knob. It's a heath bald, covered with low scrubby rhododendron thickets and mountain laurel. There are serious rock scrambles and half a dozen vista points to take in the panoramic views. I had fantastic weather with unlimited visibility.

My AT logo obsession was continuing but in a constrained sort of way. Today I photographed 15 different manifestations of the trail symbol but did not allow the Phantom to create any new ones.

Trail Magic, provided by 'Trail Angels,' is freely given, unexpected, and not-asked-for help provided to long distance AT hikers—usually in the form of food or water—sometimes left anonymously on the trail, sometimes provided by a friendly good Samaritan, often by a local resident. On Day 56, I ran across my first serious example of Trail Magic, but even better, I had the opportunity to pass on news of it to three deserving Northbound thru-hikers.

I based my hike out of Tanyard Gap. The trail northbound makes a relaxed ascent, passing a nice piped spring and an almost perfect natural root AT logo, so the Phantom did his 'deed for the day' by carefully clearing all the debris in a circle around it and adding a single stick to complete it. The Rich Mountain fire tower is open to the public. The cold wind hit me as I climbed it, but the views were well worth it. Back on the trail, I dropped down to Hurricane Gap then up Spring Mountain, almost always on an exposed windy ridge.

The trail continued, scrupulously following the state line. This section appears to be original AT because the well-worn Spring Mountain shelter near the summit was built in 1938 by the CCC. It is in good shape but with old plank sleeping platforms that are truly rustic – three spots for individuals and one for a couple. I got there at the same time that two thirty-something ladies arrived from the other direction. We chatted as they snacked and I wrote in the log book. They were on a four-day outing based in Hot Springs, doing day hikes. They told me to look for 'Rambo' and 'Spicotti', NoBo thru-hikers whom they had met the night before at the bar at Iron Horse Station. They said to tell them "Hi from the Two Cougars" if I met them. If you don't know what they meant by 'cougars,' well ... they were smiling. From Spring Mountain shelter, the trail descends in three steep steps with short climbs out of two gaps, the second being one of a bazillion gaps along the AT that are named 'Deep Gap'.

My turn-around point was Allen Gap. When I got to the road, I found a sign posted there by Trail Angels and '99 thru-hikers, the Nelsons, who have a beautiful log home 0.2 miles east of the AT crossing. The sign said they were open to serve snacks and stew and vegetarian chili to hikers between 7:30 and 5PM yesterday and today. It was 12:40 and I had until 1:15 before I needed to turn around, so I decided to check them out. Wonderful people. We talked trail and they served me a bowl of the best vegetarian chili I'd ever had. Free home-made hot food! These nice folks are perfect examples of how the trail changes people's lives. They bought this house after their thru-hike specifically so that they could stay in contact with the trail community and make a positive difference.

Back on the trail returning southbound, I finally met 'Spicotti' 0.7 miles up. He was alone and really trucking along, hoping to make it to Little Laurel Shelter before the forecast tornadic storms hit. It was already spitting rain. He'd been on the trail since February 1st, and was making good time. I relayed the Two Cougars' message, which brought no visible reaction. I told him about the Trail Angel food stop. He thanked me, said he'd stop in.

The weather was closing in with rain, some fog, and one clap of thunder. I met 'Rambo' and a friend taking a rest stop on a rock two miles further down the trail and had a nice brief chat with them, passing word from both 'Spicotti' and the Cougars and turning down an offered toke of weed. They were very nice, very young guys, and seemed quite a bit more relaxed about their thru-hike than 'Spicotti'. I hurried on as the skies darkened, but chose not to stop at the shelter as the rain seemed to be letting up. When I got back to Tanyard Gap, it was in the 60's and cloudy but the winds had calmed and there was no sign of more storms to come. So I hiked another mile south, up to the pretty meadows on Mill Ridge, former tobacco fields purchased by the forest service in 1970 and maintained as open wildlife habitat. I finished after sunset; a long and satisfying day. It was good to have some 'people stories' for a change. The 'NoBo bubble' was beginning to break the surface.

Hot Springs is more of a purely Appalachian Trail town than Damascus. Damascus gets more business from users of the Virginia Creeper rail trail than it does from AT hikers. Rail trail users rent bikes and want their bikes shuttled to more distant points. They come in cars, and generally have more money to spend. In Hot Springs, the undivided focus is on the AT, and you can see it right on the sidewalk of Bridge Street, the main street through this compact little village. There are 35 diamond shaped granite flagstones embedded in the sidewalk through town, plus two 'official' white painted AT logos mid-street at crossings.

Somehow the size of Hot Springs (considerably smaller than Damascus) also suited me. I felt as though everyone I met or casually passed was a Trail Angel or a long-lost friend. They greeted me, asked about my hike, and seemed genuinely interested. I felt welcome. I felt appreciated.

Of course there was the business of hiking more trail than just the town to get down to this day. The view from Lovers Leap down to the French Broad River and back to town is classic. To get to it, there's a pleasant stroll right beside the river for half a mile. On the way back to Hot Springs, I met a NoBo thru-hiker named 'Wood Chuck', who left Springer the same day 'Spicotti' did.

I also did a leg southbound from Hot Springs, and as I headed out, I chatted with the Two Cougars ladies, who were just completing a hike north after being dropped off by shuttle at Lemon Gap that morning. I turned around at another rustic 1938 vintage log shelter, Deer Park Shelter. This one has sleeping planks that are polished like fine furniture, purely from long use and wear. I found an ancient AT logo carved into one of the planks and took its photo. It instantly became one of my favorites of the many dozen logo shots I was collecting.

Day 58: The climb up Bluff Mountain from Garenflo Gap is the kind of climb I like. It gets to the business of "up" and just keeps going steadily for more than three miles, rising 2,000 feet of elevation at a near-constant rate. I like it because you can really get into a rhythm. And on a cold windy day such as

AT logo carved into the edge of a floorboard, Deer Park Shelter.

this day was, when ups-and-downs require constant fiddling with clothing in order to regulate body temperature, you can 'set it and forget it' when it applies to your 'thermostat.' I passed 7 hikers on the way up, and talked with five of them. They were all dropped off by shuttle at Max Patch and were headed back to their base in Hot Springs.

Max Patch is the last of the southern Appalachian balds that the trail passes over. It was a windy chilly day as I came through, but that made for great visibility. And I got to visit it twice, in the morning and evening. I camped nearby for the night and went back out in the icy wind to watch the sun set over Snowbird Mountain from the broad open summit. I wish I could have stayed another day.

Earlier in the day, between Roaring Fork Shelter and Lemon Gap, I met NC State students Alex, Holly, Tham, Steve-O, Graham, and Rebecca and their dogs Mogley, Biscuit, and Hugo. They were spending their spring break on the AT. Poor Hugo seemed locked in a one-dimensional world, and was deathly afraid of passing me. Yet he would not leave the trail to do so. Finally mustering up all his courage, he made a hilarious, crazy-eyed, full-speed dash past me.

This gang had spent the night at Roaring Fork Shelter and were headed to drafty 1938 vintage Walnut Mountain Shelter tonight. I was afraid they would

F.I.T. Wilderness

Max Patch at sunset.

find the new accommodations rather less appealing. Roaring Fork is roomy and new and in a protected valley. Walnut Ridge had accumulated snow on its sleeping platform and wind-sculpted snow drifts all around. There's no chinking between the old logs; just big wide gaps that let the wind right through. I'm betting it was a cold night for them, with a forecast low of 22 degrees. Fortunately, by midnight, the wind was relenting.

On Day 60, I bridged the gap, with the ubiquitous name of Deep Gap, between Max Patch and Snowbird Mountain, on top of which sits a white conical aviation/navigation/beacon/tower thingy. This version of Deep Gap contains the Groundhog Creek Shelter, where I met 'Selva' and 'Skezzer', two delightful guys out hiking during their spring break. Then came the climb and finally the 'payoff': some great vistas and the close-up view of that Nav Tower thingy.

On the way back to Max Patch, I met two guys out for a long section hike from Newfound Gap to Shenandoah Park, but forgot to ask their trail names. Later as I was sitting on a rock along a side slope in the woods taking a drink of water, a fast-moving hiker came by: 'just Paul ... I don't really have a trail name.' He was thru-hiking and hoped to finish before July 1st.

Paul started in Springer on February 16th, so he was making good time. He lamented that all the trail friendships he had made hadn't lasted long because nobody kept the same pace. I told him about the two Shenandoah guys—turns out they planned to stop at the same shelter that night (Roaring Fork), and Paul's eyes lit up, hopeful of a worthy set of trail companions. I wished him good luck and explained that he may pass me again somewhere north of Caledonia State Park in PA after I reach Springer and make my 'flip-flop'. I had made the same promise to a number of the NoBo thru-hikers I had met. I'm terrible at remembering faces so I had to pray I would remember them.

Weathered plastic trail sign at Garenflo Gap

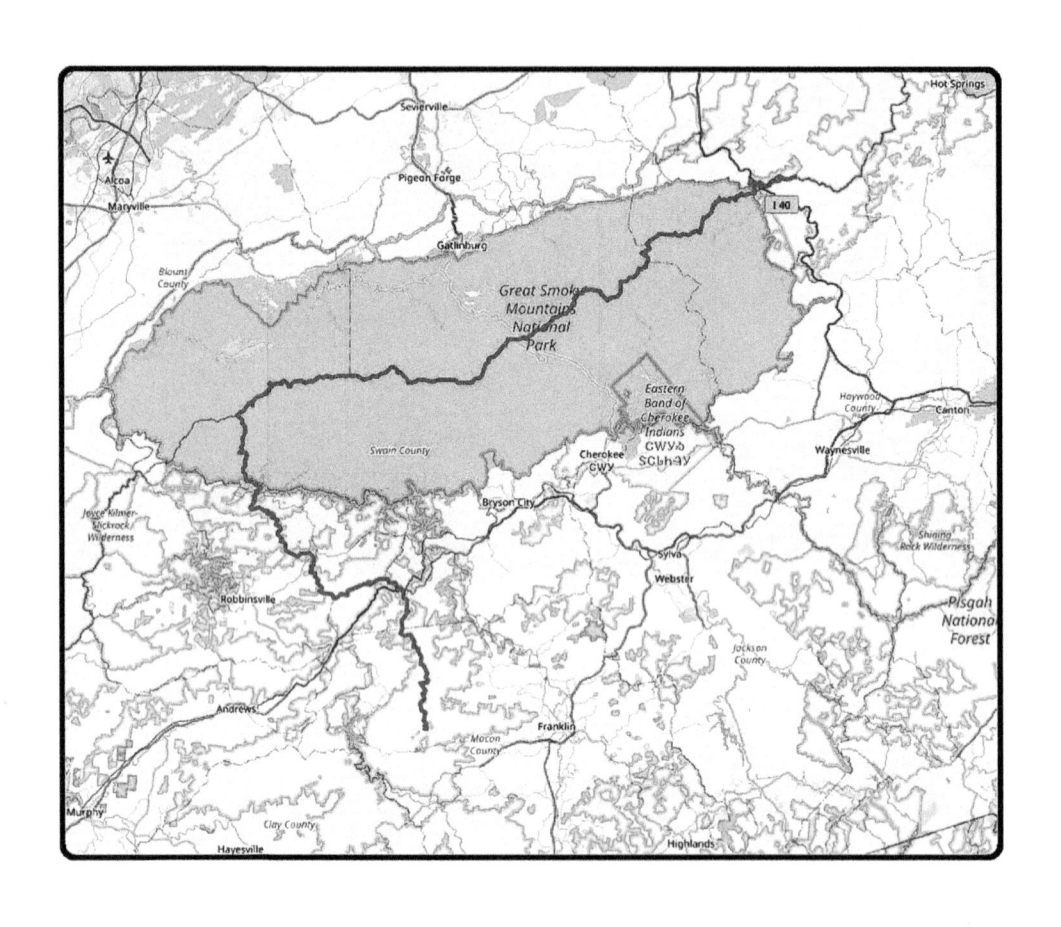

P. J. Wetzel

CHAPTER 5

Snowbird Mountain, NC/TN to Wayah Bald, NC
March 7 - 20; 125.3 trail miles one way

Okay, let's talk about the name of this trail: Appalachian. If you're a Yankee, you pronounce it 'Apple-LAY-chin.' If you live in Dixie, you insist that 'Apple-LATCH-in' is the only right way to pronounce it. Here's my take on the debate. Benton MacKaye is from Connecticut. He lived in New York and Massachusetts. He named the trail. Period. The Appalachian Trail got its name from him, so I say that the only truly correct way to pronounce its name is the way the guy who named it pronounced it.

Now hold on, dear friends from Dixie, do not despair. I'm a Yankee, born in Wisconsin, raised in Delaware and Pennsylvania. I was taught the LAY pronunciation, and prefer it. But guess what? Benton MacKaye used the LATCH pronunciation. Proof of that comes from a 1975 video of him talking about the trail that is available on YouTube. He speaks the word twice, very clearly, and there's no ambiguity about the way he pronounced it. His words were recorded at his home in Shirley Center, Massachusetts on June 1st and 2nd, 1975 when he was 96 years old, just six months before his death.

Whether he learned it that way or adopted that pronunciation, I do not know. But the mountains were named after the Apalachee Nation of first peoples and there's no dispute about that pronunciation; it's the LATCH way. Even I say it that way.

But my last word on the subject is this: pronunciations change. Common usage defines them, not some cast-in-stone unchangeable dogma. For example, in 1350, the number 'one' was pronounced 'own' as in 'alone' and 'only,' two words rooted in the word 'one'. Yet now we pronounce 'one' as 'wun.' Why don't we say 'wunly' or 'I'm all awun?' Nobody actually knows why, but sometime between 1400 and 1550, everybody who spoke English made the switch. So I bet that someday, one of the two ways to say 'Appalachian' will die out and the other will take over. Or maybe we'll go back to calling these mountains the Allegheny Mountains as many people, including John Muir, did in the 19th Century.

Right. And maybe my Dixie friends will finally stop pronouncing 'oil' as if it rhymes with 'coal'.

* * *

*"A late dispatch from Appalachia: Seeks It's on the trail,
Set to embark on Smokies Park. And therein lies a tale."*

(This is one of my 'patented' tight-rhyme Fourteeners—see the 'Crumbs' tab on my blog)

Great Smoky Mountains National Park was going to be the toughest challenge of the whole AT for my 'all day hikes' plan. There are only four access points for day hikers, one on either end (Davenport Gap and Fontana Dam), with Clingman's Dome and Newfound Gap in the middle. The trail distance between Fontana Dam and Clingman's Dome is 32.8 miles, and from Newfound Gap to Davenport Gap is 31.3 miles. Remember, I'm hiking every piece of trail both ways, so the only way through this gauntlet was to hike four days of more than 30 miles each, turning around near the mid-point of those long, uninterrupted sections.

Before tackling the first of these, an out-and-back of 32 miles from Davenport Gap, I had to do the prelude hike, a mere 14 miles from Davenport Gap to Snowbird Mountain and back.

Try as I might to 'live the moment', my mind was not on the trail that day. As I started, all I could do was gaze southward, down that dark tunnel of trail as it plunged into the park, and shudder. A sense of dread and trepidation coursed up and down my spine, and it would not go away. I felt like Dr. Livingston, about to plunge into deepest, darkest Africa. I was worried, intimidated, even scared. Tomorrow could make or break my plans. Tomorrow I must face my fears, be larger than life, hike farther than I've ever hiked in one day, and come back alive. Worse, as I finished that day's uneventful walk having not met another soul, I learned that the forecast for tomorrow looked to be deteriorating. I could be finishing both in the dark and in pouring rain.

That night I wrote in my personal journal:

My trail name is 'Seeks It.' The name derives from the 1934 George Noble bronze plaque that sits at the trail's southern end on top of Springer Mountain: "A footpath for those who seek fellowship with the wilderness." Yes ... yes ... I am one who seeks that. I am here seeking the serenity of such deep and unreachable places. I am here on the brink of the Smokies precisely for that experience. Bring it on!

I got very little sleep that night. I got up at 5:00 am, dressed, and packed extra stuff, including my Thermarest mattress pad in case I got stuck on the trail and couldn't get back in one day, as well as my flashlight as a backup for my headlamp. I was on the trail at 5:20. I would have liked to be out an hour or even two hours earlier, but getting some sleep was probably more important. It was only 0.6 miles to the first shelter and still pitch-black when I got there. It is a caged shelter, in order to keep the bears out. I went in and found nobody there, so I took the obligatory photo using my flash and signed the register.

It was a mild, windy morning with a distinct difference between the cloud-shrouded windward east-side slopes of the ridge and the very clear vistas off to the west. The clouds banked up against the knife-edged ridge lingered until around noon. The ridge gets very exposed in places. The wind was howling. I had to put on extra layers.

The climb from Davenport Gap is 4,300 feet to the high point at Mt. Guyot. But there are ups and downs, so the actual vertical climb for the hiker is more than 7,000 feet. That said, the trail is high quality, keeping to less than a 15% grade, doing the hard work of erosion control, and, in places, displaying a truly heroic effort at stone work. Much of the trail through the park was constructed by the CCC in the post-depression era.

My very favorite stretch of trail on that day's hike was a level section at the very high point (6360') while rounding the summit of Mt. Guyot. It remained

Superb CCC-built stonework, 4.4 miles south of Davenport Gap, Great Smoky Mountains NP.

a very raw windy day, but here the deep spruce woods tamed the wind. Moss abounded and no trail erosion marred my footing. There was even a delightful spring gushing pure, cold, delicious water. This point on the trail is higher than Mt. Washington in New Hampshire, and the highest point north of Clingman's Dome. It was a special sanctuary; may it always remain so.

I was feeling strong. My confidence was building. I reached my turn-around at Tricorner Knob Shelter at 12:50 pm, which meant that I'd finish in the dark, but based on the way I felt, it looked like I was capable of the miles. After all, the way back was downhill.

When the rain came as predicted, there were only little spits and spurts that barely wet the ground. For the fourth time on this adventure, the Weather Gods were with me. The rain suddenly became a downpour only in the last 30 seconds of my hike, as I was dashing back to my van in the dark at 7:30 pm.

One 32-mile hike down, three to go. I took a full rest day the next day to prepare for the next one.

Day 63 found me heading northbound from Newfound Gap at 6:10 am. I needed to use my headlamp for the first hour. The start was not a pleasant one. For a stretch of about three miles north from Newfound Gap to Charles

F.I.T. Wilderness

Trail view in the sub-alpine ecosystem near the summit of Mt. Guyot.

Bunion, this 'walk in the park' was more challenging than any section of trail I'd hiked yet. It rained an inch and a half overnight, then it froze. It probably would have been better if it had snowed. The trail through this section had been over-used and poorly maintained. There were three-foot-deep rutted, rooty, muddy sections. There were rocky scrambles where no good foothold presented itself, or if one did, it was slick with white ice—which, in the light of a headlamp on my return trip after dark, looked just like dry white rock. And then there were the places where the trail pretends it's a stream bed, some of which were frozen with black ice, while others were still soggy and flowing over the trail, daring you to find a way to avoid getting wet.

The meta-challenge was the variability of the challenges—rocks, water, ice, roots, mud, and some three-foot vertical steps up out of eroded washouts, all coming together, in varying combinations, and unceasing for miles. Now compound this with the fact that I had to walk this both ways, one of which was, as I said, after dark. In the dark, I had to pause with each step, study the next foot placement, place the foot, and repeat. Wow. Day 63's 32-mile trek ended at 11:00 pm.

Okay, those were the negatives. Thankfully the positives far overshadowed them. I got to the aptly named Icewater Spring Shelter at 7:45 am and parted the tarps covering the opening to emerge into wonderful warmth. Inside were four very friendly thru-hikers who offered me some of their coffee and chatted with me briefly. Recent college grads all, 'Green Bean' was the lone female. She was from Connecticut, 'Moses,' the tall one, was from Texas, 'Spoon' was Asian and hailed from Kentucky, and 'Huckleberry,' with the infectious smile, was a local boy from Boone, NC. He was only doing a section hike from Springer back toward home. The others were thru-hikers. We parted, promising to see each other later in the day on my return leg.

As it turned out, they caught up with me just as I reached my turn-around point at Tricorner Knob Shelter. They all came in together for their lunch break, not straggling in one at a time. This spoke volumes about their chemistry. I spent half an hour that I didn't really have talking with them. Naturally they wanted to get to know me too, and it was four versus one, so I didn't gather as much of their individual stories as I wish I could have.

From left to right: Green Bean, Moses, Spoon, and Huckleberry, relaxing and having lunch at Tricorner Knob Shelter.

Now to the scenery. What can I say? I'd need superlatives to describe both the vistas from the knife-edged ridge and the weather. I cannot conceive how either could have been more ideal. Air so still that, when standing on a precipice above a vast amphitheater-like valley dropping half a mile below, all you could hear were the distant waterfalls. Skies so deep blue that all traces of 'Smoky' had vanished from the mountains. The temperature at midday was well up into the 50's.

The following day I did the relatively short hike up to 6,643-foot Clingman's Dome, the second highest point in the east next to Mount Mitchell. The road up to the Dome had not opened for the season yet, so I had a wonderfully quiet visit to the mid-century modern 45-foot observation tower with its iconic 'floating' spiral ramp. The only sound up there was the wind. I was alone in a place that is normally crawling with tourists.

Not half a mile in, I passed four thru-hikers and stopped to chat. Two females—young 'Patches' wearing a patchwork skirt, and wiry fifty-something 'Gutsy'—had just hooked up today with two tall macho-looking 30-something guys called 'Tater Tot' and 'Big B', who said that they had started much earlier than the girls. I guess they were only together for today or a few days at most. Patches was bright-eyed and friendly and had hooked up with Gutsy quite a few days ago.

F.I.T. Wilderness

The toughest of the four 30+ mile hikes in the Smokies came next. It was the toughest because I had to end the day climbing up to Clingman's Dome and because, from Siler's Bald Shelter south for many miles, there are uncountable ups and downs, often surprisingly steep, usually short. AT long distance hikers call them 'PUDs', pointless ups and downs. Many are not actually pointless, but the biggest of today's collection, Cold Spring Mountain, is beyond pointless. The map shows that a level side-hill trail around the south flank of this peak would actually be shorter than the existing trail. Also, Cold Spring Mountain has *no spring*. It has no view either, from the top or anywhere along the slopes. It has no unusual geography, geology, flora, or fauna—in summary, no point. Worst of all, there are mud wallows on the way up the north slope, places where if you stay on the trail but try to avoid the mud, you'll fail because you will slip sideways into it. Finally, it was the toughest day because I was caught in some downpours and had to stop to change socks twice to keep my feet dry.

My turn-around point was Spence Field Shelter, which was a quarter mile off the trail, adding yet more distance. The final tally was 34.34 miles, the longest I'd ever hiked in one day. I was back at my Steel Tent at 9:10 pm with my legs feeling like lead weights stabbed through with a thousand painful arrows. I was truly bone-tired; that term is *so* apt. Muscles get tired quicker, but if you haven't actually injured them (running injures muscle cells), and if you keep them fed with sugars and oxygen, they find a way to push on. Blood, heart, lungs, and mind (if you keep a positive attitude), can keep plugging along too. But when the weariness reaches the core of your bones, the very rock (literally) on which your strength relies, then you know it has been a hard day.

The hike to Spence Field from Fontana Dam was much, much easier by comparison. Again this was partly because I did the bulk of the climbing on the outward half and finished the day going downhill. Also, the temperature was near perfect, in the 70's, and the trail was much smoother and gentler. I got to climb the rickety, rotting oak steps up old Shuckstack Fire Tower in a nerve-jangling wind. I'm not particularly afraid of heights, but this thing got under my skin. The view down to a fog-shrouded Fontana Lake was worth it, I guess. I'm just glad I didn't have to do it twice.

The thru-hiker swarm had been getting thicker every day. The crop that day numbered ten by my late afternoon-early evening survey, including a friend

Fog over Fontana Lake, view from tiny observation room atop rickety old Shuckstack Fire Tower.

I'd see on two consecutive days: 'Drop Out', who was hiking with a buddy who was only going to Hot Springs and then with a new companion. They were doing the same leg as me, all the way from Fontana to Spence Field Shelter, but only one way. Most of the thru-hikers I met settled for the ten miles from Fontana to the huge Mollie's Ridge Shelter. There the crop included four women.

My next hike was a super, super easy day. And boy, did I need the break. I hiked between the Fontana Dam Trailhead and NC 28 at the Fontana Marina and back. This little leg includes the 'Fontana Hilton' shelter, complete with hot showers. On that late mid-March day it was buzzing with early thru-hikers who had completed the first 163.7 miles from Springer and were nervously anticipating the gnarly climb up into the park.

This is a place a lot of NoBo hikers drop out. There are good shuttles available and other services, and it's a long, daunting trek to the next such bail-out point. This is where my kid brother, trail name 'Frugal', hiking with his 1970's external aluminum frame garage-sale backpack, gave up his thru-hike attempt. For him it was the isolation and the loneliness that he just didn't want to deal with. But since then, he had done many two-week sections and had hiked more than 800 miles of the trail by the time I headed out. Counting the trail miles I had done the year before, just yesterday I had passed the 900-mile mark. About fifty of those miles we had hiked together.

Day 68 was another fairly short day. I delayed my start to avoid rain and then did the climb up a ridge called Bee Cove Lead, then continued on to Cable Gap Shelter where I met a father-son team out for 3 days, carrying the same model GPS unit as mine. It was my first real hot day. It got up to at least 80 degrees.

The seven miles of trail between Yellow Creek Gap and Stecoah Gap traverse typical second-growth hardwood forest, the kind of setting you find along hundreds of miles of Appalachian Trail. Then, suddenly—nay, magically—you enter a 'Ridgetop Cloud Garden' where every tree and twig is festooned with old man's beard lichen, and with grand views of the Mountain Creek valley to the southeast and of the Smokies and Fontana Lake to the northwest.

There was more magic too—the kind of magic that can conjure a northbound thru-hiker here, exactly 10.6 miles south of Fontana Dam; someone you've already met on the trail exactly 194 miles north of Fontana Dam.

The hiker in question was 'MEATS', as in "I eat a lotta ..." though he always signs trail registers with capitals, as if the name is also an acronym. MEATS (Brandon) is from Johnson City, TN and he's the first case where my 'face blindness' got the best of me. By his account, on the morning of Thursday, February 23rd, about 8:00 am, he was heading north from Cherry Gap Shelter where he had spent a rainy night. He was out on a three-day training hike, getting ready for his thru-hike. He passed a scraggly-bearded old guy named 'Seeks It' and thought no more about it ... until today. He even remembered my van parked at Iron Mountain Gap. This was a day where I must have been tired and hurried. I have a pretty strong recollection of meeting a hiker near a log bench, which I photographed at 8:15 am. I remember speaking with this hiker briefly, but I do not remember the words said. I remembered nothing about his appearance, and yet I perfectly remember the weather at that very moment—it was in the upper 40's, very humid, with a gray dreary overcast. I've always believed that I reside somewhere on the 'spectrum'—a touch of Asperger's, maybe (related to autism)—and this seemed to be confirmation.

MEATS had been on his thru-hike for just eight days and still looked pretty clean cut. He was averaging about fifteen miles a day, with a couple of 20-milers thrown in. He had the build of a Marine and was a real pleasure to know. I wished (as always) that I had more time to get his 'back story'. And I told him I would be looking for that 'third time's a charm' somewhere up north. As it turned out, I just missed him. I'll relate the full story when I get to that day.

I was only on the trail from 11:00 am to 5:30 pm, but my NoBo tally, surely all thru-hikers, was twelve. I found myself sizing up each one of them as they passed, making a guess about whether they would make it to Katahdin, or how quickly they'd be abandoning the trail. MEATS was one I was pretty sure would make it.

Gone were the days when I would hike for more than a week without meeting another human being on the trail. I liked this kind of magic.

On Day 70, I had yet another encounter that would be repeated up north. I started before sunrise and climbed up out of an ocean of fog that shrouded Stecoah Gap and kept chasing me up the hill as it lifted. I made the two-step, 2,000-foot ascent to Cheoah Bald. If you blink as you pass the summit, you'll miss it. It's a little knob with a fire pit surrounded by logs in an open field with a wonderful open view off to the east and south; and with a little side trip through some trees, there's an even better panoramic view of the Smokies off to the northwest. But after fifty feet, you're plunging back into the woods and descending steeply.

On that descent toward Sassafras Gap Shelter, I met a small, wiry young fellow with a huge pack puffing up the hill about ten yards behind a young woman of similar age and height.

"Not far to the top," I said encouragingly, "and be sure to stop and take in the view."

He just nodded with a half-smile, half grimace.

The almost complete lack of shelter register books since Virginia was cramping my style. I was sure this pair had spent the night there at Sassafras Gap Shelter, but couldn't glean any more information about them. As I got back to Stecoah Gap after a short 13.2-mile day, I found an example of the anonymous Trail Magic that gets dropped off near road crossings. Right at the edge of the woods was a plastic grocery bag full of packaged Moon Pies and a 12 pack of Laura Lynn brand generic cola. That's the brand of the Ingles grocery store chain, the dominant one in that area. During the height of the NoBo hiker bubble, such a stash could be plundered and gone within less than an hour. I'm not saying that some people take more than their share. No, I am definitely not saying *that* ...

Day 71 was another relatively short day as I continued to let my old bones recover from the Smokies. It featured a 3,000-foot steady climb from NOC, the

Nantahala Outdoor Center on the river of the same name, to Swim Bald and back. Swim Bald is one of the 'hairy' balds, long ago overgrown with trees.

NOC was abuzz with thru-hikers as well as white water enthusiasts. The river that runs right through the center of town has a marked slalom course through some nice gnarly rapids. This was the time of year (spring snow-melt) for the toughest water. Outdoor restaurants were full to capacity. Gear shops for hikers and kayakers were doing a brisk business. There was a general store with a white blaze right on its corner with free public rest rooms. It's a thru-hiker's mecca.

Up on the trail I passed two gentlemen without backpacks who were roughly my age, and who, it turned out, were doing just what I was doing, working their way south by day hikes. They were using two cars and only hiking each stretch of trail one way. Also, they were not averse to occasionally spending an overnight on the trail. The opening of our conversation was a little awkward:

"Maintainer?" Harry asked as we approached each other.

I wasn't carrying any tools, but I didn't have a big thru-hiker-style backpack on either.

"Pardon me?" I stuttered, not sure how to answer.

"Oh are you hiking?"

"Uh … yes, I'm definitely hiking." I smiled.

Fortunately, from there the exchange got much more coherent and cordial. Harry (71) and Leo (67) were very pleasant guys, and rare kindred spirits—fellow long-distance day-hikers. Harry was built like a fireplug and had the personality to match. Leo, from Florida, was the droll one, a head taller, slender but muscular, a little more serious, a little calmer. They made a good pair. They said they had started at Damascus and were going to finish at Springer.

The hike south from the Nantahala River is a fairly steady ascent for nearly 2,000 feet and then features a steep ridge-line assault called the Jump-Off. Just below the Jump-Off, I met Harry and Leo again, coming the other way. We had just a brief chat. Above the Jump-Off, the trail presented small ups and downs for a couple miles, then an easy 500-foot ascent to Wesser Bald, the highlight of the day. Like Swim Bald, it is no longer bald and hasn't been for a long time. But this one has a big observation tower. It was a beautiful summer-like day and nearly calm. Up on top, I met three guys from Chattanooga, all about my age, who were doing a series of day hikes working northward. We hit it off and chatted for a while, then went our separate ways.

I dropped down to Tellico Gap, my turn-around point. There, while I was taking photos, a car drove up. It was Harry and Leo, come to retrieve the car they'd left there. I had a much longer chat with them at this point, as they were finished for the day. We talked about logistics of parking places ahead. Leo was calling the Forest Service about winter road closures of some of the gravel access roads just south of here. The three guys up on the tower had mentioned the same issue—the road to Deep Gap was still closed. On my way back down, I met those three guys again, now sitting and admiring the view at the rock outcrop atop the Jump-Off. We chatted for a bit, but I needed to hurry back because I wanted to get to

F.I.T. Wilderness 63

NOC before 5:00 pm when the grocery store closes. It turned out that I got there with plenty of time to spare at 3:40 pm. They had a great collection of craft beers and I had been collecting IPA bottles from local breweries. I bought a couple six packs that were new to me, but they were all out of ice, so I had to hit a gas station a mile away for that. I would usually have a beer with supper as I sat in the Steel Tent doing all my post-trail debriefing, GPS track processing, blog writing, and photo processing. Most days those tasks took me half the night; this morning I hadn't gone to bed until 4:00 am.

The next day I did the southbound leg first and counted nearly 40 NoBo hikers. At Cold Spring Shelter alone, when I arrived to take my obligatory photo, there were five hikers sitting around chatting, presumably taking a break. My count was 21 yesterday and 15 the day before. Of course I couldn't hold conversations with most of them, but today two of them struck a chord with me. Modest young 'Bootstrap' echoed my position. He wasn't comfortable calling himself a thru-hiker since he'd only reached the 120-mile mark. He had been on the trail for twelve days. Freshly retired 65-year-old 'Bird Man' from Jackson, Tennessee had been plugging along since March 1st. He had a good attitude and the patience of Job. His knees weren't strong, but I give him a good shot at making it a long way. Katahdin might be snowed in by the time he got that far, but 'Bird Man' wouldn't quit easy, as long as his knees held up. When he told me his trail name, he raised his arms and his smiling eyes lifted skyward, ready to fly to the top of the next mountain, no knees necessary. I laughed. I had to tell him about a little AT-themed poem I wrote in my favorite 'Fourteener' format. I wrote it on the occasion of photographing a little bluebird sitting on a post with a white blaze in an open field where I was doing a training hike last November near Daleville.

> I cannot fly like this small guy, who soars upon the gale.
> But that's no shake – I'd rather take the Appalachian Trail.

My turn-around was the Wayah Bald stone observation tower. There's a paved road to it and a big parking lot and public park, so it was crawling with people on this warm Tuesday. That's where I met 'Bootstrap,' and up on the tower there were several other thru-hiker types taking in the great view.

March madness, AT style, had begun. And spring was starting to bust out too. Officially it had arrived at 1:14 that morning, as the direct vertical rays of the sun crossed the equator heading north. Things were greening up down in the lowlands. On my drive down from Tellico Gap, I passed a rock wall with pink creeping phlox in full bloom on its south-facing side and ornamental Bradford Pear trees, always the first to bloom in spring, covered with their profusion of white flowers.

Spring busting out along Tellico Road

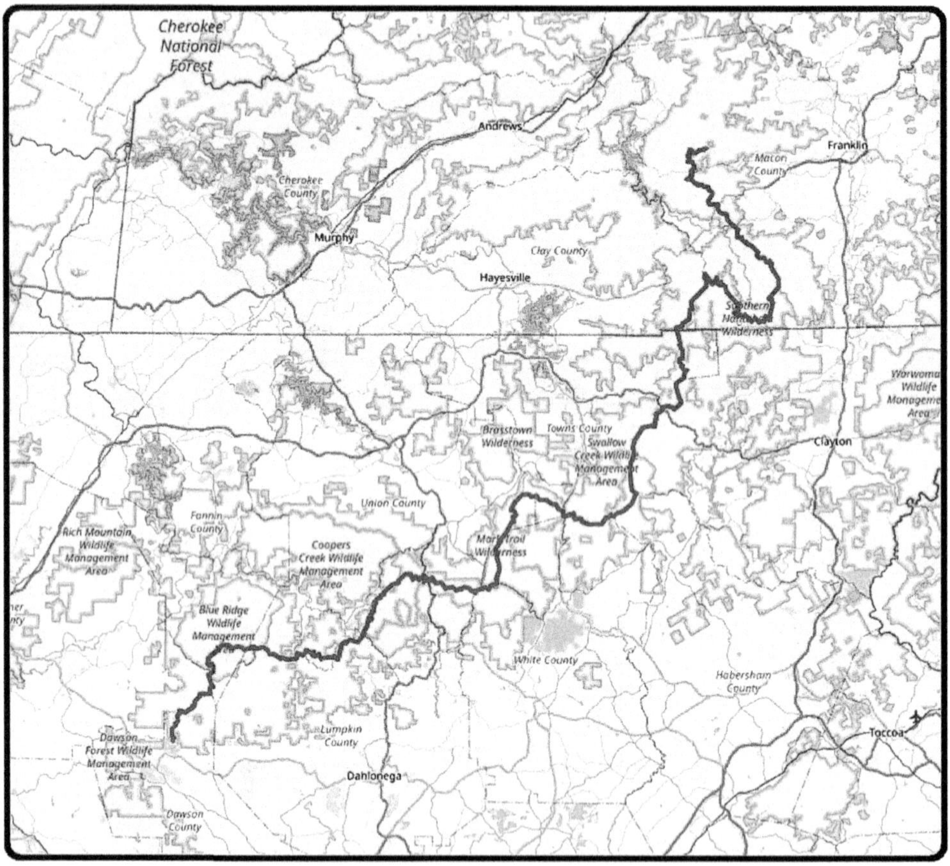
Cherokee National Forest
Andrews
Franklin
Macon County
Cherokee County
Murphy
Clay County
Hayesville
Southern Nantahala Wilderness
Brasstown Wilderness
Towns County
Swallow Creek Wildlife Management Area
Clayton
Union County
Fannin County
Rich Mountain Wildlife Management Area
Coopers Creek Wildlife Management Area
Mark Trail Wilderness
Blue Ridge Wildlife Management Area
White County
Habersham County
Lumpkin County
Dawson Forest Wildlife Management Area
Dahlonega
Dawson County
Toccoa

CHAPTER 6

Wayah Bald, NC to Springer Mountain, GA
March 21 - April 3; 117.8 trail miles one way

The hiker count on Day 74 dropped to 22. I don't know where all the slackers were that day. But in general, every day going forward until I reached Springer, I would meet more hikers than the day before. This was more or less what I had hoped for—a chance to really cut through a big slice of the 'Hiker Bubble' and meet lots of interesting folk and get a first-hand feel for the pulse of this amazing migration/pilgrimage. In retrospect, it turned out to be one of the richest social experiences of my life, and utterly unique. It is said that, on a typical day, there are 2,000 people crossing the Ginza in Tokyo at every change of the traffic light. The crosswalks are 50 feet wide. Here, every one of those 2,000 people is lined up on a two-foot-wide path in the woods, ready for you to meet and at least say 'hi' to each and every one.

Day 74 was a warm day, and the highlight was Siler Bald. This was a peak not directly on the trail, but it was maintained as an open bald by good old tractors and mowers and bush hogs. The view from the top was worth the half mile side trip. There was a thru-hiker and his girlfriend coming down off the bald ahead of me, and there was a small triangular area where the side trail to the bald merged with the AT. The side trail forked, so that NoBos would take the left fork, and So-Bos would take the right. But the guy in front of me took the right fork and then turned sharply left, so as to walk that little piece of AT between the two side trails.

View of Wine Spring Bald and Wayah Bald (with its stone tower) as seen from Siler Bald.

F.I.T. Wilderness

"Right on," I shouted, giving him the thumbs up. "Another purist. I love it."

He gave me a wave and his girlfriend called out, "I'm a purist too." But she didn't go back and do those 20 feet of trail. Maybe she did it on the way up instead.

As I crossed the highway at Wallace Gap, my brothers-from-another-mother, Harry and Leo, came by after dropping one vehicle off at Rock Gap. Today they were hiking from Wayah Gap (where I had noted their vehicle yesterday but never saw them) to here.

All of yesterday's slackers must have been in the nearby trail town of Franklin on Day 74 because I met them all on Day 75. I parked at Rock Gap and hit the trail before sunrise. I hiked the short leg to my turn-around point on the ridge of Rocky Cove Knob, just 2.2 miles in all, and then headed back to Rock Gap. I passed a handful of NoBo hikers on the way, and at Rock Gap, there were now no fewer than eleven thru-hikers gathered there, waiting for a shuttle to Franklin. When I stopped at my van to resupply, they must have thought I was their ride. Everybody seemed to perk up and swarm toward me. I had to tell them I was no shuttle driver, just another hiker like them.

I noticed a car in the lot with MD plates. I had lived in Maryland, west of Baltimore, for 25 years up until the year before. I asked those in the crowd if it belonged to any of them. An older guy said it belonged to a young red-haired woman who had taken off hiking south.

I wasted no time with my quick restock, wished the crowd good luck, and headed south on the long leg of the day. I reached the Rock Gap Shelter, which is just a quarter mile away, at about 9:30, where I met the last two hikers lingering there, packing up and talking with one another. One was a middle-aged woman named 'Blessed Child' and the other was a hiker (I'm not sure of his trail name but it might be 'UK hiker') from Bristol, England. I was hoping to talk some football—soccer to Americans. I had become a fan a dozen years ago when my daughter showed great skill at the game. I became a soccer dad and followed her career right through high school. Unfortunately, UK hiker was not a football fan at all. They both headed out, and I wrote an entry in the register and then headed on up the hill.

Just as I was coming back to the trail, the red headed woman was coming down, headed back to her car. I said I knew she was from Maryland and we struck up a conversation. She was from Frederick, just 30 miles west of where I lived and really close to the AT. It turned out that she was 'Gingersnap' who did her thru-hike last year. Now she was a park ranger/law enforcement student at a government installation in Franklin. She was set to graduate May 9th and still didn't have any job lined up. She was here leaving Trail Magic further up the trail; it turned out to be a half mile up from the shelter. She said she wanted to hike the Pacific Crest Trail next, but first needed to work for a while in order to save up money. She was very talkative and seemed to enjoy our conversation, but we both had places to go (she had a class), so we cut it off and headed our separate ways.

I learned that she was posting on Trail Journals. A week or so later, I also learned that her photo appeared on the cover of the then current (March-April

2012) AT Journeys magazine, official magazine of the Appalachian Trail Conservancy. On the cover, she appeared with five other hikers at Woods Hole Hostel, and Michael and Neville are also in the photo.

In the next few hundred yards of trail, another thru-hiker passed me. We only chatted briefly. He told me how great Gingersnap's food was and I thanked him. I barely remembered this young dark-haired slender fellow, but he sure did remember me. Another story for later, from up north.

I arrived at Gingersnap's trail magic station just as Johannes from Munich, Germany arrived, so we chatted as we pulled down the container of homemade, still warm brownies and sweet bread. There was a log book in the basket too, which we both signed. Since I had my van with me, I would normally not take food from these Trail Magic stashes, but in this case, I couldn't resist taking a brownie. Wow, it was melt-in-your-mouth delicious home-baked goodness. Johannes, by the way, would feature in another interesting tale from up north.

It was already apparent that the hiker count was going to be huge that day. One of the eleven at the parking lot said that 200 people had signed in at Springer on March 15th alone (obviously, he must have been one of them). In the end, my rough count (I lost track of the exact number) was 63 north-bound hikers.

I hiked ten miles south in cloudy, foggy weather with a tiny bit of drizzle and one shower serious enough to make me put on my poncho. The hike was largely on very smooth footing with very gradual slopes, good for making fast time. The only exception was the tough ascent and descent of Albert Mountain, which has a fire tower on top. The stairway up the tower was open but a hatch to the observation level was locked. The view was totally socked in with fog so I didn't even bother climbing it.

The weather improved and so I had great views on the way back. Big Spring Shelter, practically on the trail near the tower, was a complete zoo—an overcrowded barrio, a magnificent thru-hiker metropolis, a tent city. The cheap shack-like, particle-board shelter itself was crammed, and at least two dozen tents were scattered about the grounds. I passed hikers hauling branches and sticks up the trail to feed their fires. What a menagerie! Beyond that, there wasn't much but easy trail without views, until my turn-around point: a very short 25-foot side trail to a grand vista at a rock outcrop on the ridge of Little Ridgepole Mountain.

I checked Gingersnap's trail magic basket on the way back and found it well picked through. No brownies left, only a few sweet cakes. Back at the parking lot, I made an attempt to hike to the now dead, but formerly second largest Tulip Poplar tree in the east, but the trail was descending into a hollow and seemed very long (it turns out it was only 0.7 miles to the dead tree, as I learned later). I'm a lover of big trees, but I'd had a long day—more than 25 miles—so I gave up and turned around.

That was a full day. Day 76 turned out to be just as eventful. I passed a packed Standing Indian Shelter just a mile from the start and barely stopped to photograph the shelter. From there it was a steady gradual climb on an old road 1,000 feet up Standing Indian Mountain. A couple came out of the shelter soon after

I passed it and were following me up the mountain at almost exactly my pace, chatting as they walked. It was a bit of an awkward situation. I either had to join them and butt in on their conversation or change my pace. I decided to pick my pace up a little and soon they were out of sight, though they started catching up with me again on the way down the other side. Again I increased my pace on the totally smooth trail.

I didn't see them again until the next shelter at Carter Gap. And the story at that shelter only added to the interest. I was taking my usual photos of this shelter, one of the less easily photographed because it faces a tangle of woods, when someone from the deep shade inside asked if I was 'Seeks It'. It turns out it was 'Gutsy', who I'd met between Clingman's Dome and Newfound Gap as she was hiking northbound with 'Patches' and two guys they had just met.

Why was she here, much farther south? It turns out that Gutsy decided to get off the trail after a heart-wrenching phone conversation with her young granddaughter who missed her terribly. Apparently she's very much a hands-on grandma. She said she 'has them' two days a week, referring to her grandkids. So if she had given up her NoBo thru-hike, what was she doing here on this section of trail that she'd already done this year? She was with two friends from Florida who had begun their thru-hike March 18th. She was just offering them her hands-on support and advice and encouragement. Gutsy, it turns out, did a thru-hike back in 1996. Now she was hiking with 'Navigator' and 'JK,' who were working their way into shape. Having started with about 8 miles a day, they had worked their way up to twelve.

Navigator, I was surprised to learn, is Sandra Friend, the foremost authority on the Florida Trail. She'd written fifteen guidebooks about Florida, including the regularly updated Florida Trail Guide, and other miscellaneous books. She has a premier hiking website at 'FloridaHikes.com'. JK is her husband and her co-author on her more recent works. They had met just four months earlier, during the annual 'Big O' hike that circumnavigates Lake Okeechobee in south Florida.

It turns out that Gutsy is Sandra's hiking 'idol', at least in regards to AT hiking. They first met in 1995 through an early internet email list called "AT-L" and shared a hotel room at the ALDHA (Appalachian Long Distance Hikers Association) Gathering that fall in Carlisle PA, where they also met a number of early AT luminaries such as Earl Shaffer, Beverly "Maine Rose" Hugo, and Warren Doyle. Gutsy seemed like the kind of person who had other accomplishments that would be interesting to know about, but she was too modest to volunteer the information. About all I learned was that she has a son who lives in Fairbanks, AK.

While we were talking at Carter Gap Shelter, the couple came in who had been tailing me. Turns out, they had met Gutsy, Navigator, and JK previously, staying at the same shelter at some point—even more connections. So soon I was talking with them also. They were obviously in seriously good shape—doing 20 miles that day to get to Franklin (they started the trail on March 25th). Their trail names were 'Smoke Hawk' and 'Snake Runner'. Snake Runner is as short as Smoke Hawk is tall. Standing face to face she's looking at the middle of his chest. Her real name is Kylie and, before the end of her successful thru-hike, she changed her trail name to '4'10" to Maine.' She ran marathons. Smoke Hawk didn't admit to any pre-hike training, but it was clear he was pretty physically active, and a mentally tough guy.

Some of this information I learned at my turn-around point at the vista on Little Ridgepole where we all met again. It was bittersweet letting my five new trail friends go on north while I had to backtrack alone. But I had a feeling I would run into them again. Even Gutsy suggested she might get back on the trail farther north later in the year.

I never met Gutsy again, and I didn't meet JK and Navigator again on the AT. But when I went down to their home turf and hiked the Florida Trail in 2015, I hiked with them for several full days, had dinner with them, and got to know them much better.

At the end of the day, I also came through a patch of a southern delicacy that I had been hoping to try—wild leeks, called "ramps" here in the south. I picked and cleaned a handful and sampled them in various cold recipes and salads over the next couple of days. The flavor is a distinctive combination of wild garlic and watercress; a strong clear flavor worthy of its reputation as a spring treat.

The next day I passed another dense growth of ramps. That day's hike would take me within sniffing distance of the GA-NC border at Bly Gap. Most of the trail was fairly easy woods walking, but there were some tough short climbs that greeted the north-bound hiker fresh from Georgia. I had heard multiple accounts of the toughness of this "welcome to North Carolina" gauntlet; and I had to agree with these thru-hikers. The double-step ascent up to Courthouse Bald from Bly Gap is a serious challenge, not because of the elevation change, but because of the steepness. You start grinding as soon as you

Ramps, a delicacy found in abundance in eastern North America from Quebec to Georgia and west to Illinois. Little known fact: the city of Chicago is named for them—the plant is called shikaakwa (chicagou) in the Miami-Illinois language.

F.I.T. Wilderness 71

leave Bly Gap, and there's a false summit at Sharp Top—a short level section that leads the hiker to believe the worst is over—but is followed by an even tougher climb to a nice vista on the not-at-all-bald summit of Courthouse Bald.

As I said, after that, the trail eases up some. You drop down to Sassafras Gap and then negotiate a more gradual climb up to a pretty ridge walk with winter views of Ravenrock to your left. There is a half-mile side trail going west to the top of this impressive cliff, which I didn't take, though I should have.

Next you reach Muskrat Creek Shelter. I arrived there to find it empty—a rarity in this season of thru-hiker frenzy. I had a few minutes to read the log book, and found a typical cryptic entry from long-ago trail friend Lasher (WV→GA), whom I met twice near Blacksburg, VA back in early January. He had passed through here on February 28th, almost to his goal. Good for you, Lasher!

Then a young woman on a NoBo thru-hike arrived to take a break. She had red curly locks tucked back into a pony-tail. 'Fire Fox' was her trail name. Why is it that every female hiker with red hair gets a trail name that refers to it? We had a nice chat before I moved on.

The final story for that day was about the weather and is the fifth in the ongoing saga of finding favor with the Weather Gods. I had studied the weather forecast computer models and expected a strong chance of showers in the afternoon. I had started my hike early, in hopes of beating the storm. Thunder began rumbling over the ridges soon after noon, as I made my turn-around at Bly Gap. It sprinkled intermittently as the storms grew and multiplied. Angry black clouds gathered and loomed and dumped buckets of rain, shrouding the mountains all around me, seemingly in every direction. Thunder became frequent and lightning scary. Yet somehow the trail where I hiked stayed dry. Finally, in just the last 100 yards before I reached my vehicle, the skies opened up. If I had arrived five minutes later, I would have been soaked to the bone. I hurtled into my vehicle only superficially wet. This time the deluge went on and on; a gully-washer, a blinding downpour that wouldn't let up for a couple of hours. Such times are the big trials for true backpackers. You either stop and get out your poncho, throw up your tent, or just slog on, getting utterly drenched.

On Day 78, I crossed into Georgia and met my second AT Ridge Runner. Ridge Runners are trail angels of a special sort, paid by the local maintaining club to roam the trail, educating hikers on "leave no trace" ethics, and helping hikers by telling them about the weather, water sources, and trail conditions. They do maintenance, clean-up, pick up litter, and generally keep the shelters and privies in good order. My first encounter with one was a more anonymous meeting in Great Smoky Mountains National Park.

Today's second encounter happened on a ridge called As Knob. I passed a group of about 8 hikers who looked to be on a club hike. The last of these turned out to be Rhea Patrick, the Georgia Ridge Runner responsible for the entire 75 miles in the state. My embarrassing face blindness caught me on the way back when I passed him standing alone beside the trail looking worn out and bedraggled with his hat and shoes off. From a distance, I made a judgment that this was somebody

I hadn't met yet. So even when he spoke to me, saying "coming back the other way, eh?" the only thought that came to mind was 'how did he know that?' A minute later, after he was well behind me and probably stupefied by my noncommittal response, I realized who it was. I wanted to crawl into a hole and disappear forever.

This section of trail from Dicks Creek Gap north to Bly Gap has quite a few up and downs that aren't difficult trail but are fairly steep. I counted 44 NoBo hikers on the trail. I used a new method to keep count today: I picked up a small pebble each time I passed someone.

At Plumorchard Gap Shelter I met a couple of young guys getting ready to head out for the day, then I met them again at the state line on the way back. Their names were Anthony and Tomás, both from Blacksburg, VA. Tomás took my photo, but I failed to take a photo of them. I was too caught up in the conversation. Tomás is of Brazilian ancestry and was carrying a full-sized good quality camera. His dark hair and olive skin set off those uniquely Brazilian light hazel eyes. Anthony, on the other hand, seemed an American melting pot type, with light brown curly hair. He was carrying a small flask of whiskey with him for evening sipping; said he preferred that to beer.

Rhea Patrick, the Georgia Ridge Runner.

Tomás and Anthony were waiting for trail names to pick them rather than the other way around. That's the true thru-hiker way, yet I think most people choose to pre-empt the random process so as to avoid being tagged with a name they don't like. I chose my name the previous year so that I could start signing trail registers with it. Doing day hikes in the off season, you don't meet many people, so there's not much chance of initiating the in-depth interaction that might produce a genuine trail name. I figured if the moment was right, I could claim that my trail name 'Seeks It' refers to the unknown true trail name that I was still waiting for.

For the last few years I've leaned toward the name 'Hiking Hermit,' which is the name of one of my blogs. But that is also my own choosing, not something bestowed by a fellow hiker.

Because of a lot of rain, Day 79 was a short day. And it was the perfect day to meet the NoBo-hiking Rainwater family. This gang of Mom, Dad, and 15- and

F.I.T. Wilderness

9-year-old boys had set up their own hike-dedicated website and Facebook page that I had been following, so it was a real pleasure to run into them in person. They were headed to Hiawassee for a couple of zero days. The two boys are named Forrest and River, and being a research meteorologist, I couldn't stop myself from proffering the bad joke that they ought to have another kid and name him 'Acid,' given the condition of some of the high mountain forests they would pass through in the Smokies. It brought a laugh, thankfully. Turns out the Rainwaters never made it to the Smokies. As the weather warmed, they sent a box of winter clothing home and then got caught in a late season snowstorm and cold spell. It was then that they made a family decision to change their six-month vacation plans in favor of something a little more family friendly.

I only hiked 7.9 miles that day, south to the Deep Gap Shelter and back. Deep Gap Shelter is located in a gap called … wait for it … Deep Gap, the 'John Smith' of the gap world.

I had already hiked Deep Gap between Mt. Rogers and Elk Garden in Southwest Virginia, an ecologically sensitive flat area where they've banned camping due to resource damage.

I had parked at the Deep Gap Trailhead near Franklin, NC, and hiked a leg north from there one day and south the next.

Then, too, I remember hiking through Deep Gap near Beauty Spot on the TN/NC border. It seemed a strange name at the time because it was a pretty shallow gap.

No, wait. Deep Gap was 12.7 miles north of Hot Springs, NC. It was the next gap south from Allen Gap.

Actually, Deep Gap was the valley between Max Patch and Snowbird Mountain. There's a shelter there too, beside a creek about a tenth of a mile down an old woods road. But that shelter is called Groundhog Creek Shelter.

Wait. They removed the shelter at Deep Gap (Virginia) due to overuse and abuse, and it now sits in the Town Park in Damascus.

Yup, I had hiked through at least six different Deep Gaps already. I think that would turn out to be all of them. In New England, they don't have Gaps, they have 'Notches.'

Day 80 was a much longer day. I did almost exactly a full marathon, 26.19 miles, with lots of gaps of various names and even one 'swag'. By somebody's rule book, the 'Swag of the Blue Ridge' is apparently too wide to qualify as a gap.

My marathon took 12 hours and, besides the gaps and the swag, it involved 3 major mountains, each with about 1,000-foot climbs and each with good vistas from the top: Rocky Mountain, Tray Mountain, and Kelly Knob. I passed 27 southbound hikers on my leg north, including a group of boy scouts out on a training hike, getting ready for a trip to Philmont. And I passed 67 northbound hikers on my leg south. That doesn't include any who had already settled at Tray Mountain Shelter before I passed it at about 5:00 pm. That number was probably huge, given the huge number I'd seen camped at the summit of Rocky Mountain when I passed there about 7:00 pm. Despite this, the only real conversation I had that day was with 'Brightflower,' whom I'd expected to run into after noticing her post on the Rainwater's Facebook page. She and her husband (who was farther up the trail) were going to camp at Addis Gap. The trail footing was fairly good in most places, except for a few muddy seeps and a few bedrock sections and sections with steep rock steps. In all, I finished feeling reasonably good, considering the length of the hike.

I was now just fifty miles from Springer. The fresh 'newbie' attitudes of some of the hikers was charming. The atmosphere reminded me of my first weeks as a freshman at the gigantic, impersonal Penn State University. Everybody's a little timid, eager, trying to establish their niche and learn to fit in to their new, challenging environment. I heard debates about how much water to carry up the next mountain. Standing at the summit of Tray Mountain, overlooking the expansive vista, one hiker remarked, "Now that I'm doing this, I'm wondering why everybody doesn't want to." Eighty percent of these people would not make it, and yet the enthusiasm (or bravado) was rampant.

On the other hand, I passed a lot of huffing-puffing-struggling hikers and a few hobbling dogs, climbing mountains with pained looks on their faces, asking how much farther to the top. The poor dogs just licked my hand to get some salt. Having hiked about 1,300 miles of AT already that year, I suddenly felt like a hardened veteran by comparison. The people-watching would only get more entertaining in the coming days.

On Day 81, the weather was downright hot. I passed a lush little garden spot where spring was on full display: a noisy cascade on a south facing slope adorned with yellow flowering greenery. It was the kind of spot that invited you to stay, soak up the warm rays of the spring sun, and revel in the newly awakening season.

At 73 pebbles, today's NoBo hiker count was starting to stretch the pocket of my cargo shorts. It has to be remembered that I would hike south into this flux for only half the day. This afternoon as I was returning north, another batch of thru-hikers whom I would never meet were 'filling in' the trail behind me. The atmosphere here was certainly not like a New York City street where people studiously ignore one another. Here everybody greeted everybody else without exception, and almost always with energy and enthusiasm. I have to admit that saying 'how are you' and 'I'm doin' well, thanks' seventy-three times in one morning didn't seem as tedious as it might sound. Every face, every gear combination, had a visual story to add variation to the sameness of the verbal exchange.

Next day I would cross paths with John Muir and meet a good old fashioned roaming preacher named 'King Tutt' with Trail Magic food on tables and lawn chairs lined up to give his sermon to the unwashed.

We'll talk about Muir first. On September 22, 1867 at about noon, renowned wilderness advocate John Muir crossed over the Blue Ridge, of what he called the Allegheny Mountains, on his 'Thousand Mile Walk to the Gulf', traveling from Kentucky to the Florida Keys following the "wildest, leafiest, and least trodden way I could find." He was 29 years old and had just recovered from a near fatal accident at a sawmill in Indiana, which included six weeks of blindness.

"This affliction has driven me to the sweet fields. God has to nearly kill us sometimes, to teach us lessons," he wrote.

Dan Steyer of Oberlin College, Ohio, used Muir's personal journal entries to reconstruct the route Muir took. He published his findings in the John Muir Newsletter, Winter 2010-11 issue. His conclusion was that Muir had crossed the ridge via the 'Union Turnpike,' later called the 'Logan Turnpike,' that passed over Tesnatee Gap.

As I crossed over Tesnatee Gap for the second time on March 27th at 2:37 pm, I met 'King Tutt.' Trail Angel and Reverend Richard Tuttle, now of Nudge Ministries, Bethlehem, GA, was there with a handful of his congregation and a white canopy over his coolers and the spread of goodies on the table. He is the kind of 'listen first' evangelist who could win over hikers stopping only for the food. His way of 'witnessing' was all about respect for the individual and their views. Good for him, and bravo. The food wasn't bad either.

On this day I also had to make the 1.2-mile side trip, including 700-foot elevation drop, to the Whitley Gap Shelter. This was by far the most inaccessible shelter on the trail.

I gave up counting hikers today. My back was wearing out from bending over to pick up pebbles. Suffice it to say that there were plenty.

Day 83 had a hiker count of 83—not by pebbles but by memory, which probably means I missed some. The hike took me over rugged Blood Mountain with its CCC constructed stone shelter right at the rocky summit. I also visited the only piece of the AT that goes through a building at the Walâsi'yï Interpretive Center at Frogtown Gap. I do not call this gap Neel's Gap because that name is a pure example of white Americans trampling ancient native tradition. When the gap was named for surveyor W.R. Neel in 1922, probably by the Feds, and probably without consultation of anyone who lived in the area, it was after bulldozers had cut a highway through this gap following an 'old Indian trail'. Those 'Indians' had long ago given the gap its proper name. Walâsi'yï means 'Place of the Great Frog,' and this ancient first people's trail was steeped in layers of sacred lore and tradition; enough so that the white folks who had settled in the area named the place Frogtown Gap.

The name originates in the Cherokee legend of *"Âgän-uni'tsï's quest for the Ulûñsû'tî,"* an oral story that had been passed down through the generations by the tribe's greatest story tellers.

Âgän-uni'tsï was a powerful magician and medicine man who was sent on a search to find the great serpent Uktena. Uktena bore a magical blazing star-gem called the Ulûñsû'tî in the center of his forehead. The gem could work great wonders, but everyone knew that meeting Uktena meant certain death. Even his breath could kill. But Âgän-uni'tsï scoffed at the people, saying his magic was powerful.

Uktena was known to haunt the dark high passes of the mountains of Cherokee country, so Âgän-uni'tsï began to search them, one by one, starting in the north and working his way south. At the first pass, he came upon a monstrous

AT goes under roof at Walâsi'yï. View is looking southbound toward the back of the building.

black snake. He laughed at it as something too small to notice. At the next gap, he found a great water moccasin, the largest ever seen, but again he told the people it was nothing. At the third gap, he found a greensnake. When he showed it to the people, they ran away in fear, but he was not concerned. Next, he came to U'täwagûn'ta, which is the Bald Mountain. There he found the great diya'hälï, a lizard. Although it was large and terrible, it was not what he was looking for, so he moved on. Going further south to Walâsi'yï, the Place of the Great Frog, he found the frog squatting in the gap. When the people who came to see it were frightened, like the others, and ran away from the monster, he mocked them for being afraid of a frog; and he moved on to the next gap. This was Duniskwa' lgûñ'yï, the Gap of the Forked Antler, known today as Chimney Tops. He searched the enchanted lake of Atagâ'hï, where he encountered giant turtles and water serpents, and two huge sun perches who rushed at him but did not harm him. Next, he went to Tlanusi'yï, The Leech Place on the Hiwassee River, where he faced its resident house-sized leech who could sweep people to the bottom of the river and consume them. On he went, trying other places, always going south, until, at last, on Gahû'tï, which is the Cohutta Range of the Great Smokies, he came upon the great serpent Uktena asleep.

The legend winds its way forward through many dangerous and heroic deeds, building tension to a fantastic climax in the best tradition of oral story-telling. In the end, Âgän-uni'tsï did acquire the gem, but the Great Frog did not figure in the

F.I.T. Wilderness

rest of this story. His role in Cherokee mythology was that he could eat the sun. Whenever there came an eclipse, the people would dance and shout and scream and howl and bang on drums, making as much racket as they possibly could in order to scare him away before he swallowed it.

Two unusual incidents highlighted my traverse through this place. First, my end-of-day return ascent of Blood Mountain put me up against my 'wall.' This had happened to me once before, on a long-distance bike ride back in the 80's, so I knew what it was. Very suddenly I got so exhausted that I literally could not walk another step. I sat down on a rock and ate some Oreo cookies. Two minutes later I was fine. It's amazing how suddenly that 'wall' hits, how intense it is (every aspect of your body, including brain function, deteriorates noticeably) and how instantly the intake of food restores normalcy.

The other incident came as I walked back to the parking area down the road from the store at Walâsi'yï. I could hear a commotion as I approached a road-side parking area that had signs saying it should only be used for emergencies. People started running past me coming down from the store. At the parking area, a car full of genuine country 'hillbilly' types had stopped, and somehow one of them—an older guy with a bushy salt-and-pepper beard and a pot belly—had slipped off the steep edge of the precipice and had taken a serious fall, rolling over rocks for thirty feet and probably breaking bones. I could see him down there. I didn't see blood but he seemed unable to move. He was talking, they said, and minutes later, an ambulance roared up and took over the scene, forcing us gawkers to move on. I have to assume they got him up and to the hospital okay.

Day 84 got me to within twenty miles of Springer. Among the newbie, fully-geared northbounders whom I passed, there was an ever-increasing crop of huffing-puffing struggling folk (of all ages) with huge, heavy shiny-new packs, crisp boots, immaculate gaiters, and brand-name outfitter 'stuff' overflowing and dangling every which way.

What is it about the mystique of the Appalachian Trail that seems to send otherwise reasonable people's common sense into a tailspin? Yes, there are the fit ones, fast moving, getting on with business. "You ... you'll make it" I wanted to say a couple of times. But, from among the throngs, only a couple. And finally, there is the AT's version of Venice Beach, the 'freak show'. I passed a guy with a bongo today, and not a tiny little one either. Yesterday it was funny stuffed duck hats. Maybe some of them were just there for the party and planned to head back home next week.

In stark contrast to the gear-posers were 'The Sarasotas'—a salt-of-the-earth couple, hiking with plain old cotton duffel bags carried by a strap around their neck and shoulder. One of the bags had a crude hand-stitched seam repair. In those duffels were wool blankets.

Here were a couple of throw-backs from Granny Gatewood, circa 1955. I wasn't ten steps from my vehicle this morning when down the trail they came. Today was the fifth time we had crossed paths, because, like me, they were headed south. They had started in Franklin, took a bus from their home in Sarasota, Florida to

"The Sarasotas" heading southbound, back home to Florida.

get there. Their goal was to walk back to Sarasota, so they would keep walking south beyond Springer. Rather than take the Pinhoti and Alabama Connector and Florida Trail, which was what I would do in late 2014 and early 2015, they planned to make the trip by road walks. They said they now had the money to buy some better gear and they wanted to do more AT hiking. They're naturals—friendly, happy, at peace with themselves. It will be great to have them back on the trail.

Day 85, Friday, March 30th, was my penultimate day hike before reaching Springer. It was a calm sunny morning, already in the 60's at sunrise. I was out early enough to get a good photo of the sunrise from a vista near Woody Gap. Spring had arrived in the North Georgia Mountains. The trees were opening their buds, beginning to show little nubs of green. On the forest floor, the ubiquitous foot-high umbrella-shaped Mayapple leaves covered the ground, I saw wild miniature iris in bloom. In one place the trail was lined with the red-flowering eastern Columbine. And the birds were singing up a storm.

I did eleven trail miles that day, and that left nine for my Springer Summit Day. It would have been a total zoo here on any day during the height of the NoBo bubble anyway, but today was a Saturday. In the afternoon, the parking area

Sunrise through the still bare trees near Woody Gap.

F.I.T. Wilderness 79

on FS 42 was overflowing, with cars lining the road for more than half a mile on either side. I doubt that I was out of sight of people for even one second today.

Similarly, the road crossing and parking area at Three Forks was overflowing. That is a popular day-hike trailhead because the trail there follows a significant mountain stream, Long Creek, with some beautiful cascades, including impressive Long Creek Falls. It had poured down rain for four hours last night—to the campers' chagrin, but to the delight of lovers of waterfalls.

The Georgia Adventure Group had set up a Trail Magic canopy where the trail passes near (but out of sight of) the Hickory Flats Cemetery. This is the liveliest cemetery I know, with a picnic pavilion, overnight camping welcome, and a rest room. Yet the cemetery itself mostly consists of simple natural unhewn standing stones with no readable inscriptions.

Eastern Columbine along the AT in north Georgia.

Of course, Springer Mountain was the highlight. The trail from the parking area 0.9 miles up to the summit was half underwater (or mud) due to the overnight rains. But there's an indescribable feeling when you get to the summit, almost like being on hallowed ground. Everybody and his uncle gets a shot of themselves with the first white blaze and the 1934 George Noble-designed bronze plaque, showing an intrepid hiker with an old canvas pack strapped to his back, a broad-brimmed hat, a hatchet on his belt, and his eyes on the horizon. At the same time, you turn around and there's a fine view of the flatlands to the south.

It was about 3:45 pm as I was hanging out at that summit plaque, when a guy came by with a serious piece of GPS equipment, complete with antenna sticking up toward the sky. He said he was going to start hiking the trail for the AT Conservancy the following morning, recording a high-quality track. It was a paid contract job and he was looking forward to the challenge of thru-hiking with his ordinary gear as well as the expensive professional GPS. I asked him if he would take a moment to take my picture with the plaque, and he agreed.

We didn't chat for long, but his name was Frank Looper, trail name 'Nightwalker'.

The following day I did zero official trail miles, but hiked 16½ miles anyway—out and back on the approach trail from Amicalola Falls State Park. For a lover of

The first white blaze and 1934 George Noble plaque atop Springer Mountain, GA, taken March 30.

waterfalls, as I am, this turned out to be one of the most memorable hikes of the whole trail.

What a spectacular setting this waterfall has. It's as much a delight for its full-access walkway, complete with 605 steps, as for the falls itself. It was fascinating to look at, and I could have lingered a long time, but it was chilly there in the morning with a mist and a surprisingly strong valley drainage wind. It was much warmer once the trail took me up out of the valley and I began following the ridges toward Springer. The rest of the hike was fairly easy, with quite a few level sections, despite eventually getting me up 1,200 more feet from the top of the falls to Springer Mountain.

It turned into a seriously hot day, with temperatures getting into the upper 80's and full sunshine. At least it wasn't too humid. I got to the summit in four hours, at 11:30, and was able to take a photo of every page of the summit register log book, which only dated back to March 18th and was already roughly half full. Then I headed back down, consuming almost all of the 2 liters of water I had brought. Even the return trip had some short significant climbs. Back at the falls, it was mid-afternoon on a beautiful Sunday, so the place was a total madhouse, but I still was fully captivated by the waterfall. Again, it's the walkway/bridge giving you a perfect vantage point to appreciate the falls as much as the falls itself that makes it so special; totally worth the $5 park admission fee.

F.I.T. Wilderness

Fresh, squeaky-clean hikers, with faces displaying emotions that ranged from ecstatic to misty-eyed to scared, were lined up for their photo-op at the stone archway that is the official start of the Approach Trail behind the visitor center. Each one was surrounded by a cluster of family and friends, soaking up the attention and last-minute hugs and kisses. What a place of excitement and dreams. On one side of that arch was civilization—the world they knew. On the other side awaited adventure, hardship, and even danger—a world of discovery in the wild unknown.

Arch at the start of the Approach Trail behind the Visitor Center at Amicalola Falls State Park

PART TWO

Northbound with Spring

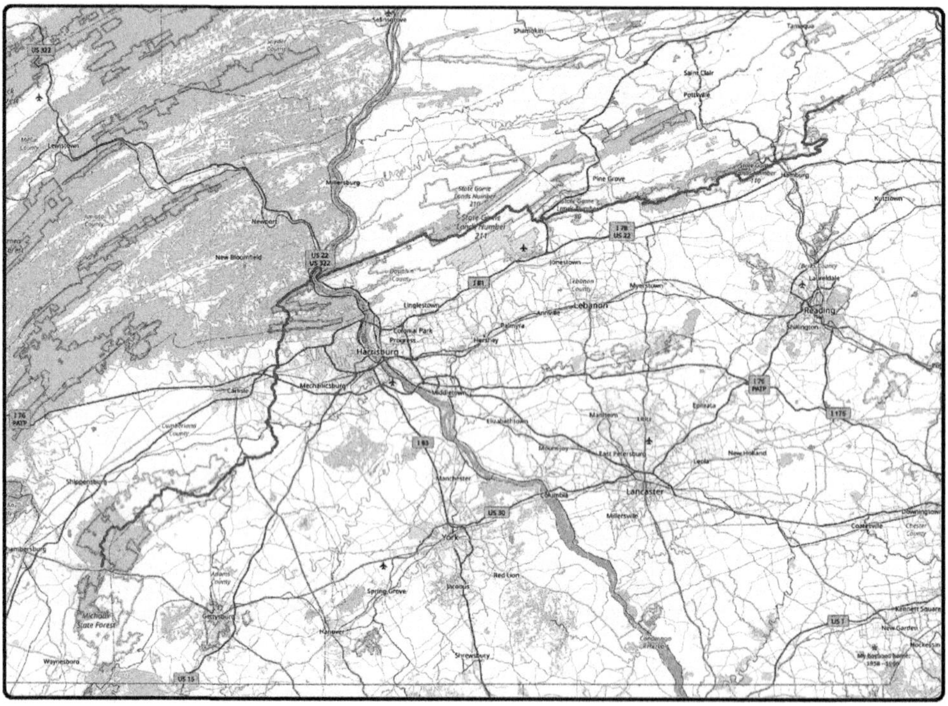
US 322
Lewistown
Millersburg
Newport
New Bloomfield
US 22
US 322
Shamokin
Tamaqua
Saint Clair
Pottsville
Pine Grove
Kutztown
I 78
US 22
Jonestown
I 81
Linglestown
Colonial Park
Progress
Harrisburg
Hershey
Palmyra
Annville
Lebanon
Myerstown
Reading
Shillington
Carlisle
Mechanicsburg
Middletown
I 76
PATP
Cumberland County
I 83
Elizabethtown
Manheim
Ephrata
Mount Joy
East Petersburg
Leola
New Holland
I 176
Shippensburg
Manchester
Columbia
Lancaster
Millersville
US 30
York
Coatesville
Chester County
Downingtown
Adams County
Spring Grove
Jacoous
Red Lion
Michaux State Forest
Gettysburg
Hanover
Waynesboro
Shrewsbury
US 15
US 1
Kennett Square
New Garden
Hockessin

CHAPTER 7

Caledonia State Park, PA to Allentown Shelter, PA
April 8 - 25; 157.8 trail miles one way

I would take only four days off to relocate from the southern end of the trail to Caledonia State Park in southern Pennsylvania. These were the home stomping grounds of Earl V. Shaffer, the first person to thru-hike the Appalachian Trail. Before World War II broke out, Earl had hoped to hike the trail with his neighbor and close friend Walter Winemiller. They both entered the war, serving in some of the worst fighting in the Pacific. Walter was killed at Iwo Jima. Earl wrote:

"Those four and a half years of Army service, more than half of it in combat areas of the Pacific, had left me confused and depressed. Perhaps this trip would be the answer."

Appropriately, it was Memorial Day, 1948, when Earl hiked through Caledonia State Park. The previous evening his father met him on the trail and drove him home, the only night during his thru-hike that he did not spend on the trail. It was a Sunday, and "crowds of people were everywhere ... hundreds of people were picnicking or playing games as I passed through to Quarry Gap Shelter." There Earl met another life-long friend, Woody Baughman, and they hiked together for several days.

It was also a Sunday and also a holiday—Easter Sunday, the eighth of April—when my footprints merged with Earl's in Caledonia State Park. The trail south of the park had been rerouted in the 1980's, but here in the park and northward it had remained on its original route. I like to think I sensed Earl's spirit as I walked the woods that day. Frank Sinatra's "Nature Boy" was number two on the pop charts that Memorial Day back in 1948, a story about meeting a young man who wandered far and wide and had gained great wisdom from his experiences.

I headed north out of the huge parking lot near several large picnic pavilions that stand right on the Appalachian Trail, and began the steep climb up Chinqua-pin Hill. Here on July 10, 1955, a bird watching enthusiast named Warren Large came huffing and puffing up the trail, trying to catch up with Emma 'Grandma' Gatewood. He had heard that this legendary woman—the first to thru-hike the AT alone—was passing through, and he wanted to ask her a few questions. They sat down on a log and talked for three straight hours.

The sense of history, the echoes of so many famous hikers, was a constant presence with me as I hiked. Their spirits all seemed alive within me, for I am old

F.I.T. Wilderness

enough to have been alive and sharing this physical world with every thru-hiker who has ever walked the trail.

It was a cold Wisconsin day in January 1948 when I was conceived. The conception was a birth control accident. Yes, in recent years, Mom and Dad had admitted that to me. Dad was still three years away from completing his graduate degree at the University of Wisconsin. They did not need the distraction of a child. But there I was; I had defied the odds. I've always felt as though some great force or strong purpose must have directed me to appear at that moment. I may never know that purpose for sure, but I know this: on April 4th, 1948, my heart was beating as strongly as the soles of Earl Shaffer's worn-out Army boots when they hit the Appalachian Trail at Mt. Oglethorpe, GA.

Then while Gene Espy was on his thru-hike between May 31 and Sept. 30, 1951, I was on the road, making a cross-country move from Wisconsin to Wilmington, Delaware, riding in the back of my dad's 1935 Chevy. We took the scenic route along the Ohio River, driving through every little river town and hamlet, as I formed my very first lasting memories. Gene Espy's thru-hike was the second one on record.

The first woman to do the whole trail in one year was Mildred Norman Ryder, who later took the trail name 'Peace Pilgrim'. Her hike was what has come to be known as a 'flip-flop'. She and her hiking companion Dick Lamb started in Springer on April 26th 1952. They hiked through Caledonia Park and on to the Susquehanna River, then 'flipped' up to Katahdin and hiked south, taking a detour to hike the entire Long Trail from the Canadian border before finishing the AT in Pennsylvania.

Mildred's hike never gained as much attention as Grandma Gatewood's, perhaps because she was a fit 44-year-old when she did her hike, and probably because she had a male companion.

Emma Gatewood's story made better drama. She was all alone. Her family didn't even know where she had gone. She hiked in tennis shoes, carrying a homemade sack draped over her shoulder. Furthermore, she was 67 years old. The press caught wind of her exploit by the time she reached Shenandoah National Park. By the time she finished, she was already a celebrity.

I've summarized what her hike means to me and to the trail in a poem I wrote, using my favorite 'tight-rhymed Fourteener' format:

Emma Gatewood: Fourteen States, the Appalachian Trail—
Two thousand miles of grueling trials. And therein lies a tale.

A test that broke much younger folk, she trekked through rain and cold—
Georgia to Maine, alone, in pain, at sixty-sev'n years old.

She hiked in Keds, and note: Instead of fancy custom pack
She stuffed her gear inside a queer old home-made denim sack.

*No bag, no tent, the year she went was nineteen-fifty-five.
It earned her fame, and some would claim she kept the Trail alive.*

*But hype aside, this truth abides: What Grandma Gatewood did
Was conquer fear and pioneer a path for countless kids.*

When I got to Quarry Gap Shelter, the place looked more like a country cottage than a hiker lean-to. It came complete with hanging baskets full of blooming pansies, a white picket fence, and a park bench. The nearby stream was neatly lined with uniform-sized rounded stones on each side, and daffodils were in bloom along its banks. The shelter caretaker, Jim 'Innkeeper' Stauch, showed up most days, judging by the entries in the log book, and he obviously applied a lot of TLC. Though he wouldn't admit it, I'm quite sure he had a rivalry going with the shelter caretaker at Tumbling Run just up the trail.

Quarry Gap Shelter was where Dorothy Laker spent the night of July 6-7, 1957. Dorothy became the second woman to solo thru-hike the AT. Meanwhile, Emma Gatewood was back out on the trail too, and not far behind her. Now 69 years old, Emma passed Dorothy a few days later, and, according to Emma's journal, they crossed paths many times that day but never spoke a word to one another. Was there a sense of rivalry there? I think so. Despite being twice Dorothy's age, Grandma Gatewood finished her thru-hike in 143 days that year. It took Dorothy Laker 162.

Day 89 was a dreary day and I was not finding inspiration on the trail, so I dug deep into my gloomy mood to write something interesting for my blog. Here's what I wrote.

"Monday April 9th.

"Curmudgeon stomped the woods. Geezer legs, gray weathered fence posts, groaned like old wood through another day.

"Numb toes, too often stubbed, met rocky bits where each foot placement needs to be custom-fashioned. Old man Pennsylvania serves up lots of these. It's nasty, weathered trail, hard hiked.

"'Rock makes for a durable footpath.' That's the official PA guidebook's answer to critics. 'Lame-ass policy, makes us *both* lame,' the old codger muttered under his breath, 'lazy a-holes could at least re-arrange some of the rocks … get rid of the damn toe-stubbing spikes.'

'Rocksylvania' gets a lot of press. 'Flatsylvania,' not so much. What PA extracts from the hiker in the way of boot killing footing it returns by having some of the smallest accumulated elevation change of anywhere on the trail.

"Photos? Get real," my blog declared. (I usually wrote the text around the best of my photos.) "I could show you parking lots. I could show you road crossings. I could show you rocks. *Of course* I could show you rocks. But I'm in grouch mode today. Grinch mode. I'll begrudge you just one photo: (I showed the twin lean-tos of Toms Run Shelters under a stone-gray sky.) This serves as a decent halfway landmark—mid-point of the AT—if only the nitpickers would stop worrying about a tenth of a mile here or there."

In 2011, the Appalachian Trail was 2,181.0 miles long (official distance according to the data book), and the halfway point was about a quarter mile north of Toms Run Shelters.

In 2012, the Appalachian Trail got lengthened somewhere down south and became 2,184.2 miles long (again, the official distance according to the data book), and the halfway point was about a quarter mile south of Toms Run Shelters.

So the old man milled about Toms Run shelters for a bit, befuddled and grumbling under his breath. And then he trudged back the way he had come.

The iconic 'ceremonial' half-way marker post.

My mood improved on day 90, but not until afternoon when the weather warmed up. I parked at the Pine Grove Furnace store (closed until April 21st), just down the road from the Appalachian Trail Museum (only open half a day on Saturdays and Sundays until Memorial Day). I hiked south into more of the scrubby woods typical of this part of the state, with lousy, rocky, low-nutrient soil. I passed the official halfway marker post and took a selfie, passed 'Halfway Spring', which seems all but abandoned, and then ascended a side slope through what has to be the ugliest section of AT I had encountered to date.

What do I mean by ugly? It looked like a bombed-out war zone. Worse, it was almost completely dominated by various invasive species, including multiflora rose, Japanese barberry, and mono-culture stands of tree-of-heaven—a badly invasive, bad smelling, super-fast-growing native of China that spreads not just by seed but by root suckers. Volunteers had been trying to eradicate the trees, so most of them were dead, blanched white ghosts—trashy standing sticks poking up through brambles and weeds and their own squalid, broken-off and blown-down slash.

Heading south, I went to revisit Toms Run Shelters on a not-just-for-foot-traffic gated road, then back to the park.

The leg north from the store took me through Pine Grove Furnace State Park, which was more like what I had expected from Amicalola Falls State Park. The landscape was pretty, but the park's natural assets were secondary to the historic old furnace and iron works and to the development of trails and lakes with sandy beaches and picnic areas. All in all, a fine getaway for locals, but nothing to go out of your way to see.

The AT then follows paved and/or smooth pea-gravel trails for more than half a mile before ascending on an old woods road. This part of the trail is a popular day hike, the destination being Pole Steeple (which, surprisingly, is not within the state park).

Pole Steeple is a pillar of rocks that is billed as the second most spectacular AT viewpoint in Pennsylvania. Unlike Pole Steeple, the other one is right on the trail (and was coming up later). But visiting Pole Steeple required a half mile side trip off the AT, and I chose not to take the detour only because I hadn't done my homework beforehand. Someday I need to go back, both for that and the AT museum.

By Day 91, my hiking joy had been fully restored. There were dogwoods and redbuds in bloom, even though today was chilly with showers of grainy ice. The heaviest of these showers even accumulated—just a little reminder that I wasn't in Georgia anymore. I traversed three bits of high ground and two flat lowland stretches; sure signs that I was getting close to the Cumberland Valley.

Of the three highland stretches, two were 'same old, same old.' And then there was Rocky Ridge. It was an unusually steep climb on either side, and it felt good to be working those muscles again; the first genuine vertical challenge since I flipped north. And on top, I found a quarter mile of gleeful trail playing among giant boulders.

If ever there was a bit of trail designed just for the sheer fun of it, the Rocky Ridge summit traverse was it. It was rock scrambling for its own sake—prepositions sans destinations: in and out and up and over and down and around. While

F.I.T. Wilderness

AT footbridge with dogwoods in bloom—the northern of two stream crossings between Old Town Rd. and Sheet Iron Roof Rd.

it didn't have to have any other purpose for being, if you were looking for a 'point' to all this effort, Rocky Ridge did offer a couple of limited winter views north toward the Cumberland Valley.

As a kid, I loved this kind of boulder rambling along the Brandywine River at Rockford Park in Wilmington, DE. Rocky Ridge connected me to that, literally. Coming down off the ridge to Whiskey Spring Road, you reach the western terminus of the 195.9-mile Mason-Dixon Trail. In 2016, I would hike that to its eastern terminus at the Brandywine Trail near Chadds Ford, PA and then hike the Brandywine Trail 20 miles south to my old stomping grounds at Rockford Park in Wilmington.

This is exactly what Benton MacKaye had in mind when he wrote his 1921 paper "An Appalachian Trail: A Project in Regional Planning." He envisioned a network of trails connecting the wilderness spine of the mountains with the urban population centers. Pennsylvania, in my opinion, has perhaps the most well-developed such network of continuous trails. Philadelphia is connected via the Schuylkill and Horse Shoe Trails, with a link to the Mason-Dixon Trail via the Conestoga Trail.

West of the AT, Pennsylvania also offers two continuous trail systems. The first goes to State College via the Tuscarora, Standing Stone, and Mid-State Trails, and further links to the Finger Lakes Trail/North Country Trail in western New York—where you can go east to the Adirondacks and Vermont's Long Trail and back to the AT, or you can go northwest to Buffalo, NY, then across into Canada to pick up the Bruce Trail and Canada's amazing 15,000-mile Trans-Canada Trail.

Pennsylvania's other connected trail system comes up from the AT at Harper's Ferry along the C&O Canal Tow Path and takes you to Pittsburgh, where you can fork west to Wheeling, WV or go northwest into the Allegheny Mountains then on into Ohio and the Buckeye Trail. From there, the North Country National Scenic Trail takes you all the way to North Dakota via the Upper Peninsula of Michigan.

I've hiked the majority of those trails now, and can vouch for the stunning variety of wilderness experience. I dream of a time when this kind of network of connected trails creates a web covering the entire nation that is as robust as our interstate highway system.

But back to the day at hand. It took an hour to go a mile over Rocky Ridge—not because it had to take that long, but because I stopped to marvel. Sometimes this trail is not about long-distance hiking; it's about living in the moment; it's about a smile; it's about stopping to smell the flowers.

Thank you, Rocky Ridge. And kudos to the trail maintainers at the Mountain Club of Maryland, who obviously had a lot of fun blazing every second rock and every third tree through this delightful maze.

Days 92 and 93 took me across the Cumberland Valley, arguably the easiest stretch of the Appalachian Trail. I passed Centerpoint Knob, then dropped down into the valley, came through the town of Boiling Springs on a paved walkway beside Children's Lake, and stopped at the ATC regional office for a chat and to get a mug shot. At the north end of the valley, I climbed up Blue Mountain,

AT regional office at Boiling Springs, PA in the Cumberland Valley. "The Cottage" as it's called, was recently upgraded from a mere office to much more of a visitor center.

stopping to rest at the sturdy stone bench inset into the side of the mountain with excellent views back across the valley.

On Day 94, I came down past popular Hawk Mountain overlook and trekked through the major trail town of Duncannon. It's a study in contrasts; some sections are decaying and trashy looking. Downtown there is the iconic Hiker Hotel, the Doyle. The bar on the ground floor seems perennially populated by seedy locals looking to have a laugh at the hiker's expense, all in good fun, of course. Along North High Street, I passed some gorgeous, if modest, well-kept homes. I turned around on the small spit of land at the confluence of the Juniata River and the Susquehanna, and made my way back up the grueling climb to Hawk Rock.

The day's hike began and ended with a country walk through a pleasant hayfield to and from the rural AT parking lot on PA 850.

At the parking lot at the end of my day, I met and chatted with a hard-working maintainer from the Mountain Club of Maryland. He was happy to get my report of trail conditions, and I was happy to hear that the extensive (hundreds of acres) hayfields on either side of the highway are publicly owned and leased back to the

Looking northbound, the AT follows the sidewalk up High St., Duncannon, PA.

local farmers for a few hundred dollars a year, with the requirement that they keep them mowed and harvest the hay about three times a year.

The AT is a patchwork of thousands of such parcels, each with its own peculiar history and accompanying issues. As hikers passing quickly through, probably never to return, it's easy for us to forget all the behind-the-scenes politicking, negotiating, and just plain hard work that goes into this remarkable experience called the Appalachian National Scenic Trail. I've happily shelled out my money to become a lifelong member of the ATC. That was my way of giving back—a woefully inadequate "thank you" for the many months of life-enriching experiences I have had on the trail.

So on Day 96, I was east of the Susquehanna River, hiking the ridgeline of Peters Mountain most of the day. Somehow it felt like I had crossed into a new regime. This, for me, seems to be the real dividing line between the north half and the south half of the trail. On the 1000-foot descent back down the switchbacks to the Park-n-Ride lot at the Clark's Ferry Bridge over the Susquehanna, I had my second "Are you 'Seeks It?'" moment. Three guys with full gear were coming up the trail northbound. The last one spoke the surprising question. He said he had been following me on Trail Journals. Wowzer, I was flattered. I chatted with 'Cool Hand,' 'Desperado,' and 'Solar Speck' for a good amount of time and exchanged photo-ops. They were from southeast North Carolina and were out for a week doing the section from Duncannon to Port Clinton.

The next day I hiked the rest of Peters Mountain and met my three new buddies again. They had stayed at the Peters Mountain Shelter, a near-palatial structure with two huge sleeping levels and a partially enclosed picnic table area. The guidebook says that the trail down to the spring has 270 rock steps, but I didn't personally check its accuracy; nor did I learn if the water source was dry. In PA, it had been one of the driest spring seasons on record, and the Keystone Trails Association had issued a no-fire order, but even that wasn't enough. That day I hiked through an area that had just burned six days before. All the undergrowth on both sides of the trail for half a mile was burnt down to the soil line, leaving nothing but black, still-smoldering ground.

When I got to the viewpoint at Shikel limy Rocks, I learned how the fire started. I passed a young five-lined skink with a short, blunt tail, sunning himself on the rock. You could tell he was a youngster of this lizard species because his lines were so prominent. His normally blue tail—the protective 'bait' meant to distract predators—had recently been snipped off, indicating he had recently been in a scrape.

One week old burn area right on the AT, a half-mile north of Peters Mtn. Shelter.

Now, you may not believe this, but the little lizard looked up at me with his steely eyes. He opened his mouth and hissed, and a stream of fire came out. He told me in no uncertain terms that this was *his* trail. He said a hiker had stepped on him last week, and it had really pissed him off. It was the last straw, he said. The result? He got back at them. He got back at them *all*. I can best summarize what had happened with this little Limerick.

The young Dragon of Shik'limy Rocks
Hates when hikers start passing in flocks.
-----Last week he, in ire
-----Set the AT on fire,
*So **now** they'll get ...*

.... ash in their socks.

F.I.T. Wilderness

Okay, maybe I'm taking a little poetic license here. But the fact is, nobody ever discovered the cause of the fire, so who knows? Maybe I'm right.

Day 98 was easy and fast. I was on the broad, flat ridge of Sharp Mountain, and there were hardly any rocks on the trail. The most notable highlight was a bright orange stream crossing the trail. The bed of the stream had been lined with acidic deposits from an old coal mine nearby.

I was passing through one of several toxic clean-up zones. Nearby Centralia, PA, a virtual ghost town, had to be abandoned because of an uncontrolled coal mine fire that has been burning beneath the town continuously since 1962. As I crossed a collapsing railroad bridge over Rausch Creek, I noticed that the water in the creek was milky white and that the stream bed was nearly as white as snow. Turns out, it was limestone sediment coming from a treatment well. They were diverting the entire flow of the stream through a bed of limestone to reduce the acidity caused by runoff from the old mines.

A more positive highlight was historic Waterville Bridge where the AT crosses Swatara Creek. Now just a footbridge for hikers, this steel lenticular truss bridge was built in 1890 and moved to Swatara Gap from Lycoming County in 1985.

Day 99 brought me up onto Blue Mountain, a ridge that the AT follows from Swatara Gap all the way to its end near the Delaware River. It was also the day I visited 501 Shelter, met Bob 'Popeye' Pyhel and learned the story of his heart attack. This is a shelter right beside a highway, so, without an on-site caretaker, it would quickly get trashed. As it was, I found it a roomy, homey place, fully enclosed from the weather, with a central skylight and bunks all around.

It was only when I wandered over to the caretaker's cabin to 'collect' a photo of the cool AT logo built into the screen door that Bob came out for a chat. He's a quiet, unassuming guy. It wasn't as if he was eager to tell me that story of his heart attack on No Business Ridge in Tennessee. But when I asked him if he had thru-hiked the AT, the story began to come out.

I made 501 Shelter my turn-around point for the day and came back the next day to finish my 'interview' with Bob. I found him working behind his cabin in his garden. We chatted for another hour. This was my 100th day hike. After a twenty-mile day, I celebrated by working late into the night, writing up Bob's story.

Day 101 was only a half day on the trail. On this cloudy, dreary Saturday, I ran into maintainer Dave Coull, out working on his section of trail north of Black Swatara Spring. He said he'd been working this well-kept four miles of trail for 27 years. Whenever I meet a maintainer, I thank them for their work, since they are often taken too much for granted by those of us who just pass through. Yet Dave insists that the pleasure is all his. It gives him an excuse to commune with the wilderness and make a useful contribution at the same time.

In the afternoon, I popped down to Oxford, PA where my mom and dad lived in a retirement community, and we had a family celebration that combined Easter dinner with birthday cake, candles, and presents for Dad, for my AT section-hiking brother 'Frugal', and for my oldest nephew, who happens to live just two miles from the AT at Lehigh Gap, which I would reach in about a week.

The next day was Earth Day, but it was hardly the bright, sunny wild-flower-strewn springtime day one pictures for that holiday; it was downright dismal. I parked at Port Clinton and hiked southbound first. I ran into a Girl Scout troop and their leaders out for a weekend camping trip. They had stayed at Eagles Nest Shelter, near my turn-around point, for the last two nights. It started raining as I turned around and just kept raining harder and harder the rest of the afternoon. It was downright pouring when I got back to Port Clinton, but by then I didn't care. I was soaked but not cold, so I strolled down Broad Street in the heavy rain, singing like a fool. Gene Kelly, eat your heart out.

It became an all-night downpour—a welcome drought-buster all over the northeast. I found 2.5 inches in the little plastic rain gauge at the Eckville Shelter that I drove by the next morning. This is another shelter on the road with a caretaker next door. I didn't meet this caretaker; too cold to come out, I guess. The temperature had dropped into the upper 30's, and the north winds were howling. There was heavy snow in the mountains …

Wait. I was hiking in the mountains.

I got lucky. I read reports of snow and ice on the trail down south where the elevations are much higher. Western PA got half a foot. But the mountains I was hiking here in eastern PA are no higher than 1700 feet. We weren't even close to getting snow.

On the other side of the luck spectrum were folks down south who had packed up their winter gear and sent it home. Among them was the Rainwater family, whom I met when they were just a week or so out of Springer. They reported on Facebook that they were okay, but had to abort hiking plans and hunker down in a shelter. This was the storm that ended their thru-hike attempt.

I waited until the rain ended and it warmed up a little before I actually hit the trail. I only managed twelve miles.

The next day was the day I actually hiked past Eckville Shelter, and I also got to visit the Pennsylvania AT's premier vista point, The Pinnacle, which commanded a sweeping view to the east and southeast. Nearby Pulpit Rock wasn't half bad either.

I met three people on the trail this day. One was a clean-cut gentleman out for a day hike. The other two were far more memorable. I first met them as they were coming south from Eckville Shelter and I was headed to it. I asked them if the road was actually the 'approach trail' to the shelter. The older of the two, taller and slender, did the talking. Yes, the road even has a blue blaze or two along it. I told them about the other shelter that has a caretaker, and the younger one, short and very stocky, quickly pulled out a page from a guidebook and confirmed its location. This one seemed to be a boy going through puberty, perhaps the older one's son?

I then caught up with and passed them on the way up to The Pinnacle and we chatted some more. The taller one tried to keep up with me, clearly eager to chat. I matched their pace to the summit and we kept enjoyable company for the distance.

F.I.T. Wilderness

We met for the third time going opposite directions near Pulpit Rock, as I was now on my return leg. There we took the time to have some in-depth conversation, and I got the basics of their fascinating story.

They called themselves the 'Transgender Couple', and they were married. We're talking here about a man marrying a woman, both of whom are transgender. I wonder what the Fundamentalist "Marriage must be exclusively between a man and a woman" set would say about this. No, actually, I don't wonder at all.

Besides facing the burden of their sex change operations, this couple would also be dealing with their age difference. Brandon would turn 22 soon, and Hailey Jo, the more talkative by far, was 37. She claimed to be having an 'off day' with her voice, and it indeed sounded purely male to me. I had assumed she was male until this third encounter. I'm a hetero guy who responds to feminine cues. I got a few from Hailey Jo, but there were more male cues than female. I have to believe that this Transgender thing is a long, tough road. And Hailey Jo, very open to discuss her situation, confirmed that her 35 years of male programming were not going to go away quickly.

This pair was planning to do a long section hike from Delaware Water Gap to Springer Mountain. They were wearing big packs and also carrying duffel bags. I knew, before long, they'd need to find a way to lose some of that weight. They weren't attempting long daily distances; just from one shelter to the next each day. I sensed that they felt free out there on the trail, and were in no hurry.

Transgender couples who are married and are both transgenders are a rarity. It was an unexpected delight to meet and talk with these two down-to-earth people in the entirely unpretentious setting of the Appalachian Trail. This is a place where such social and lifestyle considerations are secondary to the fundamentals of daily life. You don't 'Fake it 'til you make it' out here.

If only the 'real world' were more like the Trail. Civilization, especially its technology, makes us so pampered and coddled that we forget what's important, and instead focus on trivial differences between us. We have too much idle time to form pompous opinions and gaggle on about them uselessly. This is yet another reason why the Trail makes me happy. I seek fellowship with what's *really* real. I keep coming back to that Thoreau quote:

"I went to the woods to ... front only the essential facts of life, and [to]see if I could not learn what it had to teach ..."

Day 105 hit me like a ton of bricks. There was an amazing surprise encounter, and a devilish nagging problem.

I was on the trail at 8:45 am, heading north from Hawk Mountain Road, near Eckville Shelter. The climb began gradually, then the trail picked up an old woods road that climbs the steep upper half of the mountain heading westward. At the top is a nice viewpoint back to The Pinnacle at an outcrop called Dan's Pulpit. Soon after passing Dan's Pulpit, my semi-chronic neck and shoulder pain began to act up. It first appeared a while back, on that day when I threw down my two hiking sticks. I had returned to hiking with one stick, and the problem had seemed tolerable. But today it got to the point of being almost unbearable. All the rocks in this section of trail were making me stoop over to watch my footing, kind of craning my neck. While doing that, I was trying to keep a pace that was just too fast, thus stressful as well as taxing on the neck and shoulder muscles.

My immediate solution was to take aspirin, but the permanent solution was to slow down—and even stop—to rest as needed; lesson learned. By the time I was on my last few miles back home in the late afternoon, I was feeling normal again. That was where I met the first people of the day, and a memorable meeting it was. It was ATC Information Services Director Laurie Potteiger out to do a section hike with her husband Dick ('Mountain Laurel and Hardy') and their friend 'Elf'.

Laurie and Dick Potteiger, and hiking friend 'Elf' (left) near Hawk Mountain Road, PA.

I had met and talked with Laurie back in late January at the ATC office in Harper's Ferry, and she had recently posted on Facebook that she would be hiking a section of PA, so I wasn't all that surprised to run into her. But I was surprised that she remembered my name. With all the people she deals with, I thought I'd have to remind her, but before I did, it came to her—amazing. Our conversation lasted twenty minutes. They were hiking the section from Port Clinton to Delaware Water Gap, planning to arrive there at the end of the following weekend. Tonight, instead of going as far as the Allentown Shelter, they were just looking for a campsite up on the ridge. I suggested Dan's Pulpit as a great place to camp. Since they would be going north, I expected we'd cross paths again in the coming days—a treat to look forward to.

F.I.T. Wilderness

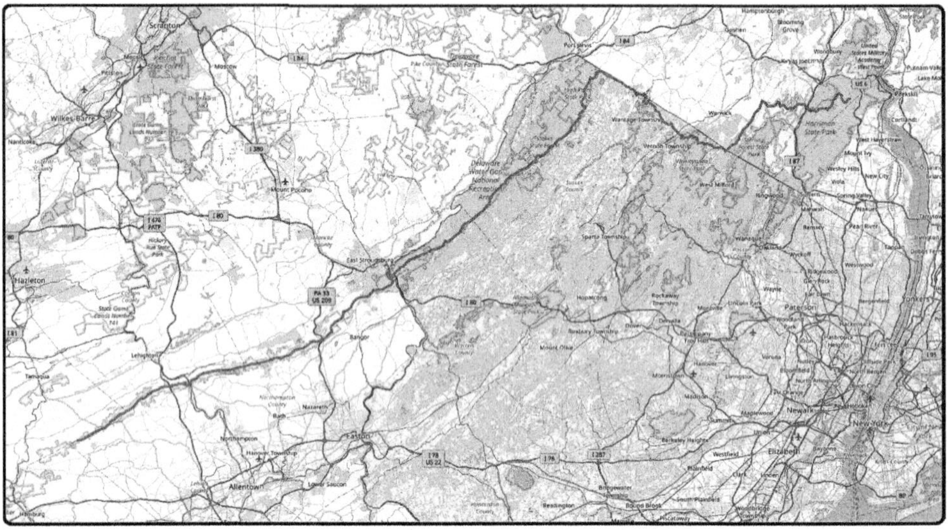
Scranton
Pittston
Wilkes-Barre
Nanticoke
Moscow
I 84
I 380
Mount Pocono
I 476
PATP
I 80
Hazleton
I 81
Tamaqua
Lehighton
East Stroudsburg
PA 33
US 209
Bangor
Nazareth
Bath
Northampton
Hanover Township
Easton
Allentown
Lower Saucon
I 78
US 22
Hamburg
Delaware Water Gap National Recreation Area
Port Jervis
Hamptonburgh
Blooming Grove
Goshen
Woodbury
Warwick
Harriman State Park
Peekskill
Cortlandt
West Haverstraw
Mount Ivy
Wesley Hills
New City
Viola
US 6
I 87
Wantage Township
Vernon Township
West Milford
Ringwood
Mahwah
Ramsey
Pearl River
Wanaque
Oakland
Wyckoff
Westwood
Ridgewood
Glen Rock
Sparta Township
Hopatcong
Rockaway Township
Wayne
Paterson
Yonkers
Bergenfield
Hackensack
Hasbrouck Heights
Clifton
Montville
Lincoln Park
Denville
Dover
Roxbury Township
Mount Olive
Hanover
Morristown
Livingston
Verona
Nutley
Bloomfield
North Arlington
Madison
Maplewood
Newark
Hoboken
New York
Summit
Union
Elizabeth
Berkeley Heights
Westfield
Plainfield
Clark
Linden
Bayonne
Kings County
I 78
I 287
Bridgewater Township
Readington
Bound Brook
South Plainfield
Piscataway
Woodbridge Township
I 95
Tarrytown
Tappan
Nanuet
Spring Valley
Suffern

CHAPTER 8

Allentown Shelter, PA to William Brien Shelter, NY
April 26 - May 13; 120.3 trail miles one way

There was some Pennsylvania-patented rocky footing and some ridiculously easy footing on the Day 106 trek between Allentown Shelter and Bake Oven Knob. The centerpiece, a place called Knife Edge, was a short traverse of the rocky ridge line. Frankly, I had walked sharper knife-edged ridges on the AT already, and definitely longer stretches of high exposed rock (Firescald Knob comes to mind). But the views were nice when you stood still, and the rock challenging when you were moving forward. There's a hard-learned rule, one of the basics of hiking: if you want to look at the scenery, stop. Trying to multi-task through challenging rocky or root-tangled footing is a sure recipe for disaster.

I ran into Laurie and gang again and we chatted for ten minutes. Laurie took more photos of me, but I didn't break out my camera. They were going to camp somewhere just beyond Knife Edge.

The next day was an exciting people day on a hike between Lehigh Gap and Bake Oven Knob. I met and chatted with Laurie, Dick, and 'Elf' again, meeting them at Ashfield Road. Bake Oven Knob—a rock outcrop with a great view just half a mile from a parking lot—was crowded with locals. The rocks sported lots of graffiti. Sadly, it's become a party place. The Bake Oven Shelter is a bit further on, and not as plagued with party people, it seemed. I stopped in there and took a photo and signed the register as usual. As I was sitting at the picnic table looking at the register, a hiker came in and sat down and dug a snack out of his pack.

"Are you 'Seeks It'?" he asked as he saw me sign the register. He'd seen my entries farther south. We got to chatting and I learned that he was a thru-hiker, the first I'd encountered since starting my leg north. He started in Springer on February 28th. While 'Samus' formerly 'Silent Sam' (he changed trail names in the Grayson Highlands area) was the first one I'd seen, he said he estimated he was the fifth. He was the seventh to sign in and get his official photo at Harpers Ferry, but had passed two of those since then.

I spent the night visiting and going out to dinner with my brother, a college friend, and my nephew, who owned a unique house built over a stream in Slatington, PA, just two miles from the trail.

The next day I made the iconic, rugged 1,000-foot climb up from Lehigh Gap to the EPA clean-up super-site on the ridge above the old Palmerton zinc

F.I.T. Wilderness   99

Grove of trees decapitated by toxic fumes from the Palmerton Plant and slow to recover.

smelting plant. Decades of toxic pollutants from the plant below had completely denuded the ridge here. The vegetation was recovering, but it still looked stunted and struggling. Some of the twisted and half-dead trees made great photo subjects. Near the end of the day I met Laurie, Dick, and 'Elf' for the fourth and last time, and later 'Samus' came by at his brisk clip—the last I would see of him too.

At the end of the day, it was back to the gang in Slatington and off to an AYCE (all you can eat) dinner at Valley Pizza in Walnutport.

The next day I started at Smith Gap and hiked the ridge of Blue Mountain for ten miles each way with almost no elevation gain and very little rocky footing. A walk in the park and not much to talk about. I didn't even have a shelter to stop at.

Lone trail tree, a sweet gum, overlooking the Palmerton Zinc smelting plant.

On Day 110 I did another twenty miles. I parked at Wind Gap and hiked south first to Leroy Smith Shelter. I got there early and met three more NoBo thru-hikers. I had a significant conversation with one of them: 'Iceman' from Kentucky. He was with two companions, 'Viking' and 'Achilles', who I had also passed and talked with briefly before reaching the shelter. They had done 33½ miles the day before and were going to do the 20+ miles to the Delaware Water Gap that day to hook up with Iceman's parents, who were considering hanging around and helping them slack-pack across New Jersey. 'Slack packing' is the term for having someone deliver your backpack down the trail while you hike with only what you need for the day. Some ultra-purists would claim it's cheating. If so, then I was cheating every day. In the final analysis, there are no fixed rules. Best to "Hike your own Hike" and give others the respect to do the same.

The privy at Leroy Smith Shelter was so clean, well-kept—luxurious even—that I took a picture. Perhaps my first and only worthwhile shot of the inside of an AT privy.

The next day was May 1st but the weather felt more like it was still April—cool and foggy but gradually clearing on a northwest breeze that brought in much nicer air. The fog and clouds lifted by afternoon and gave me a fantastic first view of the Delaware River from Mt. Minsi, my turn-around point.

It started out rainy the next morning, and while I was lying on my mattress in the back of my van in a parking lot at the Dunnfield Creek Natural Area waiting for the rain to end, I heard voices. I sat up and peered out the window to see 'Iceman', 'Viking', and 'Achilles', dressed in ponchos, tromping across the parking lot toward the start of New Jersey's portion of the AT. Like true thru-hikers, they were not letting a little rain prevent them from hiking. They were carrying full packs, so I guessed that Iceman's parents had left the area.

The 'Throne Room' at Leroy Smith Shelter.

When the rain let up to a fine drizzle, I started my day, heading first south back across the Delaware River and up to Mt. Minsi. Then in the late afternoon, I did a leg north, reaching Sunfish Pond, the first natural glacier-carved body of water along the trail, and one of the southernmost of exactly a bazillion that cover North America from there north to the Arctic Ocean.

Back in Great Smoky Mountains National Park, when I was saying goodbye to the tight-knit foursome of thru-hikers at Tricorner Knob Shelter, one of them said to me, "Good Luck, 'Seeks It'. I hope you find it."

F.I.T. Wilderness

It wasn't the right time, so I didn't explain that it's not like that; it's not a destination. I find a bit more of 'it' (fellowship with the wilderness, the intertwining of my 'self' with a deeper selfless existence) every day. But on this day, Day 112, I found a mother-lode.

As I climbed to Sunfish Pond, I was hiking in a thick misty fog. As I arrived at the large tree-lined pond—a small lake, really—the fog opened up its vistas to me. There was barely an hour of nice weather, and I was in the right place at the right time. I took the time to explore the pond and had a little lunch, and then the east wind picked up and the fog rolled back in.

North side of Sunfish Pond on a calm, foggy spring morning in early May.

Because of the weather, I had the entire place to myself, surely a rarity in this popular place. Human voices ruin the wilderness experience for me—children shouting, partyers laughing; I might as well be in the city. But today the wind was calm, the wood thrushes were warbling, and the whole expanse of the pond was laid out before me like a window into heaven.

If you are AT-hiking past Sunfish Pond, be sure to take the Turquoise Trail on the north end. It is just a tenth of a mile to a high rock point. There is no finer viewpoint from which to take in this magical setting of pristine wilderness. I had a rock seat with a backrest, a commanding view of the pond, and I felt a truly wealthy man.

I returned to Sunfish Pond from the other direction on Day 113, and had a nice lunch sitting on my 'throne' off the Turquoise Trail. The ridge walk to get there from Millbrook-Blairstown Road is one of the prettiest extended sections of ridge walking I've found—and I say that even though another day of fog and haze was interfering with the nearly constant views it presented from its glacier-smoothed, rubble-swept-aside bedrock walks. There was even the Catfish Fire Tower to climb if you didn't get enough of the vistas from the rest of the walk. When you're not on exposed ridge, you're walking through a delightful variety of woodlands, savanna-like glades, and grassy knobs that felt almost alpine.

Morning fog and afternoon heat were on tap for the next two days. I continued to enjoy the New Jersey 'balds,' open ridge areas of exposed bedrock where the glaciers scoured away so much soil that vegetation struggles to get a foothold. Both days I met 'Sun Dog,' who was doing a long section hike from Duncannon to Katahdin after doing Springer to Duncannon last year and getting sick. He was from Minnesota and was hiking in shorts and a t-shirt on a chilly morning when I was all wrapped up in a thick fleece. He said he gets up early and hikes with his headlamp to avoid the heat. This would be the last I'd see of him, but we kept in touch; a gentler man you will never meet.

Frank 'Sun Dog' Cadwell – trail completion photo he submitted to the AT Conservancy office, Harper's Ferry, posted on their bulletin board.

Another hiker crossed my path here. Her trail name was 'Kit Kat,' and she was hiking south from MA to Daleville, VA and hoped to complete the trail with further section hikes before the end of the year.

Notable flora and fauna included fields of diminutive teaberry plants (wintergreen), no more than two inches off the ground, loaded with sweet plump red fruits. I passed two persnickety porcupines—one climbing a tree and the other

F.I.T. Wilderness

Pink Lady Slippers—native Appalachian woodland flower of the orchid family.

hogging the trail, taking his good-natured time ambling along. I saw my first pink lady slipper in bloom, a temperate forest dwelling member of the orchid family. And I came upon at least half a dozen bright red-orange little salamander-like creatures called Red Efts. They are the juvenile land-dwelling stage of the Eastern Spotted Newt. These slow-moving little guys had come out in force because of all the damp weather.

To me, one of the best things about the 'people part' of my AT adventure was the unexpected repeat encounters with people. A long-distance trail is a uniquely one-dimensional world. Everybody I passed going southbound through the winter I now had a chance of meeting again as they passed me going northbound. And if, for some reason, you don't actually meet them, there's a good chance you'll see their entries in the shelter register books.

On Day 116, Tuesday, May 6th, I made the first such connection. It had been exactly two months earlier, on Tuesday, March 6th, when I met 'Just Paul from New York' between Snowbird Mountain and Max Patch.

Paul 'Parkside' Bernhardt, taken 6 May 2012.

104 **P. J. Wetzel**

Two months on the trail had transformed Paul. I didn't recognize the face at first, but Paul remembered me. He had just seen my fresh entry in Mashipacong Shelter's log book, so he knew we were close. He was worried that he might miss me—that I might be off the trail for the day already. It was 5:15 pm and he was hurrying north toward NJ 23 where a friend was waiting to pick him up for a night off the trail.

Meanwhile, I had just made my turn-around point on a short northward leg from Mashipacong Shelter. I was hurrying back south to my vehicle, hoping to get there before dark.

"Seeks It!!" called this bearded guy. I kind of stared blankly. I blamed my face blindness; he said it was the beard. I quickly remembered our meeting in perfect savant-like detail when he said his name. He had acquired a trail name, 'Parkside', which he had written in big black capitals on the back of his shirt. Better yet, he said he had met and hiked with 'Iceman' and 'Viking' and separately with 'Achilles.' I should have asked him about other hikers I met down south. I should have asked him how he got his trail name. But, as I said, we were both in a hurry. We shook hands, took each other's picture, and hurried on our way.

The Appalachian Trail does not go over New Jersey's High Point with its impressive 220-foot War Veteran's monument. I don't know why, given that the trail goes over many other popular summits with monuments and parking areas. Instead, the AT goes by it at a distance down below. There is a half mile side trail to reach it, but after giving it some thought I decided not to take the trail. I had no interest in bagging high points and, since I could see the monument and the views plainly enough from an observation deck along the trail, getting close to the granite and quartz stone obelisk completed in 1930 didn't seem important.

When the trail butts up against the New York state line, it turns right and parallels the boundary for seven miles—all the way to the Wallkill River—as if it were dipping its toes in cold water, somehow afraid to take the plunge into the Empire State. I covered this low, mostly level section of trail on Days 117 and 118, traversing through some boggy sections on a type of boardwalk called 'puncheon,' which consists of one or two long flat boards stretched across and nailed to logs cut in half, flat side up. It's a quick, cheap way to make dry trail. More of it gets laid down all the time, as maintainers find the time and capital to build it. But there was still some slogging through mud too.

The Wallkill River National Wildlife Area is one of the few extensive open wetlands that the AT passes through. You're walking on levees between shallow lakes. The government acquired this land and started restoring it in 2005; before that, it was a sod farm. The bird watching was excellent and the weather remained cloudy and dreary and occasionally rainy.

On Day 119, I reached several significant milestones. The first was the 2,000-mile mark. I had hiked 1,000 miles of AT out and back since January 1st. The second was the chance to walk the 3,950 foot-long Pochuck Swamp Boardwalk. This is not puncheon; it's genuine serious boardwalk, wide enough for a wheelchair. It was said to be the most labor-intensive section of the AT, although the new

F.I.T. Wilderness

Pochuck Swamp Boardwalk view at County Hwy 517.

granite steps on Bear Mountain, which were still under construction and which I would pass in a few days, probably now surpass that.

Early in the day, just before Pochuck Shelter, I met an unlikely looking but trail-fit hiker named Lyle (no trail name), who hailed from Michigan. We only exchanged a quick pleasantry, then I hiked on down to my turn-around at Lake Wallkill Road and visited the shelter on return. Its log book was full so I left a new one. Starting in Pennsylvania, I had made it a practice to carry with me a 50 cent, 200-page composition book and pen in a zip lock bag to leave at any shelter that lacked a register. I was using them up pretty quickly.

I was back at my starting point at 10:30, passing Lyle again. I moved my van to another parking area and got back on the trail heading north. My destination was only as far as the next road crossing, County 517. I was splitting the day up into a number of small out-and-back hikes because of all the good parking areas in the flat country. I passed Lyle again a mile or so later, and that's when we finally had an in-depth conversation. Lyle had done the entire AT from there to Springer over a number of years and was out doing an impressively long section from Culvers Gap to Salisbury, CT. (close to Mass.). I explained my hiking methodology to him and promised we'd meet again.

This section of trail had a small meandering climb then a significant descent down to the edge of Pochuck Swamp at the highway. The famous, high-cost boardwalk over the swamp was next, but I would wait to walk it until I moved my van again. I passed Lyle just after I had turned around and headed back. And that was the last time I saw him that day.

I got back to County 565 and drove down to the town of Vernon, where I got gas and ice. Then I headed back north and found the parking area on NJ 94. That's a fairly busy road and the parking area was more than half full, even on this midday weekday. The popularity is understandable when you consider that, from that lot, you can go two miles south and walk the Pochuck Swamp boardwalk and you can go a mile north and get to some impressive rock outcrop vistas on top of Wawayanda Mountain. Both of those were still on today's agenda.

I had spent an hour off the trail doing the resupply, so was hiking again at a bit after 1:00 pm. I took my good-old sweet time on the way to and across the boardwalk, really savoring the different scenery and the construction job itself. Before I got to the boardwalk proper, I crossed a railroad track where a very slow-moving train was unloading new railroad ties. The train was so slow moving that I talked with the engineer as he passed. I took photos and just sat and watched the entirely free-riding bulldozer-loader atop the open-top freight cars, precariously rolling back and forth over the piles of railroad ties (even between cars) as it picked up bundles of ties and swiveled, depositing them beside the track—fascinating.

Then I headed across a nice semi-open grassy area with lots of small walnut trees and, finally, onto the Pochuck boardwalk. There I met a lady right where I had stopped to photograph a snake and a turtle together on a log—they seemed to be staring each other down, and were oblivious to the two of us as we struck up a conversation. She was a middle-aged lady who'd had surgery for an abscess in her intestines and almost died. She had quit smoking and was, just today, out doing a first walk to try and lose the weight she had gained after the successful surgery and from the physical changes that resulted from quitting smoking. She knew nothing about the AT and started asking questions about it, so I obliged with basic answers. We then headed opposite directions until I reached the Highway 517 turn-around point. I passed her on the way back, wishing her well and encouraging her to keep on walking every day.

I was back at NJ 94 at 3:30, now with just barely enough time to complete the 20 miles required to get to the 2,000-mile mark. And to do it I had to make the 800-foot, very rocky ascent up Wawayanda Mountain first. The good vistas from the rocks are not on the AT, so I passed by without stopping to look for one, but on the way back I did catch the closest one to the AT. It was a grand vista, with the route of the AT laid out before me all the way back to the obelisk atop High Point.

Atop Wawayanda Mountain was a trail register where a sign indicated that the old route of the AT led 0.8 miles to a vista. I didn't take that. The trail descended a few hundred feet to a very pretty stream running over big boulders and bedrock, then there was a small climb and descent to Barrett Road where I passed a small parking area. On the north side of Barrett Road, the AT takes an old woods road up to a minor summit and there leaves the old road and heads down into the woods. That minor summit was 0.3 miles beyond Barrett Road, and it was where I turned around. At 0.2 miles beyond Barrett Road, the numbers from the data book say I passed my precise 2,000-mile point, though I would only have completed the 2,000 miles when I had walked back the other way to my van to end the day. Jeez, I'm such a numbers geek.

On the return hike, I stopped near the short side trail atop Wawayanda Mountain that leads to Pinwheel's Vista and bushwhacked to a viewpoint of my own choosing, which included the Pinwheel's Vista rock outcrop.

Then the rocky descent to the base of the mountain featured two unpleasant issues. The first was a quick shower that got heavy enough to force me pull out my poncho and put it on just in time for the rain to end, making me feel like a fool.

F.I.T. Wilderness

Then I passed a gentleman in his late 30's and slowed down as we struck up a conversation. He was actually very interesting and had done a lot of hiking on the AT and elsewhere around the U.S., but I was tired and feeling a little downtrodden by my poncho episode, and by the descent on the big rocks, and by the 20-mile day, and he was one of those people who seems to love to talk more than converse. I finally had to make an excuse that I needed to hurry.

He wished me well and I said it was good talking with him. As I left him, he pulled out his cell phone and proceeded to exit stage rear, phone to ear, yapping away yet again, oblivious to nature's evening voices along the very pretty field-walk at the apron of Wawayanda Mountain.

I inhaled deeply, lifted my eyes to the sky, spread my arms out to either side, and invited nature to return to me. And thus I resumed my solitary pilgrimage, setting down more Footprints in the Wilderness.

There was one last episode from that day's hike. At midnight I woke up with some pain in my left ankle. I had developed a pain in my lower left shin quite early in the day, something I hadn't had before. That spot was sensitive, but it became clear that it was actually caused by favoring the long-standing minor pain from a turned ankle. So now I realized that I had indeed aggravated my left ankle sprain that I first developed near Damascus, VA (though that was ultimately caused by the broken ankle, never repaired by the orthopedist back in 1986). This time I knew exactly how I had tweaked the ankle. It was while I was off trail two evenings earlier. I was trying to flatten an aluminum soda can by stomping on a shoe placed over the can. In other words, I wasn't wearing the shoe, just using it as a cushion to flatten the can with my stocking feet. My foot came down crooked, and the pain immediately told me I had done damage.

So I now had that classic story to tell—I had hiked 2,000 miles on the Appalachian Trail in 119 days, and then turned my ankle trying to crush a soda can.

Fortunately, the injury was not serious enough to drive me off the trail—or maybe it was. Other things were piling up on me that I wasn't even aware of, more than just that ankle. The weariness I felt while walking with the talkative gentleman proved to be a symptom. It all came to a head over the next four days.

New Jersey was a 9-day state. The full plunge into New York state happened on a glacier-scoured bedrock spine overlooking Greenwood Lake. It was deceptively difficult trail. On paper the elevation profile looks nearly level, but there are interminable small scrambles up and down and over and across the variable bedrock surface.

The people stories abounded. Early in the morning, I met Lyle for the 8th or 9th time. At the state line marker, I met 'Chief,' a toy boxer four-legged hiker type, and 'Chief Daddy,' who was an outfitter, guide, 2008 AT thru-hiker, and 2010 PCT thru-hiker. He was from Atlanta but now lived in Manhattan, and was just out doing some circuit hikes locally. While we chatted, two young guys arrived, and they turned out to be doing thru-hikes. 'Goose' and 'Blue Grass' and I crossed paths and talked twice more that day. They seemed well-grounded and all-around pleasant young men.

Did that description of those early-20's-ish guys make me sound old? Well, I felt old by the end of the day. The hiking had been especially physically demanding. I wasn't able to log the miles I had planned, so I had to turn around short of my target in order to avoid hiking these precarious little bedrock scrambles in the dark.

I told myself that, with a good night's sleep, I would be fully recovered by morning, as always, and ready to hit the rest of that bedrock ridge-spine walk and whatever else the AT had to throw at me down the trail. I was ignoring the accumulating problems; I was in denial.

Day 121 had me covering the rest of the rugged scrambles along Bellvale Mountain, and then continuing east to Mombasha High Point. The toughest parts of the hike were Cat Rocks and the Eastern Pinnacles. Both offered blue-blazed bypass trails for wet conditions, lazy or tired or less adventurous hikers, and those who want to leave their packs at the end and then go back and scramble the rocks without the extra weight. It's nice to have choices, but for me, of course, there was only one choice, since I intended to religiously pass every white blaze in both directions. And, once again, doing the trail twice paid dividends. The first time over Cat Rocks I didn't notice the nest of ravens with the four nearly grown but unable-to-fly youngsters looking very uneasy as I snapped their photo. I didn't notice the brightly colored milk snake that slithered across the trail right in front of me. And I didn't notice the bear family. Four of them. A mama, a papa, and two cubs. This was not my first bear sighting, but it was my first serious bear encounter. First off, I saw the mama and two yearling cubs only after they had noticed me first. The cubs scrambled right up trees, but the mama wanted to run. She was making some soft, murmuring vocalizations, as if saying, "No, kids, not the trees. That's a human—a spear thrower, a gun wielder. Get down and run. Follow me."

The trail must have curved around, because I saw the mama and kids again, and this time they were with a scary-huge male. And this time I had stopped to pee and was standing stock-still when I saw them approaching, so they hadn't spotted me. I hid behind a tree and got out my camera, hoping to catch a great photo of the big male. But he was coming straight toward me—too close. Camera in hand, I lost my nerve, and never got the hoped-for photo. I stepped out boldly, making a deliberate noise, and they all bolted.

That day was the first time I met legendary hiker 'City Slicka' who remained on the trail almost continuously for the next decade. This day he wasn't going anywhere, though. He was in his sleeping bag at Wildcat Shelter, taking a zero day, and not seeming too well thanks to the tough trail that was also wearing me down.

That night I didn't manage to get to bed until after sunrise. I spent an hour on the phone with my son who was job hunting in New Mexico, and way too much time blogging and writing. I got a couple quick hours of sleep and was on the trail by 10:00 am, already exhausted.

Of course today would be the day I had to hike Agony Grind; it figures. Actually, I found that short stretch of steep trail much less daunting than its name suggests.

The highlight of the day was a chance to hike with a blind hiker who was faster than I was. The story starts after I had made a descent of a nasty bit of rocky cliff—a scramble requiring use of the hands. There I met Lyle again. He said he was taking a short day. While we were chatting, a local who was a frequent hiker in the area came down, going in my direction with his dog, Eli. As the three of us were chatting, I noticed another pair of hikers coming down the rock scramble, seemingly talking about every hand hold and every move of their feet. Well, that's because one of this pair was Andres, an accomplished blind hiker, and he was being talked through the gauntlet by his friend Chuck. Their normal mode of travel was for Andres to hold onto the center of Chuck's backpack for direction and support if needed. He would sometimes stumble, but their pace was easily three miles per hour, which was hard for me to match. It seemed totally remarkable to me that those two had just done that brutal Class 3 descent down the virtual cliff. We all chatted and then Lyle headed up the cliff and the rest of us hiked more-or-less together.

Chuck and Andres were hiking on the clock, and turned around at 11:30. I said farewell to them and got a photo. Then I talked with the local, now taking a rest stop on the ascent to Mombasha High Point. That was my turn around point. Back to Agony Grind to make the descent to the New York State Thruway. At the bottom, I found Lyle chatting with another hiker who was being supported by his dad at the intersection of NY17 and Arden Valley Road. I ended the day there. I had only done twelve miles, but that was all I was good for that day.

Chuck (left) with expert blind hiker Andres.

I felt like a zombie as I returned to my van. I just plunked down in the van and slept like a log for four straight hours into the evening. Then I woke up momentarily for a natural break, and went back to sleep, sleeping even more soundly. But I was now far behind on my trail debriefing, GPS and photo processing, blogging, journaling, and writing the daily email to keep the family abreast of where I was. I was torturing myself. As dawn came, I had to resupply with gas and ice.

Vintage 1928 Fingerboard Shelter, right on the AT.

I was finally on the trail just before 9:00 am; and this day was to be my Waterloo.

I passed Fingerboard Shelter and turned around for the day at William Brien Shelter. Fingerboard was built in 1928 and is the oldest shelter on the trail. William Brien was built in 1933. Both are stone structures in the Adirondack style with the bases of their walls flared out several feet. A nuclear bomb would barely phase them.

And today I traversed the infamous Lemon Squeezer in a very peculiar mood. My attitude had been getting increasingly out of balance the last few days, almost bipolar. Here's what I wrote on my blog about this famous bit of trail.

"The Lemon Squeezer is actually a gauntlet made of three eccentric bits of trail. Besides the ever-narrowing, uncomfortably skewed crevice, there's a cave passage somewhat like Virginia's 'Guillotine' or Grayson Highlands' 'Fat Man Squeeze.' And finally there's a seriously difficult 8-foot vertical rock face with no hand-holds. You have to pull yourself up with your arms. This is the most challenging bit of rock scrambling on the AT. I'm 6'2", so I could reach the lip at the top, yet I barely had the strength to pull myself up. If you're short and have no companions with you, it would be literally impossible. Instead of any climbing aid, the trail offers a blue-blazed bypass route labeled 'Easy Way.'

"NO! NOT ACCEPTABLE!!!

"A blue blaze bypass of any sort is verboten, totally out of the question for the trail purist like me.

F.I.T. Wilderness

"To the purist, the white blaze is a sacred trust. It is, in some real sense, like a religion. There can be only one 'TRUE PATH!' Here the AT trail builders had violated that trust.

"In my opinion, blue blazed bypass trails are the road to perdition. Verily I say unto you, brother hiker: Take thee not that first step onto the 'easy way,' or before you know it, you'll be using blue-blazed short cuts just to save time. Next you'll be road walking, hitch-hiking, skipping whole sections.

"Hell, why not just drive the entire route? Google Maps tells me it takes less than 24 hours by car from Amicalola Falls State Park to Baxter State Park. Wave at some white blazes as you whiz past them on I-81. Groseclose and Troutville, VA; Cumberland Valley, PA.

"Start early, you'll be done by midnight. Big deal. Been there, done that. Send in your application for your 2000-miler certificate and move on to the next whoop-ass challenge. Who's yo' daddy? Talk to the hand ..."

The thing is, I actually meant it. That blue blaze 'Easy Way' caused something in me to snap. Why in the f*** was I doing this? What, after all, was the f***ing point?

I had to get off the trail. I did not even really know why. I could see practical reasons, physical reasons, and even spiritual reasons, though they weren't at the heart of the issue. The weather forecast looked lousy, with rain promised for several days. My physical condition had somehow deteriorated, and I didn't understand why. My mental condition was getting seriously out of whack, and the next day marked the threshold of a very special personal holiday, which I call the 'Lost Day.'

It is rooted in a made-up religion of a far distant future species of human descendants that I'd been writing about in an epic fantasy/sci-fi tale. I had been working on this story, and on building the world of these people, since the late 1960's. Among other things, I had developed a new calendar system in which the New Year began on May 15th (the Return of Green); and in which every four years, the old year ended with a 'Lost Day,' holiest day of the four-year 'Tally.' The associated religion involved Ancestor worship and a deep reverence for the Earth such that this distant-future culture lived an enlightened stone-age existence, completely in harmony and balance with the planet.

The day after tomorrow at sunrise, the Lost Day was to begin ... and end. Here are a few more details from my "mythopoeia", my world-building notes:

"The 'Tally,' the four-year calendar cycle, represents the fundamental spiritual cycle for self-improvement and growth. Each Tally concludes with a special atonement day when our innermost being is laid bare and open before our Ancestors and Protectors. At the completion of each Tally, one day is unaccounted for. There are forty-three Ides to the Tally, each being thirty-four days long. The symmetry is perfect: 43 × 34 is 1,462, which is one more than the number of days in four years containing one leap day. So, the new Tally must begin a day earlier than the holy Keepers of the Tally would "expect." That day is lost to men, but for cosmic symmetry it is not lost to our Spirits. And so, the first Ide of the new Tally is devoted to the "reaching out" to touch that Lost Day that was hidden from our conscious mortal minds by the Ancestors. Though lost to consciousness, the Lost Day is an integral part of our spiritual whole.

"On the Lost Day, while the Spirits hold all living beings (and indeed, all the moving planets and stars) in a deep sleep or trance, they move among the living, taking an accounting and reaping the spiritual harvest that each one of us has cultured through our deeds and our prayers—the emergent 'Knowledge,' the 'Good and the Noble' in us, fashioned out of the raw Chaos by our thoughts and actions. This harvest represents our worth to them, because it is what sustains and impels the very current of reality—the 'Great Stream'. So, the greater the harvest we provide, the more influence we have on nature's course, and therefore the more favorably the Spirits will regard us through the coming Tally."

I was in no condition to face that spiritual harvest. I packed up and drove home.

Park Like setting above Island Pond on Fingerboard Mountain

The infamous Lemon Squeezer

The "Easy Way" and the 'impossible' white-blazed route above the Lemon Squeezer

PART THREE

The End of Doubt

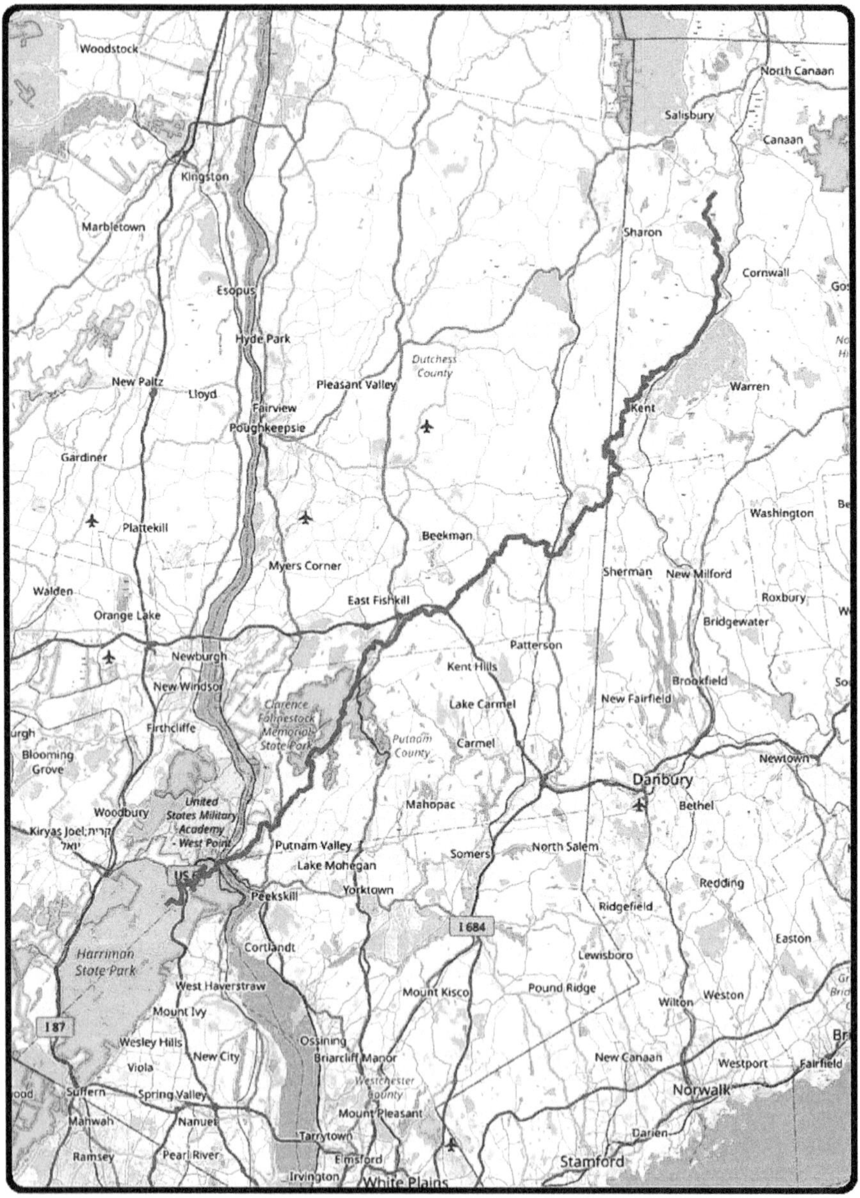
Woodstock
North Canaan
Salisbury
Canaan
Kingston
Marbletown
Sharon
Cornwall
Esopus
Hyde Park
Dutchess
County
New Paltz
Lloyd
Pleasant Valley
Warren
Fairview
Poughkeepsie
Kent
Gardiner
Washington
Plattekill
Beekman
Myers Corner
Sherman
New Milford
Walden
Roxbury
East Fishkill
Orange Lake
Bridgewater
Newburgh
Patterson
Kent Hills
New Windsor
Brookfield
Clarence
Fahnestock
Memorial
State Park
Lake Carmel
New Fairfield
Firthcliffe
Putnam
County
Carmel
Blooming
Grove
Newtown
Danbury
Bethel
Mahopac
United
States Military
Academy
- West Point
Woodbury
Kiryas Joel
Putnam Valley
North Salem
Somers
Lake Mohegan
Yorktown
Redding
Peekskill
Ridgefield
I 684
Easton
Cortlandt
Harriman
State Park
Lewisboro
West Haverstraw
Mount Kisco
Pound Ridge
Wilton
Weston
Mount Ivy
I 87
Wesley Hills
Ossining
New City
Briarcliff Manor
New Canaan
Westport
Fairfield
Viola
Westchester
County
Suffern
Spring Valley
Norwalk
Mahwah
Nanuet
Mount Pleasant
Tarrytown
Darien
Ramsey
Pearl River
Elmsford
Stamford
Irvington
White Plains

CHAPTER 9

William Brien Shelter, NY to Sharon Mountain, CT
May 17-28; 92.5 trail miles one way

On the drive home, I asked myself: Had I realized how hard it had become? Did I really like to hike *that* much? Was I ready for it to get tougher when I reached New Hampshire? Can a 63-year-old man hike the entire Appalachian Trail in both directions—4,368.4 miles—in a single calendar year? Had anyone my age or older done it? Are there enough road access points in the tough sections of the White Mountains and Maine, in the 100-Mile Wilderness, to accommodate my out-n-back, no-nights-on-the-trail, day-hike approach? Was hiking the infamous Mahoosuc Notch twice even possible for me? Had I been delusional right from the start? Was I on a fool's errand?

It took me three days to figure things out. I realized I had pushed myself too hard. I was dreading the future rather than anticipating it. I had lost too much weight and had been trying to get by on way too little sleep.

At home I slept more than half of every day, did the necessary chores, and ate like a pig. I got out my maps and spread them out on the bed. I studied them in detail, picked through all the various sources of information I had in maps, guidebooks, and online. And I figured it out.

The White Mountains can be hiked in small chunks using side trails from access points. Some of the days would include only a few miles of AT hiking. Most of these would require 2 to 4 miles of off-AT hiking both ways, but they would insert me into otherwise long sections with no direct road access. In the 100-Mile Wilderness of Maine, there are private toll roads that provide plenty of access points. The primary ones are the Katahdin Iron Works Road and the network of five branching roads accessed from Jo-Mary Road.

I satisfied myself that the entire 796.6 miles of trail I had left to hike to Katahdin could be split up into day hikes that would almost never be more than 20 miles. And the 20 milers were on easier sections of trail. It turned out that Great Smoky Mountains National Park was the toughest challenge of the whole AT, and I was done with that.

I could do this. The Lost Day had come and gone in an instant like the ephemeral Green Flash at sunrise. The New Year of my spiritual calendar had arrived, and I was ready for a fresh start.

Telephoto view of the NYC Skyline from ridge of Black Mountain, Harriman State Park.

Panoramic viewpoint with rustic bench along the AT near Bear Mountain summit.

P. J. Wetzel

I got back to New York and was on the trail by 11:00 am on May 17th. The day's hike got me to the west side of Bear Mountain on the very oldest portion of the AT, officially opened on October 7th, 1923. It was a bright clear day, and as I crossed over Black Mountain, I had a clear view of the New York City skyline, 37 miles away. West Mountain Shelter, a half mile off the AT by a blue-blazed side trail, sits on a high bluff with a stunning view of a wide swath of the Hudson River and adjacent countryside.

I hit the meandering, extremely heavily used trail over Bear Mountain on Day 125, and came down some of the newly installed, hand-cut solid granite steps, designed to last a thousand years from the looks of them. The project was begun in 2006 and completed in 2018, and it involved the placement of more than 1300 steps, each weighing in at about half a ton. At the stone tower on top of Bear Mountain, I was roaming around taking photos when a couple appeared sporting tiny packs. They stopped to fill water bottles at a fountain and I struck up a conversation. Ultra-light and ultra-fit, 'Swivel' and 'Spiral' left Springer March 20th and were already on Bear Mountain. I shared the descent of the granite steps with them, and got a photo, and soon they were gone like a summer gust.

The very busiest part of the Appalachian Trail, and also its lowest elevation, comes as the trail passes through Bear Mountain State Park Zoo. I came through in the morning, but on the way back in late afternoon I found the gate closed. I had to take the blue blazed trail around the zoo, which meant I would have to come back another day to walk that piece of trail.

Next on the agenda was the walk across the Hudson River on the Bear Mountain suspension bridge, opened on November 27th, 1924. Hikers used to have to pay a nickel toll to cross, but it has been free to pedestrians since some time in the 1990's.

I hiked on up past Saint Anthony's Nose, didn't take the half-mile side trail to the view, and turned around at the US 9 trail crossing, which came complete with a 24-hour full-service deli and pizza shop.

Bear Mountain Bridge, with Anthony's Nose looming across the Hudson River, taken near the lowest elevation point on the Appalachian Trail.

I went back and hiked Bear Mountain Park Zoo southbound the next morning, then hiked a pretty bland section through hilly country with lots of road crossings. The highlight of the day was stopping for a long chat with the 'Hiking Humanitarian' and his wife. It turns out that Kirk and Cindy Sinclair were walking from Cape Henlopen, Delaware to their home in Norfolk, CT via roads and the AT. They had just completed a continuous year-long thru-hike of the American Discovery Trail, doing it west-to-east. They had started on a Pacific Ocean beach at Point Reyes, California a year ago that week and had walked the entire length to the Atlantic Ocean. They had also hiked other trails. Kirk had done the 'triple crown,' meaning the Pacific Crest Trail and the Continental Divide Trail, as well as the AT. He had done the AT twice (1978 and 1983) as well as various other shorter trails—20,000 miles in all. Here was a humble, pleasant couple, at peace in the woods, but super-stars in my estimation. It was an honor to have a chance to meet and sit and chat.

The weather continued to be glorious. It was as if my new positive attitude had extended all the way to heaven. I had bright blue cloudless sky for each of the last three days, mild to warm temperatures, and low humidity. I was taking it slower, watching my diet and my sleep, and loving what I was doing.

The next day took me past Canopus Lake with nice views at a few points, but mostly wooded trail as I traversed the ridge beside it. The weather remained nearly perfect but was getting a little hotter. I had distant views of the Catskills from a bare-granite high point, and the following day brought more such views of the Fishkill River Valley, The Hudson Highlands, and the Shawangunks in the foreground.

That was the day I passed through the unusual RPH Shelter, which is more like a small house or cabin than a shelter. Avid hiker Martin 'The Edge' Hunley was there. I had met him on the trail a couple times before, but today he didn't seem to be hiking, but doing maintenance around the shelter instead. I didn't get a chance to get much of his story then because he was talking on his cell phone, but he was clearly local to the area and spent a lot of time hiking up and down the AT from there. It turned out that he was meeting a couple doing a section hike and was going to be their shuttle driver for the next several days.

The next day's people encounters were notable for two very different reasons. The first was one that has haunted me ever since. About 1:00 pm, just as I was emerging at the I-84 overpass, I ran into an older, smallish, bearded man who I had passed a couple times yesterday but hadn't stopped to talk to. This time he was without his backpack, compass in hand, studying the trailhead bulletin board. He seemed a little frantic, and upset. When he started to ask me his question, he was incoherent. The words made no sense to me. He was pointing to his compass and to me, very perplexed. Finally, he pulled out a card which explained that he had aphasia as a result of a stroke. The problem with this impairment is that he couldn't express his question, and similarly could have problems understanding my answer.

I'm pretty sure that he was disoriented by the road walk and wasn't sure which way was northbound. But it wasn't clear to me, and so I was not sure if I helped him. I worried about where he had left his backpack, but it would seem difficult for him to mistake where he had come from (south) versus where he had not yet been (north). If this wasn't the case, he had no business hiking alone on the AT. As I repeatedly pointed northbound, saying "Appalachian Trail North," he seemed to suddenly have an 'aha' moment and articulated it pretty well. "Okay, right!"

I left him and went toward my vehicle parked a quarter mile down the road, but saw him still going back and forth at the intersection, as if still confused. Here's what I was worried about: he had seen me hiking northbound at one point and southbound at another, and now he was seeing me walk down the road. I was very afraid that I had been the source of his confusion and that it was beyond his capacity to work it out. Gosh, I hoped not ... but I did wonder. I never saw him again.

I turned around for the day at Nuclear Lake, named because, until the 1970's, it was the site of a former nuclear testing facility.

On the way back south, I passed a guy who, upon seeing me, immediately asked, "Are you 'Seeks It'?" This turned out to be 'Bomber', the guy I met below 'Gingersnap's' trail magic site near Rock Gap, Franklin, NC. Once again my 'face blindness' was painfully evident. I studied the guy's face intently and could not recall him. He told me where we met, and it came back to me. He was the guy who passed me praising the amazing brownie he had just eaten. I do not remember any more of the conversation, though I told him I had just met 'Gingersnap' as she was coming back from delivering said brownies. I do not remember him saying

Eric 'Bomber' McKinley and his stiff-necked companion.

his trail name or me saying mine. Either he had inferred my name from register books, seen my blog or Trail Journals posts or Facebook posts, or we had a much more extensive conversation than I remembered. I suppose it is possible I had been 'peopled-out' by the long conversation I had just had with 'Gingersnap'. That does happen to me.

Anyhow, back to that day's meeting with 'Bomber'. I checked my records for the date of our first meeting: March 22nd. He was the second person I had met from down south (the other being Paul/'Parkside') and both of them were two months *to the day*, between encounters. Bomber was headed to the Telephone Pioneers Shelter and would get there just before sunset. He wanted to spread out all his stuff to dry it out, so I didn't want to delay him, but we would stay in contact through Facebook. His real name is Eric. After he completed his thru-hike, he went into the Air Force; he had already enlisted before he started his hike. He specialized in disarming enemy explosive devices, thus the trail name. He also did a lot of sky diving. He had climbed really high mountains in South America too, which, unlike playing with live bombs and jumping head-first out of perfectly good airplanes, was something we had in common.

Day 130 started along NY 22 where I parked near the Appalachian Trail Metro-North stop, only used on weekends and holidays. This is the only railroad stop on the AT. Beyond the tracks, I traversed nearly a half mile of spanking-new boardwalk over Swamp River and its attendant broad swamp. There's even a beaver pond with a huge lodge right near the boardwalk. Climbing up over Corbin Hill, I met 'Bomber' again. We had a very nice chat and took photos. At the bottom of this field walk, the trail passes the Dover Oak, a huge old white oak of massive girth right beside West Dover Road, County Highway 20. A six-hundred-foot climb brought me to the Telephone Pioneers Shelter. The name has no historic significance, other than it was sponsored by the local chapter of the Telephone Pioneers of America when it was built in 1988. While signing the shelter register, 'Day-Glo' and 'Blue Bird' popped in for a break. They were section hiking from

Appalachian Trail Train Station, note resident on duty marked by the red ellipse

Resident caretaker of the train station. Sadly, sometime in the following five years this birdhouse was removed and has not been replaced.

122   **P. J. Wetzel**

the Delaware Water Gap to North Adams, MA. I headed on out for the second half of the ascent to the ridge top, where the rock outcrop I spied on the field walking earlier now presented me with a great view of where I had just hiked. I could even spot the Dover Oak.

There was a beer can-littered illegal campfire site right near the viewpoint, the trashiest spot I'd encountered anywhere on the AT. Underage drinkers come up here a lot, and they are *not* going to pack out the condemning evidence. Finally I reached my turn-around point at Nuclear Lake well ahead of schedule. It was a calm, humid, summery late morning. I had a chance to linger there and appreciate the abundance of wildflowers, which no doubt glow in the dark.

South end of Nuclear Lake, NY.

On the hike back, I ran into the late-60's-ish couple that 'The Edge' was shuttling; very pleasant people. I was especially impressed by their smiling eyes. They were excited to learn of my way of hiking. The next day would be their last day on the trail for this year. Each year since 1990, they had hiked a section, starting in Springer and steadily working north. Next year they hoped to do all of CT and MA. I finished this 12.8-mile hike early, and I might have headed out to do another leg, had it not been for the fact that I was deliberately taking things a little easier since my 'watershed' experience a few days earlier.

The following day I crossed into Connecticut, my tenth AT state. I was on the trail at 6:50 am and hiked a 3½-mile leg north. In the past, I have always loved

F.I.T. Wilderness 123

open-meadow and pasture walks. This morning's hike started out with a mile of that, but on this morning it was a pain because the grass in the successive fields kept getting higher and higher until it was nearly waist high. Worse, it was all soaking wet with dew. At first, in the lower grass, I was having reasonable success keeping my feet dry, but across the final field of waist-high grass, that was impossible, so all the care and energy I spent keeping my feet dry was wasted. That's what really bothered me – the pointlessness of all my effort. I went through three pairs of socks on this 3.5-mile leg, then returned to my van, changed socks again, and did some resupply before driving to the next trail access point. Fortunately, by then, the dew had evaporated.

Wiley Shelter had sagging fiberboard floors that didn't look very comfortable. I got out the register and was starting to read through it when a hiker came in, hiking northbound, and sat down at the picnic table with me. I was reading the register and trying to talk with him at the same time—telling him that the pump, the shelter's water supply, was out of order but that there was a small stream running across the trail right in the same area—when the last register entry caught my eye. It was 'MEATS'! He had signed the register today. That was the hiker from Johnson City, TN, who I had met twice down south.

Well, the hiker I was talking to turned out to be a thru-hiker also, named 'Salty', and he had met 'MEATS' back in Duncannon, but had been behind him since then after taking two zero days. He said he saw MEATS' entry in the Telephone Pioneers Shelter. He had apparently stayed there the night before. That meant that he had to have passed me somewhere that day. But even with my two hours off the trail for resupply, I had picked up the trail seven miles further ahead. Had MEATS made a super-early start? Given the warm weather and 5:30 sunrise, it was certainly possible. Anyhow, it turned out that MEATS had somehow passed me by.

'Salty' was from Grasonville, on MD's eastern shore, practically a neighbor. He had met Beth/'Patches' and had heard of or met several other thru-hikers that I knew. He was a nice kid, early 20's, and had a broad face with a bush of curly brown hair, but kept himself clean shaven.

On Day 132 I crossed from New York into Connecticut, for the second time. The trail dips back into New York after 5½ miles in CT in order to climb Schaghticoke Mountain. A nice chunk of that day's hike was along the Housatonic River past the historic 1842 covered bridge named Bulls Bridge. Based on the languid strains of Charles Ives' symphonic poem "The Housatonic at Stockbridge", I had expected a quiet, lazy river, so I was surprised to find noisy rapids and pleased to see them lined with yellow blooming water flag iris. Here was another beautiful import from Asia via the early European settlers. Just like the ubiquitous orange daylily that blooms in June and July all over eastern North America from Manitoba to South Carolina to Arkansas to Nova Scotia, this is technically an invasive species.

At Tenmile River Shelter, I signed the last page of the register book, so I left a new one. There was a pack and belongings inside and a minute later a hiker came up from the spring. It was 'Wisconsin', who only had nine miles to hike today to where a friend would pick him up. He was a mechanical/electrical engineering student at the University of Minnesota who had done the trail south of here in two big sections during summer breaks. That summer he hoped to get to Katahdin before school resumed.

On the way back along the Housatonic River, a man of Indian descent (meaning the Asian subcontinent) wearing crisply pressed black dress pants, spit-polished black leather shoes, and a starched whiter-than-white dress shirt approached me and asked, "how far?"

"How far to what?"

"To the end of the trail."

So I got to pull out that classic shock line. "That way? It goes to Georgia. The other way, to Maine."

His reaction was satisfyingly amazed. He was looking for a short day hike so I suggested that the big iron footbridge over Tenmile River would be a good destination for a pleasant walk.

At midday I was back in my van, parked at the Schaghticoke Road trailhead. I spent two hours on the phone dealing with an idiot at the Bursar's Office at the University of Maryland, trying to resolve an issue regarding my daughter's fees and tuition. It wasn't until 2:30 pm when I stepped out of the van, ready to hike again. Just then a car came up with Maryland plates. It turned around at the intersection and stopped. Out popped 'Salty'. He hadn't told me before, but he was taking two zero days. His wife was driving the car. We chatted for a minute or two and noted that we'd probably not meet again on the trail as he roared on north.

The next day was Saturday, the start of Memorial Day weekend—the traditional kickoff of the summer season. And the weather got the memo; the temperature soared to 90. It had not yet reached 80 in that necka-the-woods that year, so I wasn't used to it. It was the kind of day when you have to take a break and sit by a cold mountain stream and soak your feet. I let my bottled water soak there too, then had a super-refreshing cool drink.

I did nearly eighteen miles on Day 134. The highlight was St. John's Ledges, a seriously steep climb and rock scramble. It took me 20 minutes to negotiate that 1/8-mile bit of trail. Otherwise almost the entire day was a peaceful stroll along the Housatonic River. At Steward Hollow Brook Shelter, I signed the register book and thumbed through it, noting some familiar names. Paul/'Parkside' had passed here May 12th, 'Iceman' and 'Viking' two days before that. So all of them were already more than two weeks ahead of me.

Memorial Day in the woods. I paused to remember a few friends and high school classmates who had given their lives in service to their country in Vietnam. The weather was hot and beautiful, and another cascading cool stream called Hatch Brook was a perfect rest stop while I let my water bottles cool. Roger's Ramp, a narrow, tilted slot between house-sized boulders, was more fun (for me) than the Lemon Squeezer. It suffers from an image problem because it just isn't a very 'sexy' name. It was very similar to Lemon Squeezer, yet steeper, and had a similar blind approach from below, passing under the overhang of a gigantic boulder. And it had a similar tilt, just enough to make it a challenge when carrying a backpack. I did fourteen miles and had time in the evening for a big meal to keep my weight up, and for a good night of rest.

Summer had arrived. The lazy hazy long days, when the air feels soft on your skin and smells of humus and dew and rich green life. I had finally learned to pace myself properly. I had hiked 2,200 miles so far that year, more than the entire length of the AT in five months. Without realizing it at the time, I had just completed half the day hikes it would take to reach my goal.

I felt like a trail veteran, and it felt good, amazingly good.

It was beginning to dawn on me that I had missed my calling in life. Purposeful long-distance walking in wild places was what I was meant to do. Nowhere else had I felt such peace and contentment. Emma Gatewood said much the same thing back in 1955, and so have many others. I think many of us who love long distance hiking have something in common, and it is this: something in our past has steered us toward the wild and away from human entanglements. The human experiences we're trying to escape can be highly varied. For Earl Shaffer, it was his 4½ years in the army fighting in the Pacific theater in WWII. For Emma Gatewood, it was decades of spousal abuse. For David Miller, author of the annually updated *AT Guide* and of his memoir *AWOL on the Appalachian Trail*, it was a bleak and unrewarding job. I could go on and on.

For me? I've spent a lifetime thinking about this. It was much deeper-seated, almost Freudian. I was a first child and a birth control accident, as I've mentioned already. During those critical first two and a half years of my life, my dad and mom were ridiculously busy with dad's PhD studies and his dissertation, which dad wrote and revised by hand and mom typed up on an old mechanical typewriter, making seven carbon copies, erasing and correcting every error by hand. As a result, I was often left alone to learn the ways of the world on my own, without, I believe, enough physical contact, enough hands-on attention. Don't get me wrong, my parents loved me dearly: I was breast fed; my mom had read Dr. Benjamin Spock's 1946 classic book on child care, and constantly referred to it. She was as thoroughly modern and up to date as any Harriet Nelson '50's housewife in America.

But U.S. Government pamphlets being distributed at the time warned against "excessive" affection by parents for their children. Worse, our family was of stoic German roots, rarely showing or expressing emotion.

Dr. Spock's advice was "Trust yourself. You know more than you think you do." Unfortunately, my mother's instincts were rooted in generations of dysfunctional mother-child relationships. She herself had been an only child. She grew up with two working parents. Her mother worked the evening shift at the telephone company. Her father came home late in the afternoon from his auto assembly plant job and went straight for the beer. She often said that she 'raised herself' so it was natural that she expected me to do the same.

Her own mother's understanding of how to raise children was even more sullied. She was orphaned as a young teen and handed over to older siblings who didn't want her. She was a true 'Cinderella' until her husband rescued her from the situation by marrying her when she was seventeen.

In other words, my mom knew only poor examples of how to nurture, and she had precious little time to do it. They hadn't planned to start a family until my dad graduated and got a job.

And so, from my youngest days, I took to exploring nature on my own. I remember watching a little red-leaved Japanese Maple seedling sprout and grow in my backyard near the fence row. I observed with fascination as a gash in the bark of a young Norway Maple along that fence line healed itself through the summer. I hunted for four-leaf clovers in the lawn. I thought that was the way everybody lived. I got my nurturing from Mother Nature.

As I grew up, I was forever surprised when someone tried to show me kindness. I understood what it meant to be valued and appreciated on an intellectual level. My mom was always praising my little advances: counting to one hundred, reciting my ABC's, learning to read. But I did not have a clue what it meant emotionally. I was Peter. I was a rock. I was an island.

In school, I excelled during the era when group activities were rare, where achievements were based on individual effort. I got a great job at NASA that I thought was my ideal career setting. I had earned a PhD and so was given the latitude to do independent research, and I was studying the interaction between the earth's land surfaces, its vegetation and soil, and the lowest layers of the atmosphere. I loved that work, translating the relationships I saw in nature into computer code that made its way into weather prediction models and climate models. I published scholarly papers that are still being cited today.

But I hated the parts of my job that called for people skills, competitive interaction, management. There was always that implicit pressure to climb the 'corporate ladder.' All I wanted to do was climb mountains.

As a grad student in Colorado, I roamed the mountains whenever I could. When I moved to Maryland and took the NASA job, I used my leisure time to work with nature in my backyard. I became an avid daylily hybridizer—learning the workings of the language of DNA, and learning what folly it is for humans to try to manipulate Nature's Code for their benefit.

I was always most comfortable out there at the interface between myself and nature, and uncomfortable in the other direction, at the interface between myself and 'civilization.' I was at my happiest when I was laying down footprints in the wild; seeking that connection that had nurtured me from the start.

Unfortunately, it took me sixty-three years to figure that out.

Fortunately, I figured it out.

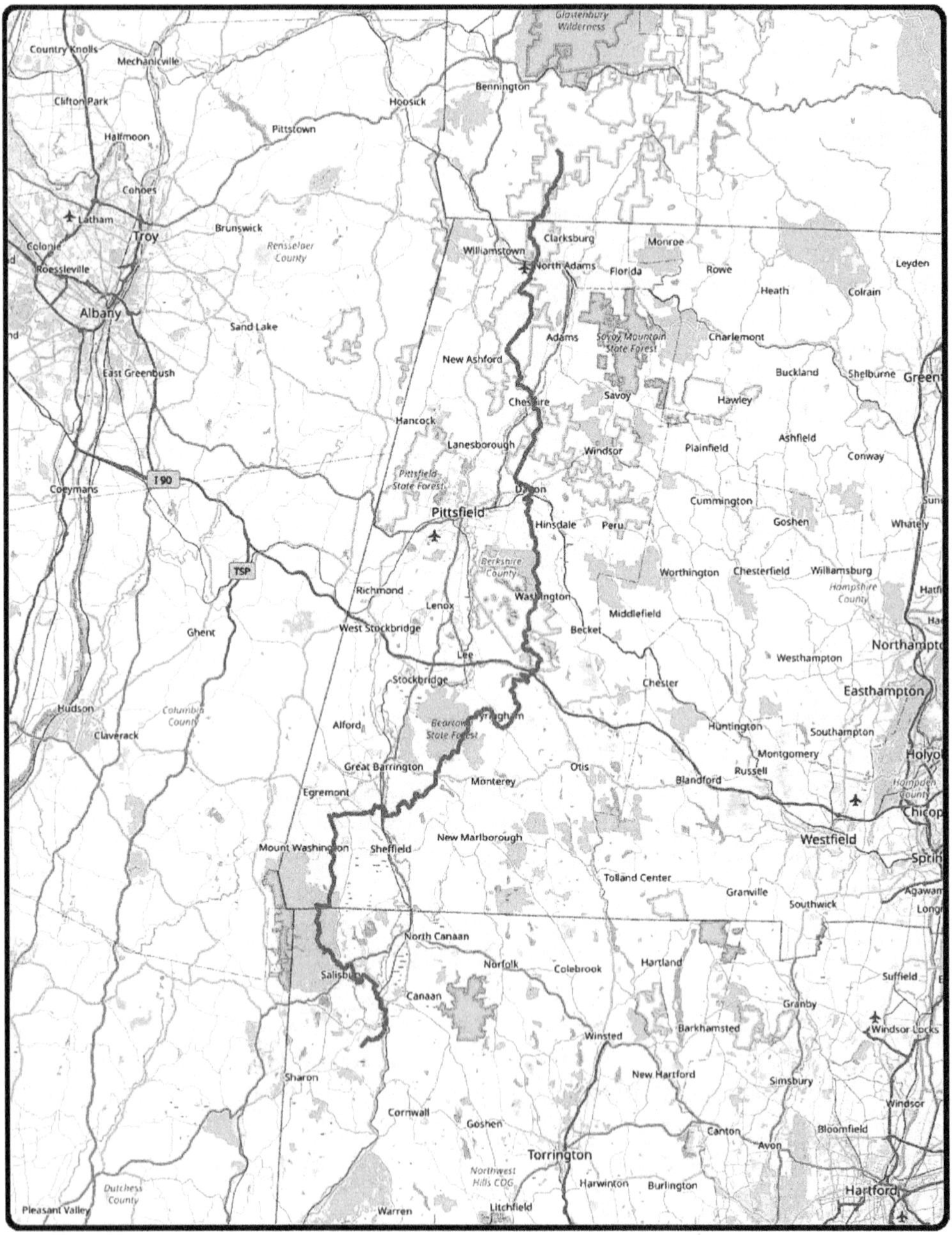
Glastenbury Wilderness
Country Knolls
Mechanicville
Bennington
Clifton Park
Hoosick
Halfmoon
Pittstown
Cohoes
Latham
Troy
Brunswick
Rensselaer County
Colonie
Roessleville
Albany
Sand Lake
East Greenbush
Clarksburg
Monroe
Williamstown
North Adams
Florida
Rowe
Leyden
Heath
Colrain
Adams
Savoy Mountain State Forest
Charlemont
New Ashford
Buckland
Shelburne
Savoy
Hawley
Cheshire
Hancock
Ashfield
Lanesborough
Windsor
Plainfield
Conway
Pittsfield State Forest
Dalton
Coeymans
I 90
Pittsfield
Cummington
Hinsdale
Peru
Goshen
Whately
TSP
Berkshire County
Worthington
Chesterfield
Williamsburg
Hampshire County
Richmond
Washington
Lenox
Middlefield
Ghent
West Stockbridge
Becket
Lee
Westhampton
Northampton
Stockbridge
Chester
Easthampton
Hudson
Columbia County
Alford
Beartown State Forest
Tyringham
Huntington
Southampton
Claverack
Montgomery
Holyoke
Great Barrington
Otis
Russell
Monterey
Blandford
Egremont
Hampden County
New Marlborough
Westfield
Mount Washington
Sheffield
Tolland Center
Granville
Agawam
Southwick
North Canaan
Norfolk
Colebrook
Hartland
Suffield
Salisbury
Canaan
Granby
Winsted
Barkhamsted
Windsor Locks
Sharon
New Hartford
Simsbury
Windsor
Cornwall
Goshen
Canton
Bloomfield
Avon
Torrington
Northwest Hills COG
Dutchess County
Harwinton
Burlington
Hartford
Pleasant Valley
Warren
Litchfield

CHAPTER 10

Sharon Mountain, CT to Consultation Peak, Long Trail, VT
May 29 – June 12; 118.1 trail miles one way

The story of the Appalachian Trail begins with the story of the Appalachian Mountains, an ancient chain of peaks and ridges that run from Alabama to Newfoundland, Canada, and even on across the Atlantic to Ireland and Scotland. It is one of the oldest and most complex geological stories on the planet.

It all began 13.8 billion years ago with the Big Bang. Well, actually *everything* we know began 13.8 billion years ago with the Big Bang. Why the Big Bang produced a blob of hot quarks and gluons, nobody knows. It could have just as easily produced a horde of pink Easter bunnies streaming out of a rabbit hole, but it didn't. Scientists can't explain it.

One proposed explanation is that the physics of our universe came from a parent universe. Alan Guth, MIT professor and cosmologist, first showed back in the 1990's that it is possible to create a child universe 'in a test tube.' The baby universe would inherit the properties of its parent universe, subject to quantum mutations, but would disappear from the parent universe and be entirely separate and autonomous once formed. Such an 'evolution of universes' would neatly explain why our universe is so specialized and conducive to life. Yes, boys and girls, deep down in the rabbit hole, there is a Mama Easter Bunny.

Wherever they came from, the quarks and gluons began consolidating into stars a mere hundred million years after the Big Bang; a blink of an eye really. Some of the stars exploded, leaving behind the 'heavy' elements necessary for rocks, trail running shoes, and pink bunnies.

Some of the rocks got together and formed the sun and the Earth and another big ball called Theia. A hundred million years later, Theia and Earth collided in the "Big Splash". The coincidence of the timing is just astounding.

Besides producing the Moon, the Big Splash left a big mess on Earth. It took some time for the mess to clear up. The first continents were forming while it was still too hot for liquid water on the surface. And the oldest of those continents was called the Slave Craton (now part of northern Canada around Great Slave Lake). This is where the oldest known rocks on Earth come from; they're about 4 billion years old. The oceans didn't start forming for another quarter billion years.

For the sake of keeping my readers' eyes from glazing over, I'll fast-forward from there. Chunks of continents floated around, crashed into each other, split apart again, in seemingly endless random fashion. Wherever two chunks crash together, ranges of mountains get pushed up, and that's what happened in proto-North America.

What we now call the Appalachians reached their height of splendor 325 to 260 million years ago when what was to become Africa butted hard up against proto-North America, forming the super-continent Pangaea.

This was the time of the great swampy forests of club mosses, 150 feet high, which produced most of North America's coal. The green tunnel was in place, and the earliest ancestors of dinosaurs, alligators, and mammals, none more than a few feet long, were there to hike it. Overhead, dragonflies with 2½ foot wing spans ruled the skies.

Back then the Appalachians were as high and rugged as the Alps or Himalayas are today. It's impossible to say with any accuracy where the highest peak was or how high it might have been. But an AT thru-hike would have been one seriously epic trek. This was the start of the Jurassic period. Some of the hikers were real trail hogs, like Diplodocus, more than 100 feet nose to tail, weighing in at up to 125 tons.

Africa started separating from North America more than 200 million years ago, leaving Florida and the Atlantic coastal plain behind. The mountain-building party was over. From that time until today, erosion has patiently chipped away at the Appalachian peaks, one grain of soil at a time, until today the best we have is 6,683-foot Mount Mitchell.

The Jurassic was a hot period, seven degrees Celsius warmer than our world. My hike on Tuesday, May 29th probably would have been considered typical back then, but for me it was the hottest day yet. It never got below 70° F overnight and soared to 95° in the cloudless afternoon. That's 35°C to the rest of the world. The trail took me through the town of Falls Village and offered more hiking along the Housatonic, though I was rarely in sight of it except when I crossed it—twice each way—on two bridges with two very different stories. The US 7 bridge was brand new, built in 2010. The one-lane 1903 iron structure of Water Street Bridge in Falls River was so old and worn out that it was closed to auto traffic. The best

The new US 7 bridge over the Housatonic, complete with wide AT sidewalk.

view on the river was north of there at Great Falls. All that splashing cool water looked really tempting, but I had miles to go. I managed almost twenty despite the heat.

On Day 137, I passed Rand's View and Billy's View. Rand's was grand; Billy's was just silly—badly overgrown and barely a view at all. Giant's Thumb was a strange monolith in the woods with an almost Celtic standing-stone quality. The reverential circle of logs around it for seating added to the effect.

I passed 'Wisconsin' twice that day. First, on the way out, I passed him slogging along, hoping to get to Riga Shelter. He looked tired, laboring up the trail. On the way back, I found him curled up in his sleeping bag right on the trail just a half mile shy of US 44. He said he could go no further. He was feverish and said that every joint in his body ached. I asked if he needed me to make a call or get help, but he declined. His father was on his way down from Dalton, MA.

I worried about 'Wisconsin' all evening. But his story has a happy ending. Five days later, he passed me on the trail, perky and chipper as could be. Turns out, it was Lyme Disease. I've had that twice and never had such a severe reaction. The prescribed Doxycycline had him feeling fine in no time, and he was once again headed for Maine.

The next day I left Connecticut behind and entered Massachusetts, as I passed through one of my favorite spots on the trail: cool, secluded Sage's Ravine.

To get there meant traversing the most rugged part of Connecticut's section of trail over their version of Bear Mountain. Views from the stone monument on top were spectacular on this bright clear day. The north face of the mountain presents a serious rock scramble. That was where I met an intrepid father carrying his 35 pound, 4-year-old daughter up that 900 foot near-cliff in a kid-carrier backpack. Great way to share your cardio workout with your young-un.

At the state line register book, I found many familiar names. 'Parkside' had come through May 14th; 'Samus' and 'Achilles' on the 10th—both wrote that they were glad to be back in their home state.

Great cliff views and ridge top bedrock walks were the features of Day 139. Race Mountain was my favorite. There you walk right along the edge of a steep escarpment ... okay, a cliff ... with numerous grand vistas and the blue glimmer of Twin Lakes off to the southwest. The day began and ended with the tough ascent and descent of Jug End. There was a great view north and east, with Mt. Greylock poking up in the distance. This piece of trail featured the most uncompromisingly tough footing, with sections of sloping bedrock without knobs or footholds that required good gripping soles. I would have hated to try this gauntlet in wet weather.

The next day it was all lowland walking in the vicinity of the ATC's Kellogg Conservation Center at South Egremont, now called the April Hill Conservation Center and no longer owned by the ATC. I also rambled past the site of the last battle of the 1787 Shays' Rebellion, in which 4,000 rebels almost overthrew the U.S. federal government. Well, that's an exaggeration, but the clash revealed the weakness of the United States government as organized under the Articles of

Confederation, and directly led to the convening of the Constitutional Convention in Philadelphia, starting May 25th of that year.

It had rained all morning, and my half-day afternoon walk took me through swampy areas thick with mosquitoes. I got to high ground and escaped the skeeters only to run into the first of the year's deer flies. Then it was back through the torture chamber of mosquitoes.

My favorite spot on Day 141 was Ice Gulch, a deep cleft in the bedrock—twenty feet wide with fifty-foot sheer vertical walls—and probably named because it retains ice in its shady areas into late spring. It's a short walk south of Tom Leonard Shelter where the log book featured entries from a number of the early NoBo thru hikers I had met, including 'Iceman' and the ultra-light hiking couple 'Spiral' and 'Swivel.'

Then, on the way back, at 2:40 pm, a vicious thunderstorm rolled in. I was on the ridge at the end of East Mountain, four miles from safety and very exposed. I could see the gray curtains of rain out over the Housatonic Valley. A sudden cold downburst came whipping through the trees. I knew the rain was not far behind. I needed to get off the slippery bedrock and out of that exposed position fast. I found a spot in the wind-shadow on the lee side—a nice flat rock to sit on, a few pines at my back. I ripped the poncho out of my pack as quickly as I could and got it on. Thirty seconds later and little rivulets were already forming on the trail. I hunkered down, nestled inside the poncho, and hoped the storm would blow itself out. The lightning flashed all around me. Thunder pealed across the sky and thumped the air, but it could have been worse. Soon the wind was subsiding. Fifteen minutes later, the downpour had tapered off to a light steady rain and the thunder had rolled off to the east. And so I began the four-mile trek back through newly-formed pools and rivulets to my cave, my wickiup, my yurt … my two-ton transient home-place, thankfully out of the elements.

I guess it was the adrenaline, but I felt alive, more so than I did most of the time. Ten thousand generations of ancestors were sharing their wisdom with me: "This is how we have lived since the dream time. It is not easy. It is not comfortable. It is real." I was walking the path of the hunter-gatherer—alert, seeking that which the trail might provide; seeking a fuller understanding of The Provider. This … THIS … is the oldest profession (despite the prostitute jokes): the hunter and gatherer of nature's provisions. This is who I am, at the deepest level.

On Day 142 I hiked The Ledges, catching some great views to the west and southwest. I visited the two Mt. Wilcox shelters but at the southern one, I missed the new shelter and only visited the old CCC built log lean-to. If I had not met 'Sawdog', the Ridge Runner—one of two for the state—I never would have realized my mistake. He was installing a new register box at the north shelter. We chatted while I signed the new log book. So on my way back, I revisited the south shelter and photographed the new one that I missed. Since it was part of my core mission to visit every shelter, I would have kicked myself later if and when I realized I'd missed it. I also met a pair of thru-hikers who knew other thru-hikers I'd met. 'Maverick' knew the other 'Maverick,' who I had met, and he and 'Tetris' also knew the other 'Maverick's companions 'Goose', 'Blue Grass', and 'Groundhog'. These were guys who were probably well up the trail now, because I had met them just before the 'watershed' when I left the trail in southern New York.

The next day I met 'Patches.' Our last meeting had been near Newfound Gap in Great Smoky Mountain National Park. She was hiking alone, still wearing her signature multi-colored patchwork skirt. She was the third hiker I had crossed paths with twice, months apart. These long-distance connections were a real prize for me, even though they were usually brief. We had a great chat, caught up on each other's progress, and talked about some other mutual connections we had accumulated since we last met. She said she had been hiking with 'Spoon' until recently, part of the quartet I had met down south in Smoky Mountain Park.

Upper Goose Pond Cabin was the first New England style hut. It's more than just a roof and a platform to sleep on. Caretaker Nancy, from Maine, said she cooks pancakes for everyone for breakfast, free of charge, though donations are requested. The bunks have mattresses. The propane stove

Bethann 'Patches' Swartz with her signature patchwork skirt.

in the kitchen is available for everyone to use. There's no electricity but there's a canoe and a rowboat the hikers can borrow to go out on the pond. I spent a fair amount of time talking with Nancy, since it was the middle of the day and nobody else was around. She's a slight woman, probably less than 100 pounds, with short cropped black hair and a big generous smile. She said caretakers rotate, so she was only there for a week; apparently lots of people want the job. She was a good listener and eager to show me around. She had me sign the register and give her my Facebook contact and blog URL, and she did indeed follow me the rest of the way through New England. The register showed that 'Patches' was one of eight hikers who had spent the night there last night.

On Day 145, I hiked from US 20 east of Lee, MA north past October Mountain Shelter and back again. That took me over Becket Mountain (nice climb, not too hard) and along the ridge that connects it to Walling Mountain on trail that pass-

F.I.T. Wilderness

es through some nice semi-open woodland. Lots of sky was visible but not much of the surrounding countryside. Walling Mountain had the first significant stand of spruce-dominated forest on the trail since the isolated stands above 5,000 feet down south. I suspected that this marked my transition to the 'north woods' and away from the familiar deciduous hardwood forests.

Not far from scenic Finerty Pond, where the mountain laurels were coming into bloom, I met 'Spoon.' We had a great chat and caught up on each other's adventures. Spoon still misses hiking with 'Huckleberry' (the section hiker who left the trail when he got home to Boone, NC), 'Green Bean' (she got off the trail when her husband graduated from college and had not yet returned), and tall, long-legged 'Moses' (who they all realized they were slowing down, so they let him push north at his own pace. He was about two weeks ahead by then, according to shelter log books). When I met them together down south, they seemed to be a tight-knit group who enjoyed hiking together. Obviously that was a correct impression on my part, since 'Spoon' still considered those days his best on the trail.

In the middle of a scrubby woods that was thick with mosquitoes, I also met 'Grey Goose,' a 52-year-old thru-hiker from Knoxville, TN. We had a nice chat and I learned that he was taking a zero day tomorrow to meet up with his wife, so I told him we'd probably pass each other again. He was such a gentle soul. While we stood there talking, being swarmed by mosquitoes, he would gently flick them off his skin. Me? Smash! I was out for revenge—primed for the kill.

At October Mountain Shelter, where I turned around for the day, the shelter register had entries from 'Samus' (May 13th), 'Iceman' and 'Viking' together (May 15th), and 'Parkside' on May 16th. It was now June 7th; these guys were surely well into the White Mountains by that point, getting close to Maine.

Warner Hill is not much of a hill, really, but more of an open grassy top, and it provided me with a fine view of Mt. Greylock on Day 146. Indeed, the trail was nearly flat all day, so I made good time, finishing nineteen miles by 4:00 pm.

The next day I made my way through the trail town of Dalton and up over North Mountain. My turn-around was at the excellent vista point called The Cobbles. It has a commanding view of the town of Cheshire, the

View of Mt. Greylock from Cheshire Cobbles.

town's forest-lined reservoir, and of course Mt. Greylock. I love turning around at scenic points like this because it gives me a chance to come back and see it under different conditions the next day. Back in Dalton, I had a big AYCE dinner at the Old Country Buffet.

I summited Mt. Greylock on a beautiful sunny day. It was hot in the lowlands, as I hiked through the town of Cheshire, but up on the summit, at almost 3,500 feet, the weather was perfect. On a clear day like this, the rule of thumb is that the temperature cools 5°F per thousand feet of elevation (or 10°C per km, for those of you not stuck in the 19th century). Greylock is half a mile above Cheshire, so at least twelve degrees cooler.

It was a Sunday, so the mountain was crawling with tourists, but the grassy summit is a big place, so it didn't feel crowded. Hang gliders were set up in a line along the south face of the summit, waiting for the wind to pick up. I climbed the tower, took in the views, then stopped in at Bascom Lodge to check it out and sign the register. I didn't bother with the restaurant there, since it was surely overpriced; you pay for the spectacular view. Again today I had the luxury of such a great viewpoint as my turn-around. I would be back again tomorrow.

It was much more peaceful the next morning at 10:00 am when I returned to the summit after the long climb from North Adams. In the afternoon, I headed north out of North Adams and did another 1,500-foot climb up to some rocky ledges at the intersection with the Pine Cobble Trail. The pinkish-white mountain laurel blooms were at their peak and the weather was hot but bright and clear; ideal conditions to bring out the contrast between the flowers and the leathery dark green evergreen foliage. I returned to North Adams at the end of the day, weary but happy.

On Day 150, I finished a short piece of trail in Massachusetts and started the trek up the Long Trail of Vermont. Conceived in 1909, the Long Trail pre-dates the Appalachian Trail, though it is far from the oldest piece of foot trail that the Appalachian Trail 'piggy-backs' on. Construction of this 273-mile trail took place between 1910 and 1930,

Northbound AT, approach to the tower at the summit of Mt. Greylock, MA.

F.I.T. Wilderness

overseen by the Green Mountain Club. The AT uses the southern 105.2 miles of the Long Trail, which continues north to the Canadian border.

I ran into 'Grey Goose' again, fresh and clean and happy after a couple days off the trail with his wife. It was a day of green tunnel walking in the Green Mountain State. I made my turn-around at Consultation Peak. I knew I was there because there was a little sign on a tree that told me so. No views there, but no complaints either. The legs were on automatic pilot; the mind was ever alert to the sights, the smells, and the sounds around me.

We humans are a walking species. I would argue that walking is our defining trait. The thing that led to our success—that distinguished us from our ape cousins—was getting down out of the trees and walking on two legs, thus freeing up our arms and hands for tool use, and therefore demanding that our brains master that new art of making and using tools.

Sadly, over time, we have taken this ability to craft hand-gadgets to the extreme. We've learned to accomplish everything sitting down, and our bodies suffer for it.

"Sitting is the new smoking," says James Levine, a professor of medicine at the Mayo Clinic. "The chair is out to kill us."

"Walking is the best possible exercise," wrote Thomas Jefferson in a letter to Peter Carr, dated August 19th, 1785. "Habituate yourself to walk very far. The object of walking is to relax the mind. You should therefore not permit yourself even to think while you walk. But divert your attention by the objects surrounding you."

Thoreau scoffed at the concept of walking as exercise for its own sake. In a lecture first delivered at the Concord Lyceum on April 23rd, 1851, and later published in *Atlantic Monthly,* he said "…the walking of which I speak has nothing in it akin to taking exercise, as it is called, as the sick take medicine at stated hours—as the swinging of dumb-bells or chairs; but is itself the enterprise and adventure of the day."

I'm on his wavelength. I can't stand treadmill walking, though I did use the machine during a couple of intensive months as I got in shape for South America. I don't even like to walk the same trail too often. This was an important reason I showed up out here on the AT. I got tired of the trails near my home in the Maryland suburbs west of Baltimore. I hiked round and round the wonderful fire roads and woods trails at Liberty Reservoir, which was right outside my door. But eventually, I got sick of it and started ranging out farther and farther west, hitting the Catoctin Trail, and finally doing some local pieces of the AT. I started ranging farther and farther up and down the AT until it became a "thing"; and the "thing" grew into an obsession. By now, there at the threshold of the nation's oldest long-distance trail, this habit of walking in places new and wild had become, and has since remained, my primary "enterprise and adventure of the day."

Long Trail sign at the Vermont-Massachusetts border

F.I.T. Wilderness

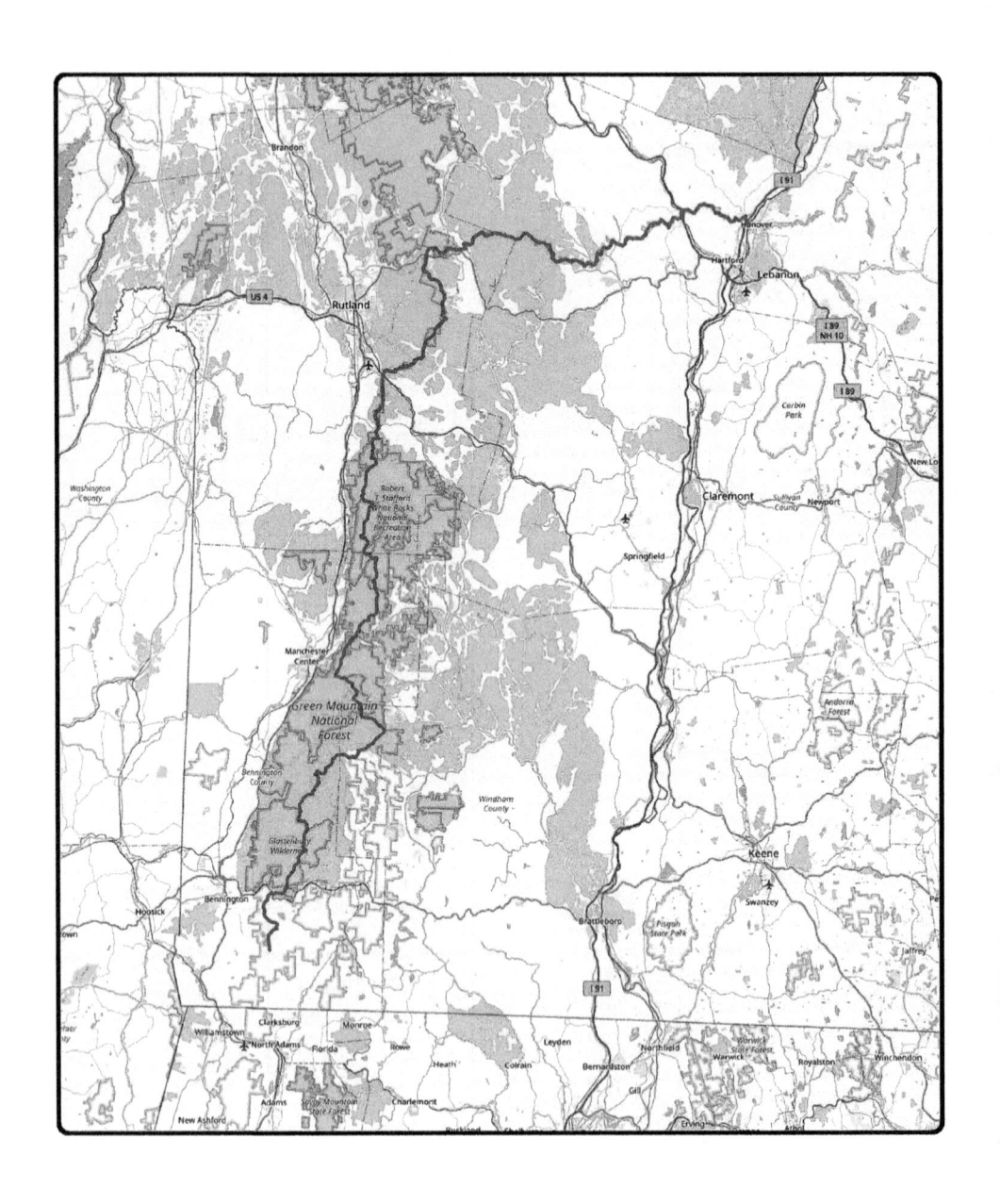

P. J. Wetzel

CHAPTER 11

*Consultation Peak, Long Trail, VT to Hanover, NH
June 13 - July 3; 142.8 trail miles one way*

    I ended the last chapter with glowing testimonials to the pedestrian life. But we all know that every rose has its thorns, every lollipop has its stick, every piece of cake leaves its crumbs. Hiking a rugged natural trail in the woods is full of inherent hazards, and I would be neglecting my duty if I failed to report this side of the story.
    The trail abuses us. The hiker takes a few knocks every day. I painfully stub my toes, usually on protruding rocks, at least once or twice every day. I'm talking about 'jamming' them—an impact strong enough that it sprains the ligaments, causing swelling and pain that lasts from minutes to hours. To avoid toe stubs and ankle sprains from landing awkwardly and twisting the foot, I concentrate on where I'm placing my feet. The rougher the trail, the more I'm watching where I put my feet. All too often the result is that I end up smashing my head against an unseen overhead branch or getting slapped in the face by a clot of wet leaves. Being very tall and not having great balance, I tend to fall at least once a week; like flat-on-my-face fall.
    Falls happen much more often at the end of the day, when we're tired and losing concentration. There are four common causes for falls: one: you're not watching your footing carefully enough and trip on an obstacle. Two: you're not watching your footing carefully enough and step on a slippery slanted rock or root. Three: you're not watching your footing carefully enough and step on loose gravel or wet leaves (or even an accumulation of acorns) that slip out from under your foot. Four: STICKS!
    Who would imagine that a simple 18-inch-long loose stick on the trail could be such a serious hazard? Trust me, it is. The offending stick is oriented roughly length-wise along the trail. You don't even notice it. You step on the front of it with your forward foot. This subtly lifts the back end of it while holding the front end firmly in place. Your trailing toe catches the lifted back end of the stick while the front foot prevents it from moving, causing the back foot to trip just as your body weight has shifted in preparation for that foot to move forward and take your weight. The result? Fail. Fall.
    People who haven't done a lot of hiking might think this is a joke; think again. Loose sticks are ubiquitous on all but the most manicured or heavily-trampled trails. When you are taking ten million steps, a tiny statistical minority of these

sticks are bound to set up this bizarre hazard. I've lost count of how many times this has happened to me in my 22,000 miles of hiking. Novices will need to trust me on this one. The long-distance hikers are merely nodding their knowing agreement.

Falls cause cuts and scrapes that need attention. Don't neglect a cut; out there in the woods, sanitation is not the same as at home. Infections can happen quickly and can get out of control. Constantly wet feet and footwear that is too tight are the main causes of blisters. A hiker's feet swell when s/he hikes all day; so always buy shoes at least a half size larger than your 'city shoes'. A full size larger is not too much.

Every hiker has experienced the knee pain that can come from going steeply downhill too fast. It gets to the point where we would rather be hiking uphill just to relieve the discomfort. The ligaments around the knees suffer the worst. I've found two ways to walk that prevent this. The first is a sort of duck-waddle. The key is keeping your upper torso bent slightly forward at the waist, not standing up straight. Project your knees slightly outward rather than forward as you pick up your feet. This looks stupid, but you'll have the last laugh as those hot-shots—chortling under their breath as they pound down the hill—are forced to take a zero-day the next day to heal their knees. There's another way that probably looks even stupider: walk sideways. Some people even resort to walking backwards downhill. Everybody is different. I no longer have any discomfort going downhill because I've developed the habits that work for me. Where there's a will, there's a way.

Now here's a related issue that is a matter of personal preference. There are hikers who swear by 'Vitamin I': ibuprofen. They consume it in prodigious quantities, and some of them may be the ones pounding down the hills chuckling, their pain masked by the drug. I don't know if they're doing themselves long term harm, but I would rather not take the risk. The human body is a finely tuned machine, designed through millions of years of field testing. It is self-correcting, self-repairing, and provides a whole 'control-panel' of sensory cues that tell us what's going wrong and even how to fix it, as long as we learn to read the signals. Listen to your body; learn its rhythms. There are actually hundreds of subtly different ways to walk. During this AT adventure, every time I took a pill, I've mentioned it here; there were no more than three times. For me, 'natural' is the best and only way to go.

The Green Mountain State is a great one for 'going natural'. There is only one state in the union that has a smaller population: Wyoming. My first full day on the Long Trail took me from Consultation Peak to the highway that leads west to Bennington. There were more beaver ponds than people. One recently flooded area had several hundred feet of puncheon uselessly floating in knee-deep water. There was a crude trampled path around that was hard to find, but it was there—not the work of maintainers, but of a lot of bushwhacking hikers. Did I pass every white blaze here? Both ways? Shut up.

The next section of trail ran twenty-two miles through the Glastenbury Wilderness, part of Green Mountain National Forest. Wilderness areas have no road access, and, in fact, do not allow any form of motorized equipment. Maintainers aren't even supposed to use chain saws. In some wilderness areas they don't even mark the trails with paint blazes. You're on your own. The federal law establishing these rules, The Wilderness Act, was signed into law by Lyndon Johnson on September 3rd, 1964, and includes this poetic definition:

"A wilderness, in contrast with those areas where man and his own works dominate the landscape, is hereby recognized as an area where the earth and its community of life are untrammeled by man, where man himself is a visitor who does not remain." — Howard Zahniser

    I would be tackling this pristine region in two consecutive 22-mile out-and-back hikes. The first of these took me thirteen hours. Most of the trail was fairly easy, but there was a lot of climbing—up from the narrow notch at the highway, an elevation of 1,400 feet, to the 3,700-foot summit of Glastenbury Mountain. There's a fire tower there (far predating the wilderness designation), and today's weather allowed for some of the most spectacular views I'd yet seen on the trail, because there were so many ranges of mountains and individual peaks visible, and few signs of humanity. I visited two shelters and met more than twenty hikers—most of them northbound thru-hikers—but only had time for a few brief chats. The NoBo bubble was catching up with me.

    The next day, coming in from the north end of the wilderness, I passed many of the same hikers. Among them, I had the most in-depth conversation with thru-hikers 'Whistler' and 'Two Cents.' We talked about trail names. Whistler said he took his name from the famous painting, 'Whistler's Mother.' 'Two Cents' leaves two pennies at every shelter he stays at. But from what I could tell, he was not at all shy about also expressing his opinions, just sayin'.

    At the Kid Gore Shelter, deep in the designated wilderness, I paged through the register book and saw some long lost 'friends. 'Moses' had come through May 24th, saying he had finally met some familiar faces, after having hiked solo since Waynesboro, VA. I was surprised to see an entry from 'Fire Pit' who I had not seen or heard from since near Hot Springs. 'Wisconsin' had passed through five days earlier.

    The next day was the 154th on the trail. My turn-around point for the day was in the heart of Lye Brook Wilderness, but the highlight of the day was the fire tower atop Stratton Mountain, overlooking the major ski area and lots of wild country. The ski area gondola to the summit runs all summer on weekends and was free to hikers. The summit tower had a register beside it, where I found 'Parkside' had checked in May 20th and 'Spiral' and 'Swivel' on the 28th. Checking in much more recently were 'Salty' and 'Patches'.

    During the day I passed and chatted with thru-hiking couple 'Alien' and 'Swiss Miss' from— where else?—Switzerland, here on a six-month visa. And for the second day in a row, I chatted with 'Whistler' and 'Two Cents'. 'Two Cents' planned to not only thru-hike the AT but also do the entire Long Trail. And though I haven't mentioned them so far, I once again met and chatted with section hikers 'Match Box' and 'Twisted Knickers,' two wonderfully spirited ladies whom I first met coming out of Dalton about a week earlier and had passed nearly every day since. They were out enjoying twelve days on the trail, and their pace going one way was close to mine going out-and-back, so I had little doubt I'd see them again.

Finally, while I was hanging around the Stratton tower, the caretaker came out of his little hut all decked out in tight fitting clothing—long sleeves and pants drawn tight at the cuffs, gloves, and a hat with a full bug net tucked into his collar—declaring his contempt for the black flies.

They were pretty thick that day, and had been the day before as well, always only at the highest elevations. I had thought they were just ordinary gnats; I hadn't really paid them much attention.

I asked the caretaker, "These things bite?"

He was flabbergasted. They eat him alive, he said. They've been known to kill livestock.

It was my turn to be flabbergasted. Yes, black flies are notorious. Why weren't they bothering me? All they did was buzz by me. A few would land on my skin and crawl around aimlessly until I smacked them. Most didn't land on me at all, or landed and took off again. I must have some sort of naturally repellent scent. I wish that was true for the skeeters.

The following day was Father's Day. I have two great kids, and, since we're far apart, our tradition is to chat on the phone. I took a short hiking day in the vicinity of Manchester Center and spent the second half of the afternoon shopping and chatting with the kids. I went into the Eastern Mountain Sports outfitter there and bought a piece of equipment that has been my most important one ever since. This was a large nylon belt pack that I bought to carry food and water on hot days when quick and convenient access is a big advantage. It even began to replace my backpack. Twelve years later, this piece of gear—much repaired and expanded in volume by the repairs, and still fully functioning—is usually all I carry on my day hikes.

Half of Day 156 was spent in the Peru Peak Wilderness. The other half was spent getting to and from it through the Bromley Mountain Ski Area. In the morning, the summit of Bromley was badly socked in with fog, and finding the trail on that grassy open summit was tough. On the way back, the grass had filled with a profusion of summer wildflowers. Where were they in the morning? All tucked up tight and waiting for the sun.

Big Branch Wilderness was next. These wilderness areas along the Long Trail are strung together like pearls on a necklace. This was the day I met 'Corky,' hiking in her brown Crocs. I ran into her as I had just made a wrong turn and was backtracking. Once I righted myself, we were both going the same way so we climbed the next hill together and had a nice chat about her footwear. Most hikers carry a pair of Crocs with them to use as camp shoes, to let their feet air out and relax.

They're so lightweight that few people consider it a problem to tote them along on the outside of their packs. If they're so nice and light and let your feet air out and relax as you go, why not hike in them, Corky asked?

Corky is from Front Royal, VA, and although I've never met her since, I have to claim her as one of my greatest hiking 'mentors', simply because of her footwear. About a year and a half later, on my next long-distance trek—North Carolina's 1,175-mile Mountains-to-Sea Trail—I started hiking in orange Bistro-style Crocs and have worn them exclusively ever since, with the one exception being when I'm hiking in more than three inches of snow. I've now logged well over 12,000 miles in Crocs and see no reason to ever return to the trail runners I used on the AT. Wearing those trail runners, every evening the first thing I wanted to do when I got off the trail was rip them off so my cramped, sweaty feet could air out. When I'm hiking in Crocs, I just keep them on even when I stop.

Some people might wonder about ankle support, which Crocs obviously don't offer, and worry about feet slipping around in them on uneven surfaces. My response to that is that they're more like hiking in bare feet, while avoiding the danger of cuts and thorns. They're just a more natural way to go. Some readers may know about the Rarámuri, the indigenous Mexican tribe of long-distance runners in the Copper Canyon area of the Sierra Madre Mountains, in the southwestern state of Chihuahua. Their preferred footwear is a simple flip-flop-like sandal made of a piece of automobile tire strapped to their feet with a couple of leather thongs; simple, natural, and very comfortable.

I took a few days off the trail as summer officially began in the Northern Hemisphere. I had some business to take care of at home. On my way back toward Vermont, I decided, on a whim, to stop in at the AT Conservancy headquarters in Harper's Ferry. Exactly why I went there, I'm not sure. The 'excuse' I used was that I wanted to avoid Friday afternoon rush hour traffic through DC. Yes, I hate the 'urban blight' traffic that much. But it seemed that I was somehow 'meant' to drop in there. Two stunning events prove that: one very good, and one very sad.

The good news came first. As I wandered in the front door at 12:30 pm, I met thru-hikers the 'Troverts': Cynthia Harrell ('X Trovert') and her husband, Woody ('N Trovert'). They had just hiked in on their way north. I mean, what were the chances!!!??? Cynthia is practically family. She is the little sister of one of my brother's good high school friends. We had been following each other's AT thru-hike attempts since the previous winter when we learned of our common plans. Woody is a retired park ranger for the National Parks System. There were some other big wigs there in ranger uniforms, and Woody was being treated like royalty.

Cynthia and I got to visit, chatting about old times and new. In the course of the conversation, Cynthia happened to mention fresh news of a thru-hiker who had drowned up in Maine. She thought the trail name began with 'P'.

No. No. "Not 'Parkside'?" I asked, incredulous, and dreading the response.

"Yes, that's the name," she said, and my mind went into a reeling swirl.

I checked with staff there (Laurie was in a meeting and was unavailable), and checked the hiker photobook, and everything confirmed it. The staff eventually came up with the following news release:

BOWTOWN TWP, Maine — Officials on Monday identified the man who drowned over the weekend while through-hiking the Appalachian Trail.

Paul Anthony Bernhardt, 20, of Flushing, N.Y., had hiked nearly 20 miles on the trail Friday, June 15th, and was trying to swim across a small cove near the outlet of Pierce Pond in Bowtown Township when he went underwater about 35 yards from shore.

Rescue personnel eventually found Bernhardt's body in nearly 15 feet of water but couldn't immediately retrieve it.

Game Warden Sergeant Glenn Annis and wardens Josh Bubier, Dan Carroll, Kris MacCabe and other volunteers were able to retrieve the victim at 11:30 p.m. Friday.

Pleasant Ridge Fire and Upper Kennebec Valley Ambulance personnel also were at the scene.

Paul 'Parkside' Bernhardt was the first person I met twice along the trail, both south and north. And now he was gone. That early in the season, the water at Pierce Pond was surely ice cold. He probably cramped up. 'Achilles' was there, along with several others, at the Pierce Pond Shelter and heard his cries for help. 'Achilles' dove in to try to rescue him, but was too late.

What still brings me to tears is the simple fact that Paul would never make it to Katahdin, that his thru-hike was the last thing he knew. I can only hope that it made him happy. And judging from our last meeting on May 6th, I believe it did.

The rest of my time at the ATC office was kind of a blur. I talked with Cynthia and Woody some more and got photos with them, bought an ATC hat, and eventually got to talk to Laurie, to whom I promised to send my full-resolution photos of Paul. I looked through the photo album to find faces and names I recognized and signed the register. I left about 2:00 pm and, as I drove on north, one thought kept screaming in my head: why couldn't it just have

Paul clowning around, claiming his first pose (page 104) was too 'generic'.

been some anonymous kid whom I had never met?? It's awkward and yet understandable, I suppose, how we react so differently to bad news about strangers versus the same news about a friend or acquaintance.

Among the six other hikers who were there at Pierce Pond Shelter that evening, I had met four—'Achilles,' 'Spiral,' 'Swivel,' and 'Drop Out.' 'Catwoman' and 'Germanator' were also there. They all headed down to New York for Paul's funeral. Then they all returned to the trail, carrying a small tin with his ashes. The 'Parkside Fellowship' stuck together through the Hundred Mile Wilderness and summited Katahdin together before noon on Friday, June 29th where they held a small memorial and gathered for a group photo.

The AT Conservancy was kind enough to award Paul a thru-hiker 2,000-miler badge and certificate posthumously. It was the right thing to do.

I was back on the trail Sunday, a day later than planned. The Vermonters care about their trails, and they love to hike. This Sunday the weather was perfect and the locals were out *en masse*. I was hiking a very popular two-mile stretch of easy trail between Danby-Landgrove Road and Little Rock Pond. The pond was smooth as glass that morning under a crystal cerulean sky, and the walk to it follows babbling streams nearly all the way. When I got back to the ample parking lot, it was full to overflowing. I was able to turn my parking space over to one lucky noon arrival, but many others had no such luck.

The afternoon fare was White Rocks Mountain. The summit offered a nice view on this clear afternoon, but for me the white rock 'cairn city' that people had constructed at the junction of the side trail with the AT held my interest more. Some of the constructions seemed to defy the laws of physics; others were just works of art.

Day 159 took me high over Clarendon Gorge on a swinging suspension bridge that had been built in 1974. The gorge, and every other stream in this part of Vermont, was scoured clean by all-time record floods produced by Hurricane Irene in late August 2011. The bridge over the gorge is anchored in bedrock high above the water, and took the storm easily, but reading old accounts from the earliest hikers—specifically Emma Gatewood and Earl Shaffer—this crossing of the Mill River presented problems, as the old bridges kept washing out. Emma made her way across the river wading the raging current chest-deep, roped between two strong young men.

Hurricane Irene had washed out other bridges and sections of trail. The next day I had to take a road-walk detour around the worst of it. I learned later that many hikers were pushing through the weeds and fording the streams on the closed section of trail and were getting through fine, but this information came too late for me.

This was also the day I climbed Killington Peak and it was a miserably wet rainy day, though nothing compared to the hurricane of the previous year. From Governor Clement Shelter on up to the summit, the trail was open, but some streams had to be forded where bridges had been in place before the hurricane.

Somebody had thrown a nice new 2x8 over one stream, just stretched across the water on the gravel. It was better than no bridge, that's for sure.

Up on the upper reaches of the mountain, above 4,000 feet elevation, it was foggy and cold enough that a bit of ice was accumulating. The wind was ripping at my clothing. I still decided to make the nearly vertical climb to the actual summit—a hand-over-foot scramble over slippery wet rock and even slipperier mud. Up top, I met a family who had scrambled up ahead of me. They had come from the ski area. We all enjoyed the panoramic view of the wall of fog ten feet in front of our faces, and then returned the way we had come. The shelter down below was my turn around point and all the way back, JC the rest of the way was more slogging through mud and over wet roots on treacherous, steep side-slope trail. It was memorable, I'll say that.

I had turned around at the summit of Killington in the hope that on my return the next day up the north side of the mountain, I'd be able to catch the views. But it was not to be. The morning brought intermittent rain and when I got to the Cooper Lodge Shelter below the summit, it was so foggy that I didn't even consider making that gnarly climb up to the open summit.

Of course, on the way back down, the sky began to clear. At least I could catch the decent views from Churchill Scott Shelter about halfway down.

Early the next day, just north of US 4, I bade farewell to the Long Trail and struck out eastward toward New Hampshire. The weather had turned magnificent, so I at least got some great views *of* Killington Peak, if not *from* it. At Thundering Falls, there was a short reroute due to 'impassable boardwalk' caused by flooding from Hurricane Irene. At the other end of the reroute, I met two NoBo thru-hikers coming out of the closed boardwalk section. 'Pretzel' and 'JC' said it wasn't all that bad. The boardwalk was tilted and off its moorings in places, but hardly impassable. But the white blazes had been painted on the road walk, so I told them I was obligated by my 'mission' to hike that both ways. We had a great conversation. They had figured out who I was before we spoke a word, saying that they had seen my van with the AT stickers at several trailheads. After they headed on up the trail, I walked that closed, now blue-blazed boardwalk section both ways too.

Matt 'Pretzel' Mason was one of those hikers whose life took new directions because of the AT. After his thru-hike, he took a job at the Walâsi'yï

Pretzel (left) and JC at the closed, flood-damaged boardwalk.

Interpretive Center at Frogtown Gap in Georgia, and worked there for many years. He thru-hiked the Pacific Crest Trail in 2015 and recently (2019) moved to Bozeman, MT and thru-hiked the Continental Divide Trail.

The main thing that distinguished Day 163 in my mind was the scary drive up sketchy Stony Brook Road to its rocky, gated end where the AT crosses the road and where the town of Notown is, was, or might never have been. There are no buildings in Notown, and nobody lives there. Far as I can tell, nobody has *ever* lived there, but it is listed as a 'Populated Place' and shows up on Google Map searches. One explanation for this is that every parcel of land in Vermont is included in a 'town,' which is like a township, a subdivision of the parent county. Maybe this piece of Vermont was so remote—located right at the border of Windsor and Rutland Counties—that it somehow slipped through the cracks and wasn't specified as belonging to any town, so some map maker long ago just marked the area as belonging to 'No town'. Could be. Maybe not.

The next day I visited the roof of the private cottage near the trail called Luce's Lookout. Its views of the upcoming White Mountains are probably every bit as good as those from Killington. The weather was clear, visibility unlimited. At Wintturi Shelter, I looked through the log book and found an enigmatic entry from 'Cody Coyote', written just four days earlier. He's the quiet kid I had encountered sitting smoking a cigarette near the memorial to the hermit Nick Grindstaff down in Tennessee on February 9th. I only knew his trail name because of his entry in the log book at Iron Mountain Shelter. The entry at Wintturi said, "Don't really know where I'm gonna go today. Turning my mistakes into GOLD!" This kid had a story, probably an interesting one; and I wish I knew it. Had he been hiking north all this time?

The trail between Woodstock Stage Road and Joe Ranger Road passes mostly through rolling farm land and includes a lot of pretty meadow walking. The weather was getting hot, but still bright, and allowed nice pastoral views from high points on Dupuis Hill and Arms Hill, barely 500-foot climbs. The privy at Thistle Hill Shelter was a piece of work. It had its own name, Cloudland, and featured a panoramic 360-degree view from waist level up, and a gazebo-style seven-sided sunroof of some sort of translucent white plastic or fiberglass. It was one of the modern composting shelters, set three feet off the ground, and required people to add compost to their 'deposits.' Apparently this privy used to be located at a privately run shelter on 1,000-acre Cloudland Farm, located near the crossing of Cloudland Road. There was a sign for a 'Cloudland Shelter' there and an old beat-up privy with two crescent moons painted on the door.

Day 166 brought me to the threshold of the long road walk through Norwich, CT and Hanover, NH. I had easy trail and a bit of road walking through West Hartford and its newly opened general store with a 'Welcome AT Hikers' sign and a coat-rack to hang backpacks on the front porch.

At the end of the day, I had time to pause and contemplate what was to come. I wrote in my blog:

"New Hampshire is here. I will cross the Connecticut River into the "Live Free or Die" state tomorrow. I've been both looking forward to and worrying about the White Mountains for a long time.

"It's going to take this old man a significant effort to get through the Whites by means of day hikes. I don't walk fast anymore. Three problems conspire to slow me down. First, I can't push off with my left foot because of the instant, then long-lasting pain that produces. It's probably arthritis. The base of the left big toe is chronically swollen. The original condition is decades old—believe it or not, it's a 'gardening injury.' Second, I have to baby my left ankle because of several episodes of sprains, down near Damascus and then recently stomping on that soda can. The old 1984 broken ankle is at the root of that one. And third, I can't use my chronically bad left knee for more than simple support—no hard pulling. It's Chondromalacia, caused by repetitive stress from hard bicycling. I basically walk on one leg.

"Yep, this old soldier has accumulated war wounds that slow him down. The climbs that I face in the White Mountains are steeper, longer, and tougher than anything I've faced so far. They will make or break this adventure. I won't know if I can do it until I get to it. The same was true for the four 30+ mile days I had to do in the Smokies. And that's encouraging. I wasn't sure if I could do those days until I actually put leather to dirt, or in this case Carbon Rubber to granite.

"One thing is fairly certain: it's going to take a long time for me to make it through the White Mountains. So on a day like today, when the trail was smooth and fairly easy (no elevations above 1,600 feet), I wanted to make some distance. I did more than 20 miles today.

"I will miss Vermont. End-to-end, Vermont has become my favorite Appalachian Trail state. It was more of the same today, not spectacular, just very pleasing. There were a few views from high meadows, almost like the balds of the south, and one pond. Otherwise I was in the woods all day, enjoying the warm but tolerable weather and the sights, sounds, and smells of summer."

Now as I looked up the trail, just as I did back in Davenport Gap, I could see only a big dark, scary, green tunnel into the unknown.

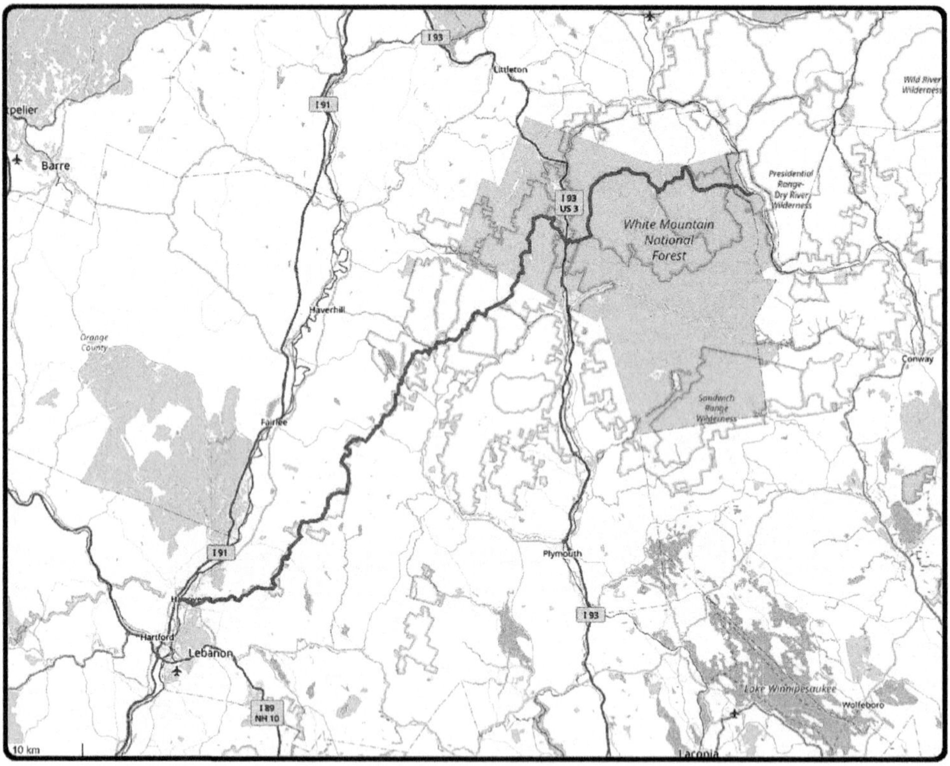
I 93
Littleton
I 91
Barre
Wild River
Wilderness
Presidential
Range-
Dry River
Wilderness
I 93
US 3
White Mountain
National
Forest
Haverhill
Orange
County
Conway
Sandwich
Range
Wilderness
Fairlee
I 91
Plymouth
I 93
Hartford
Lebanon
I 89
NH 10
Lake Winnipesaukee
Wolfeboro
Laconia
10 km

CHAPTER 12

Hanover, NH to Crawford Notch, NH
July 3 - 16; 97.3 trail miles one way

Since 2007, there has been no more energetic, pro-active Trail Angel than Betsy Maislen, aka 'Short 'n Sweet.' Back in 1993, she and her husband built a house on a lot near where Northbounders come out of the woods onto Elm Street in Norwich, VT. I'll let her own words tell the story from there. This was from a completely unsolicited email I got from her on June 1st:

Seeks It,
You are having an amazing journey! I've been following your Trail Journal for months now. My husband and I live right on the AT in Norwich, VT. I know you don't spend any nights out in the woods but I'd like to offer you a chance to stay at our home when you come through our neck of the woods. We live at 230 Elm St in Norwich, and if you Google the address, you'll see we really do live RIGHT on the AT (it's the 3rd house on the left after you come out of the woods at the top of Elm St). You'd be more than welcome to park your car in our driveway for any hikes you take in this area as well. There's not much space at the trail head just up the road from us. Also, the AT has its longest road walk on the entire trail right here in Norwich/Hanover, about 5 miles in all. Not sure how long it will take you to make your way to VT from CT. The only thing I ask is that you give me a head's up when you are getting close so we can be sure we are around and haven't decided to take off on a hike in the Whites for a weekend.

As a little bit of back ground, our son thru hiked the AT in 2007, in his gap year between high school and college. Since then, my husband and I have been section hiking and have now covered about half of the entire AT. Just went south and hiked from Amicalola Falls to Fontana Dam the first 2 weeks of May. It was beautiful!

Our Trail Angel status didn't begin until our son did his thru hike though. That's when we learned so much more about the AT community and began to have a sense of just how much a stay in a home with a meal, a hot shower and laundry could mean to a hiker.

Best of luck as you come north! I would look forward to meeting you.

Short 'n Sweet
Elizabeth Maislen, APRN, CTTS
Cardiothoracic Surgery
Dartmouth Hitchcock Medical Center

Betsy is one of those people that just overflows with caring and kindness. She now leads, trains, and recruits a network of volunteers helping hikers in the Norwich-Hanover area called simply 'Appalachian Trail Trail Angels.' It didn't seem to faze her when I replied that I was concerned about being distracted from my 'mission.' I had turned down other opportunities to stop in with friends and former schoolmates. Staying in her house, as with staying in motels, was actually a significant inconvenience for me. I'd have to pack stuff I kept stowed in the van, carry it in, unpack it, use it, pack it up again, and return it to its proper place in the van. Even when I went home to take care of business, I found myself based out of my van more than out of my permanent residence.

No, that talk went right over her head. Betsy emailed me twice more as I approached, each time repeating her invitation to be her guest, to stay at her house when I passed through. Just give her a little advance notice, she said. That was the kind of distraction I wanted to avoid—making an 'appointment' meant predicting where I'd be, which I never knew from day to day, even hour to hour. I tried to make it clear to her that I looked forward to stopping in as I passed through, but I avoided giving her any indication of when I would actually walk down Elm Street.

It happened on Day 167. I parked my van along Main Street in Norwich, near the Norwich Green and the Episcopal Church, and was out hiking at 6:00 am in a cool soupy fog. I had just a short leg to hike south, up Elm Street and half a mile through the woods to my turn-around point at a power line clearing. As I walked up Elm Street, I kept an eye out for the trail exit on the left and for 'Short 'n Sweet's' house on the right. I knew it was three houses down from where the AT comes out of the woods, but I was going the wrong way to be able to count. I noticed a girl with a day pack at a mailbox. She looked like a kid waiting for the school bus, but it was July. Before I could ponder that paradox much longer, the girl started walking down the road toward me. As she passed, she looked at me oddly and asked, "Are you 'Seeks It'?"

I hesitated, nonplussed. "How did you ...?"

"I'm Short 'n Sweet. Betsy Maislen."

I was thinking 'no way.' I was expecting some grandmotherly type, not a fit young woman.

We chatted only briefly because she had to get to work. Apparently, every Tuesday she walked the five miles to her job as a nurse at the big hospital outside of Hanover. Nearly a two-hour walk, hence the early start. What she had been doing at the mailbox was setting out a cooler of goodies, a register book in a ziplock bag, and a Tupperware 'Compost bucket' for trash.

What were the odds of us crossing paths this way? Nearly astronomical.

I headed on up to the power line clearing and was back, passing her house again at 7:00 am. I stopped to check and sign the register book. There were entries from many of the people I know: 'Achilles', 'Patches', 'Tetris', 'Bomber', 'Pretzel', 'Spiral' and 'Swivel', and more. I wrote a long entry describing my meeting with Betsy, and while I was there, her husband Bill 'Gray-Beard' Schults approached me before driving off to work. We talked for a while, mostly about the people in the register. Then I headed back to my van and the northward leg.

That took me across the controversial concrete-orb-festooned Ledyard Bridge over the Connecticut River and across the state line into New Hampshire. Hanover, home to Dartmouth College—the seventh oldest college in the U.S. and originally opened to educate the 'Indians'—is the only place along the AT that I would call 'urban.' The Main Street drag, which the trail follows for three blocks, was lined with shops and stores and restaurants—three- and four-story brick buildings shouldering one another. It was packed with cars and bikes, milling crowds of shoppers and students, and folks enjoying their lunch on benches and at restaurants with open-air seating.

In the right frame of mind, one could consider that a refreshing change from the "footprints in the wilderness" theme.

Thing is ... the trail routers seemed to have deliberately avoided the fine network of woods trails that skirt both Norwich and Hanover on their south sides. In Hanover, there's the River Trail along the Connecticut River and Mink Brook that connects up with the Quinn Trail through the Mink Brook Nature Preserve. Cross Lebanon Street at the end of the Quinn Trail, and you go straight into the woods and back to the route of the AT. This would involve almost zero street walking through Hanover. On the Norwich side, there's a trail down that power line right-of-way to the Unitarian Universalist Church, then once you cross Christian Street, you're in Dresden Athletic Fields. With a tunnel under I-91, you'd access a whole network of trails along Bloody Brook beside the river to Foley Park, which abuts the bridge over the Connecticut River. Again, almost zero street walking through Norwich. The only road walk required would be the bridge itself. I do not understand.

I headed on up over Velvet Rocks on some wet slippery footing, visited the unusual transparent-plastic roofed shelter by the same name, and made the return trip on a warm sunny afternoon with the slippery footing now dried out and firm.

The next day was a warm day. Even up on the summits where it was cooler, the humidity clobbered me. I sweated until my clothes were soaked. There were three 1,000-foot ascents to do—Moose Mountain both ways and Holt's Ledge where I turned around. I stopped in at 'The

Holts Ledge.

F.I.T. Wilderness 153

Spruce Moose,' formally the Moose Mountain Shelter, built entirely with hand tools back in 2004. The Dartmouth Outing Club was clearly having way too much fun making up and posting their signature orange and black trail signs. The trails through this section are blazed with orange-and-black horizontal stripes as well as the official two by six-inch white blaze. The orange and black apparently dates back to before the AT.

I did a very short hike on Day 169, not because of bad weather but because of logistics. I got a second look at Holt's Ledge and captured a view of its steep rampart and fine view on digital film. I stopped in at Trapper John Shelter where there was an outdoor fireplace bigger than the shelter itself, apparently part of an old cabin.

The climb over 3,230-foot Smarts Mountain was the main event of the following day. The morning climb up to Lambert's Ridge brought me to a view of a frozen tsunami of fog. It looked like a breaking wave; it never moved. On the way back, it was gone.

The observation deck atop Smarts Mountain's fire tower gave me my first view of Mt. Washington, 47.78 miles away as the crow flies, and my last view of Killington, 41.81 miles in the other direction. Thank goodness for the bright clear New England summer air.

My turn-around was at the Hexacube Shelter, hexagonal in shape, set on Mt. Cube. Did you know that another word for a cube is 'hexahedron?' Did you care? I wrote in the shelter register: "My GPS is telling me the elevation profile on my map is all wrong. Got my butt christened in a slippery mud hole. Somebody's put a hex on my cube."

One section of steep solid granite on the climb to Smarts Mountain included half a dozen hewn log steps, followed by half a dozen stone steps, followed by fifteen re-bar ladder steps drilled into the solid rock. This was my first taste of the kind of rugged trail the White Mountains would throw at me.

Coming back to Hexacube from the north, over Mt. Cube, was memorable for a distinctive type of glacier-smoothed bedrock. It was nearly pure quartz with no grain. The weather was humid and damp, so the cold rock was sweating. It was every bit as slippery as ice, and I didn't even trust my footing on level places, let alone any even slightly sloped surface. I made it through the worst gauntlet very slowly. Behind me a hiker, being equally careful, suddenly had his feet slip out from under him and he took a nasty fall. I sympathized. It's happened to me often enough. It's always more embarrassing when somebody is there to see it.

I hiked north to the trailhead on NH 25C for an afternoon leg. There was a seriously difficult stretch—a swampy mile and a half that was on rounded, sometimes slippery stepping stones—that was infested with ravenous mosquitoes on this cloudy humid day. I didn't look forward to the return trip. I stopped in to check the site of the Ore Hill Shelter, which a vandal had burned down the previous fall. Apparently, to this day, the shelter has never been replaced. The sun was coming out so I had hopes of it chasing away the skeeters, but by the time I got back to the swampy section, a dark cloud had moved overhead and it began to sprinkle. Great. Just what the mosquitoes were hoping for. I made my way through it as quickly but as carefully as I could but ended up just as itchy on emergence as I was on the way out.

Gnarly Webster's Slide and gentle Mount Mist were the highlights of my hike to the Mt. Moosilauke trailhead off High Street at Glencliff the next day. There was no bridge over wide, calf-deep Oliverian Brook beside NH 25, so it was shoes and socks off time and a cooling ford each way. There is now a bridge there, built for vehicle access to a quarry and a private home. A lot of hikers probably bypass this short bit of trail anyway, and hike the road to the town of Glencliff for resupply, then up High Street. The guidebook suggests that the post office there is "a prudent maildrop for northbounders to pick up cold-weather gear before entering the high country of the White Mountains."

Summit cairn on Mt. Moosilauke. Mt. Washington is visible in the distance, far right.

On the way back south, as I entered the woods beyond NH 25, I found new trail magic had been dropped off since I passed in the morning. There was a good assortment, including cold beer, something rarely included in these anonymous drops. I normally leave these for the true backpackers, but here I had to indulge. I grabbed one Rolling Rock—nice taste but weak compared to my preferred IPA— and one Clif Bar.

Day 173 was a truly epic day; so much so that of the 270 day hikes that comprise this adventure, this one ranks as my favorite, with the hike from Carver's Gap to Hump Mountain, NC a close second. What tipped the balance here was the variety.

The geographic feature of the day was 4,802-foot Mount Moosilauke, the first place on the AT that northbound hikers pass above true timberline. So, there was a true 'bald' here, hiking across the tundra under the open sky. That's my favorite kind of hiking. That's why the Roan High Balds hike rivaled today's experience. My second favorite kind of hiking is trail that brings the hiker up close and personal with waterfalls. There the approach trail up from Amicalola Falls, with its 605 steps, wins the day. It was my third favorite hike of this excursion, even though it's not officially on the AT. On the north slope of Moosilauke is the Beaver Brook Cascades—more than 1,000 feet of waterfalls in steps. The trail is always near them. It was heaven.

It was a tough day-hike, going both ways up and over Moosilauke between the High Street trailhead and Kinsman Notch. Once is enough for a good day-

F.I.T. Wilderness

hike. The total elevation gain was close to 6,000 feet doing it twice, and the Beaver Brook side is notorious for its extreme challenge—rock and boulder scrambling much of the way. But I honestly didn't even notice how tough it was; I was having such a great time. It didn't hurt that the weather was perfect—bright blue sky with unlimited visibility, not even much wind.

Favorite view of some of the 1000 vertical feet of trail-side cascades of Beaver Brook.

Coming north out of Kinsman Notch the following day, there was plenty of tough trail again. It started with a grueling 700-foot climb out of the notch in the first half mile. Much of the rest of the day combined little and big climbs and descents. I was averaging little more than one mile per hour for the first five miles to the Reel Brook side trail. The mile of further trail to Eliza Brook Shelter gave me a break. Eliza Brook Shelter was falling apart, so the AMC had a new one built in a shop and had the parts airlifted to the site where it was completed just the previous October. It still had that new-wood beige color, and the logs fit to one another like Inca stonework.

From there the trail followed Eliza Brook with some very nice waterfalls right by the trail. Then, crossing Eliza Brook, it started heading straight up the side of the mountain. There were lots of well-built stone steps but they felt more like a ladder than steps, and the walk felt more like scrambling then hiking. My turn-around point was Harrington Pond. This is an ultra-remote, gorgeous little shallow lake with sphagnum moss fringes—floating mats growing out over the water, very reminiscent of the lakes in northern Wisconsin where my family vacationed when I was a kid. As a backdrop, Harrington Pond has a steep rocky cliff, part of Kinsman Mountain. The AT goes right up that cliff. Growing in the bog around the lake were millions of carnivorous pitcher plants with their strange red and green blooms and in the open water area millions more yellow water lily blooms.

On the way back, I began to notice the areas where moose liked to browse on the mossy undergrowth. The tell-tale piles of oval-shaped marble-sized moose droppings were everywhere.

I started the day at Franconia Notch the next day, at the Flume parking area, and hiked south over the double peaks of North and South Kinsman, scrambled down the virtual cliff to Harrington Pond, and had to scramble right back up, using hands for what seemed like several hundred feet of near-vertical climbing. I don't have a fear of heights in any clinical sense, but this bit of 'trail' gave me weak knees. This isn't hiking; it is hard class 3 or maybe class 4 climbing.

The summits of Kinsman are not quite high enough for tundra, but all the trees are stunted and there was plenty of exposed rock. The weather cooperated again today; it didn't just cooperate, it was perfect. I felt like I was traipsing through killer panoramic views of White Mountain National Forest for hours.

This hike also gave me my first exposure to the Appalachian Mountain Club's famed hut system, which dates back well into the 19th century. I stopped in at Lonesome Lake Hut for a look on the way back, when the place was mostly empty except for the 'croo,' the hard-working college kids who cook and keep the place clean, and who carry all the supplies in from the highway on their backs—60 or 70 pounds of it at a pop.

View NE to Franconia Ridge from Lonesome Lake.

Day 176 was another big day. It marked the beginning of a multi-day traverse through 27.7 miles of rugged high peaks with no road access. I was going to chop this up into five day hikes, so forward progress was going to be slow.

Back in Great Smoky Mountain National Park, I did 30+ mile days to hike through two similarly long sections from either end to the middle. But Smoky Mountain Park has a policy that no trail in the park can be steeper than a 15% grade. In the White Mountains of New Hampshire, if anything, the rule seems to

F.I.T. Wilderness

be 'the steeper the better.' So I had no hope of covering this segment in two long day hikes from either end.

On the other hand, in the Smokies (with the possible exception of a trail up from Cade's Cove) there are no reasonably short access trails that could usefully insert a day hiker into the middle, whereas here in the Whites, there is an abundance of access trails of four miles or less in length. So that was the plan: bite off two chunks at either end and then do the middle via side trails.

Today I took the bite from the south end, starting at Franconia Notch. This was the cream of the crop, because it contained nearly all of the tundra walking above the timber line—nearly 2.5 miles of glorious tramping along Franconia Ridge, surrounded by nothing but the sky and the infinite horizon.

The weather continued to be utterly perfect—cool and comfortable at these altitudes with blue skies, a few puffy afternoon clouds, and visibility virtually unlimited. There were plenty of other hikers on the trail, but here in the Whites in the middle of July, the atmosphere was very different. This wasn't an Appalachian Trail crowd. Few of the hikers one meets are thru-hikers. These were summer vacationers out to enjoy the rugged outdoors for a week or two.

Franconia Ridge, view of the AT connecting Mt. Lafayette with Mt. Lincoln in the distance.

My turn-around point for the day was 5,260-foot Mt. Lafayette, where the Greenleaf Trail intersects with the AT, leading down to Greenleaf Hut. The next day I came up to Greenleaf Hut and got to pass over Mt. Lafayette twice more, in the morning and afternoon. I bet not many people can say they summited Mt. Lafayette three times in two days, coming up from three different approaches. I did only 3½ miles of the actual AT this day, going to the summit of Mt. Garfield, because of the nearly 3 miles each way I had to hike to get to it. The 'broken record' of perfect weather was playing again. There was no wind. I was soaked with sweat as I hiked the saddle between Garfield and Lafayette in the afternoon.

My access route to the AT for Day 178 was via the four-mile Gale River Trail. I did 3.9 miles of AT, first going south to Garfield Ridge Shelter where I met and chatted with the caretaker. Turns out, he was a hiker I met twice yesterday. This was another new shelter like Eliza Brook, built in a shop and air-lifted to the site. The hand-crafted woodwork was stunning. There in the shelter register book was another entry from Cody Coyote: "Turning my mistakes into GOLD!!!"

It was a Saturday, and Galehead Hut was crawling with people, even in the middle of the day. I signed the register and then headed up the trail toward South Twin Mountain. It was only 0.8 miles away but the information at the hut said it would take an hour. That was meant for average people, not fit hikers, but it was a very steep climb, ascending 1,100 feet in that distance. Near the bottom, I was having my regular 'feed' and trying to walk very slowly so I could eat without breathing hard. I didn't usually stop while eating because I found that I'd stiffen up and get chilled. I was paying too much attention to how good the Oreo cookie tasted. Suddenly a foot slipped on a sloped dry granite rock. It wasn't a bad slip but was just enough to propel my face smack into the up-thrust root of a toppled tree. I had cuts on my chin and my lower lip was bleeding freely where two teeth went through it. Rather than hurry back to the hut for first aid, I opted to go on. The bleeding didn't last more than a few minutes.

I made it to the summit of South Twin before my chosen turn-around time, designed to get me back to the van by 7:00 pm. I enjoyed the open summit for a few minutes despite the hazy conditions. There was enough of a breeze that it cooled me off some after the hot climb. As I sat relaxing, a lady and two young boys came up from the other side. The lady asked if I had water. Her kids were dehydrated. Pretty seriously I suspect, because they gulped down the half-liter bottle I gave them in seconds, very thankful. I'd refilled my empty water bottles at the hut, which is why I could give them my last unopened water bottle. Then I headed back down. On the upper part of the Gale River Trail, I met a female 'croo' hiking up to the shelter with a light load, just a 25-pound crate of vegetables. She was taking a break and seemed interested in talking, so I chatted with her for five minutes.

Okay, let's talk about my trail food and how I ate it. After 3,000 miles of hiking, I had pretty much settled into a routine. Individually wrapped string cheese sticks were the first of a trio of items. I kept them in my cooler in my van, and carried only enough to cover the length of the hike. I preferred the jalapeño version when I could get it. These perfectly complemented my other trail staples: Flavor-Blasted Goldfish crackers and Oreo cookies. I made a custom mix of one quarter Pizza flavor and three-quarters Extra Cheddar flavor Goldfish that I blended as needed and carried only what I'd need for the day in a zip lock bag. The good old original Oreo cookies ("Milk's favorite cookie") bought in family packs, go in another zip-lock bag. Occasionally, I had a craving for meat and carried a can of Spam or a tin of Vienna Sausages.

On the trail, to avoid 'hitting the wall', I had a feed every 2 to 2½ miles of hiking, depending on trail difficulty. I feed on the move, preferring not to stop and let the old bones stiffen up. Each 'feed' consists of one jalapeño cheese stick, one full mouthful of flavor-blasted Goldfish crackers, and two to four original-recipe Oreo cookies.

Although both Goldfish Crackers and Oreos contain a surprisingly generous helping of fiber, I also carried and consumed five Sunsweet prunes a day. I love the flavor of prunes and they kept the cheese from clogging up the old tubes.

My insertion point the following day was at Zealand Falls Hut via the 2.3-mile Zealand Trail. I had that done at 7:30 am and passed the hut while they were serving breakfast. It was a total zoo. I moved on without checking the register, since I'd be back later. A 1,500-foot climb took me to the side trail to Zealand Mountain. The map showed a 'vista' icon but there was nothing but trees. The only distinguishing thing about this rounded peak in the woods is that it is one of 48 '4,000-footers' in New Hampshire, so people flock there just to bag it, to check it off their list.

Another one of these was Mt. Guyot, which has the same name as the 6,000+ foot mountain in Great Smoky Mountain National Park and was named for the same Guyot—Swiss-born Princeton University professor of physical geography and geology Arnold Henry Guyot. There's even a third Mt. Guyot on the Continental Divide in Colorado.

I took the long tough 0.8-mile side trail down to the Guyot Shelter, since it was an official AT shelter. Along the way I met a guy working on a big cairn. He turned out to be Joe Roman, the caretaker of the shelter and campsite. He had built a comfortable stone seat into the cairn and was working to cap it off with a large, very pure white quartz rock. We talked for a while and I took his picture sitting in his 'easy chair.' Joe is still actively working and teaching and hiking in the Whites.

I parked at Crawford Notch on Day 180 to finish the 27.7-mile gauntlet. It was the easiest of the days. I climbed 1,600 feet on easy trail to picture-perfect Ethan Pond and visited the slightly leaning shelter there; the walls could use some cross-bracing. After that, the trail joins up with the old Zealand Valley Railroad bed and soon crosses North Fork on a big wooden footbridge with laminated beams for support. Most of the hiking on the railroad bed is incredibly easy, yet it is the only

Joe Roman with his 'easy chair' cairn, slopes of Mt. Guyot, NH.

place I fell today—sightseeing instead of watching my footing, and tripping on a root.

Crawford Notch is named for the family who moved to the area in the 1790's and opened it up to tourism. They were inn keepers and guides. Ethan Allen Crawford and his father Abel cut the Crawford Path to the summit of Mt. Washington in 1819 and it has been in continuous use ever since. The AT follows much of this route.

Perhaps the most prominent current 'inn' in Crawford Notch is the posh Appalachian Mountain Club's Highlands Center Lodge. After the day's hike, I decided to splurge and checked in for a three-night stay in a private room with a private bath on a plan that excluded dinner but included the buffet breakfast.

Luxury! I took a hot shower, slept for hours and hours, and took a genuine 'zero day' the next day. I had a great AYCE breakfast soon after the buffet opened at 6:30 and then went back for a second breakfast at 9:30. My body was thanking me. The past five days had been tougher on it than my ever-optimistic mind had been willing to admit.

I went out, bought a pint of my favorite ice cream—Häagen-Dazs White Chocolate Raspberry Truffle—and ate it all. I decided that Heaven is in the freezer aisle. That brand name, by the way, is a completely bogus one made up by a Polish-Jewish couple from Brooklyn. *Feged aboudit.* I took another long shower and slept and blogged and slept some more.

The AMC Highlands Center

F.I.T. Wilderness

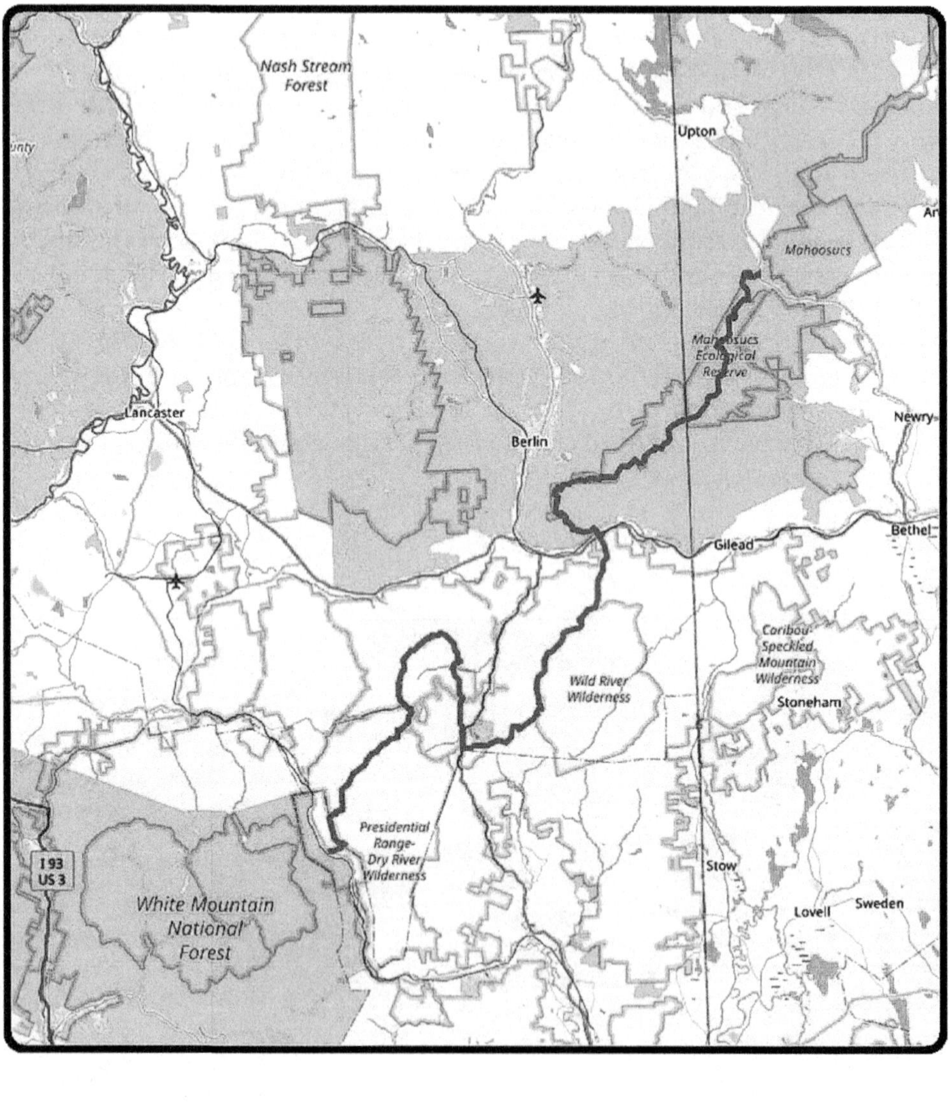
Nash Stream Forest
Upton
Mahoosucs
Mahoosucs Ecological Reserve
Newry
Lancaster
Berlin
Bethel
Gilead
Caribou-Speckled Mountain Wilderness
Wild River Wilderness
Stoneham
Presidential Range-Dry River Wilderness
I 93
US 3
White Mountain National Forest
Stow
Lovell
Sweden

CHAPTER 13

Crawford Notch, NH to Grafton Notch, ME
July 18 - August 3; 78.2 trail miles one way

After another indulgent breakfast at Highland Center, I was on the trail the next day at 8:20 am.

The climb up Webster Cliffs gave me the willies. Steep and tough and nearly constantly on exposed ledges—or requiring me to clamber up rock faces with hands and feet—it featured no less than fourteen vista points, or should I say "chances to plunge to an untimely death." The first of these was just below 3,000 feet and the last was at the 3,800-foot summit. I felt more like a bird soaring over the stunning views than a hiker.

From the summit of Mt. Webster, the trail finally leaves the brink behind and negotiates a broad saddle to Mt. Jackson by means of short level sections. These were punctuated by even shorter rock scrambles either up or down, seemingly randomly distributed. It wasn't too hard, but was uncomfortable because of the short tough bits. Mt. Jackson has an open summit with a nice view across the broad saddle that connects it to Mt. Pierce. In that saddle, the Mizpah Spring Hut was gleaming like a beacon from a couple miles away. It's a nice multi-level hut, clean and relatively quiet that day. Unlike most of the huts, it doesn't have any great views, but in less than a mile you climb up to Mt. Pierce where there is tundra and the first really comprehensive view of the trail and ridge leading to Mt. Washington.

That was my turn-around point and the point where the AT joins Crawford Path.

The next day would be my first of two summit days, reaching 6,288-foot Mt. Washington.

I had been to Mt. Washington twice before. In the summer of 1970, a college friend and I drove to the summit while on a 45-day driving tour covering most of North America. Then on March 13, 2007, I made a winter ascent up from Pinkham Notch in crampons, as part of my training for South America.

The winter ascent followed the Lion's Head Trail, the most popular winter route to the summit, but not even usable in summer. It immediately tests the climber; I think they do that on purpose to weed out the weaklings who have no chance of summiting. After an approach on snow-cat roads, we stopped and put on crampons and traded our hiking poles for ice axes. Immediately the trail became nearly vertical. I was caught totally off guard, expecting the worst would be far up above the timber line.

F.I.T. Wilderness

For several hundred vertical feet, we were doing some serious scrambling up 60-degree slopes in snow that was two and three feet deep. There were roots and branches and small trees to grab on to and the ice axes were also constantly in use. Finally, the terrain got less "technical" but remained very steep, all the way up to the tree line. The whole route is only four horizontal miles to climb more than 4,000 vertical feet, and probably half the horizontal part was on that snow cat trail at the bottom.

It began to snow lightly as we reached timberline and made the assault of the Lion's Head rock formation. The going had been tougher below; now there were just one or two difficult spots. From Lion's Head, we traversed across a very gently sloping, nearly level, broad ridge with great views down to Tuckerman's Ravine on the left. That ravine is a popular place for spring skiing because it collects a few hundred feet of deep drifted snow. There were people climbing ice and snow cornices there, doing technical training.

Our traverse was very exposed to the SW winds of 30 to 35mph, and I wasn't dressed in enough layers to handle it. Mount Washington is notorious for bad weather and especially wind. The highest wind gust recorded at the weather station at the top is a brisk 231 miles per hour. I stopped at the base of the steep slope that would continue all the way to the summit and put on a couple more layers.

We reached the drifted-over parking lot at the top at noon and the actual summit at 12:10. I got my pose beside the summit sign with three-foot-long wind-deposited rime-ice 'feathers' jutting horizontally off the observation tower behind. Visibility was excellent despite the ongoing spitting snow.

Winter climbers are not allowed inside the summit buildings; only the weather observers are there this time of year. But there is a sheltered area at the entrance to the visitor's center where we could sit out of the wind. We had some lunch and talked and then headed back down at 12:45. We saw no other people until we were half-way back down. We were way ahead of the other parties coming up that day.

The weather was a bit nicer on my first AT summit day. Temperatures hovered in the mid 40's at the top, with winds about 30 mph. I did the summit in reverse—starting at the top. I had shelled out the $25 to drive the summit road, parked, then hiked down Crawford Path to Mt. Pierce, past the iconic Lake of the Clouds Hut, and then doing the summit climb at the end of a fourteen-mile day.

All day I was above timberline and had unlimited visibility. As I got back to the summit at 4:30, a cloud hovering just above the peak began to lower. The wind was beginning to drive wisps of fog past me, so I snapped a few quick photos before I lost the chance, then headed into the crowded snack bar and shop area—what a different world. After a day spent in the wild, I was assaulted with yelling kids, crying babies, screaming parents, and general all-around din and babble. I bought a t-shirt and headed down the mountain.

The next day I spent another 25 bucks and drove back up there to hike the whole Presidential Range to Mt. Madison and back. I couldn't have had a better day. The temperature broke records—it was above 50 degrees at the summit of Mt. Washington all day and I was even too hot at points. The wind was literally calm, the sky was clear and blue, and visibility was again unlimited.

The hike took me past Madison Springs Hut, first built in 1888 but rebuilt several times, and now a bright, clean, modern place. I actually hiked a little past the summit of Mt. Madison before turning around, and so I got back to the parking lot at Mt. Washington at 6:15. They shoo everybody out of the parking lot by 6:45, so I didn't have much time to spare.

Early morning on Mt. Washington, before the crowds. Summit sign and observation deck.

Now a note that brings me great sadness. Sometime around 2020 the official route of the AT was switched to the Gulfside Trail, which bypasses the summit of Mount Washington. The summit is now a side trip. The AT never gets above about 6160' or about 130' short

View of the 'Great Gulf' rimmed by the highest peaks of the Presidential Range – Washington, Jefferson, Adams, and Madison. Only the last two are visible, top center.

of the summit. That is lower than the elevation reached at Roan High Knob in North Carolina, and therefore only the 5th highest point on the AT's actual footpath. I understand the change. The AT has been rerouted away from a number of busy trails near parking areas that have become badly over-used. And yet I felt a sense of loss, almost grieving, when I learned of this particular change.

So, the big buzz was over—the most intense part of the Whites—but there was still a whole lot of tough trail ahead. Day 184 was a Saturday, and every hiker in the state seemed to have converged on Pinkham Notch Visitor Center and Joe

F.I.T. Wilderness

Dodge Lodge. The parking lots were overflowing. I did the climb up to Mt. Madison and back on a lot of easy level trail, but at the end was a 2,000-foot rocky ascent within a mile of trail. I got back to the visitor center early and talked to the AMC people staffing the information desk. Despite the crowds, they always take the time to answer your questions and then check to make sure you got the answer you needed. I was asking about the four shelters I would visit tomorrow, and trying to design the most efficient route to hit them all. These four are all on the slopes of Mount Adams and are run by the RMC, the Randolph Mountain Club. While they are officially AT shelters (which is why my 'rules' required me to visit them), they are all more than a mile from the trail. I would be coming up from below to visit them all. My rules did not include having to hike specifically from the AT to each shelter, just to visit each shelter.

The friendly staff gave me detailed directions, times—everything I needed—and I even went ahead and bought the thick White Mountain Guide—a guidebook with complete maps covering every trail in the White Mountains area.

I did do a small piece of the AT the next day before hitting the Lowes Path to the four shelters. I hiked less than a mile from the Pinkham Notch Visitor Center to the Wildcat Ridge trailhead parking area where I would launch into a twenty-mile section of remote trail with no intermediate road access.

Then it was off to 'waste' the day tramping around the north slope of beautiful Mt. Sam Adams, climbing to Crag Camp, The Perch, Gray Knob Shelter, and The Log Cabin. That last one was the first I visited and the least noteworthy; it was just a typical lean-to shelter. From there, I got on a trail called The Randolph Path, which is described as being built by a man who thought his trail should be able to be hiked by ladies in their full-length skirts. Thus, it was never steep, though decades of erosion had left some pretty tough rock barriers to scramble over, especially on the steep side-slope as you got close to The Perch Shelter. After visiting The Perch, with its great views of the valleys to the north, I took the Perch Path up heavily rocky footing to the high point of the trail where the Perch Path ends at the Gray Knob trail. That had me descending gradually to the very nice, almost hut-like Gray Knob shelter, where a sign said that the caretaker was out. From there it was another 0.4 miles to the fabulous Crag Camp Shelter, which is very much like a hut. There I talked to the caretaker and soaked in

Interior of Crag Camp Shelter

the amazing views of the slopes of Mt. Adams with Mt. Madison in the background. The shelter had huge two-story picture windows and could house 20 in three bunk rooms with a huge living area. What a palace! Then it was down the Spur Trail to a very brief bit of Randolph Path just to cross a stream, then down the King Ravine Trail until it intersected with Lowes Path, which I took back to my van.

View of Mts. Adams, right, and Madison, left, from front porch of Crag Camp

It was a surprisingly fun day because of the varied trail and scenery and the lack of crowds.

The next day it was back on the real AT. The climb up to Wildcat Ridge was a lot like the climb out of Carter Notch—nosebleed views from exposed ledges down to the deep notch directly below.

Here's what the AMC guidebook says about this trail:

"The sections from Lost Pond Trail jct. to E Peak and from A Peak to Carter Notch are very steep and rough, and there are several ups and downs and other steep, rough sections along the rest of the trail that make it more difficult and time consuming than one might infer from a casual glance at the map or the distance summary."

And here's a sample of the south-to-north detailed trail description:

"...Lost Pond Trail enters on the left and the trail shortly begins the very steep climb up the end of the ridge (use care on all ledge areas). The first pitch up rock steps and a ladder leads to an outlook across Pinkham Notch. After a tricky traverse and a fairly difficult scramble up a rock chimney, the trail crosses a ledge with an excellent view of Mt. Washington ..."

I was really glad I bought the AMC guidebook. The seemingly innocuous five Wildcat Peaks were just as described—gnarly tough. Finally came the steep descent to Carter Notch and the hut there by the same name.

That's where I turned around. And then I had to run that gauntlet all over again.

On the way back, I was delayed briefly when I lost my bandana and had to backtrack to get it. A couple of hikers had picked it up, so they saved me some further hiking; I thanked them for that. Then about ten minutes later, I lost the trail at a vista ledge and started going the wrong way. I don't know why I didn't realize it, but it was only a minute later that I ran into the hikers who had retrieved my bandana (they were a bit slower than me). That was the only time in 3,000 miles of hiking up to that point, that I found myself going the wrong way on the trail.

The next day I would have to access the middle of this section via Nineteen Mile Brook Trail, a 3-hour climb, 3.6 miles each way. During the morning, as I climbed up along the brook which had been scoured by Hurricane Irene, I was flabbergasted to meet Beth ('Patches') coming down from an overnight stay at Mt. Hight. She was in trousers, not her signature patched skirt. That's because she had finished her thru-hike twelve days earlier (which I knew because I had been following her blog). In it she said that she was going to do some random hiking around her beloved Whites, so meeting her was not entirely unexpected. But it was on a side trail, not the AT. It took her a minute before she remembered me, but then we had a long conversation. A lot of trail talk, but there were many things I thought of later that I wished we had talked about. Beth went on to work at a local ski area for the next couple of years.

I climbed on up to Carter Notch and resumed the AT northbound, climbing 1,500 more feet to Carter Dome and continuing past several summits to my turnaround at Middle Carter. On the way back, I stopped in at the Carter Notch Hut to use the privy and fill water bottles and chat with the 'croo' for a minute, then made the long descent back down Nineteen Mile Brook Trail. I had kept a stiff pace most of the day, and I really felt it by the time I finally got back to the van at 6:45 pm. I was so tired that I didn't want to do anything but sit. I felt like crying. After about twenty minutes of just taking it easy, I began to feel human again. I reminded myself of those dark days back in southern New York where I had overextended myself. Once again, I had been losing weight, despite eating all I could. With all the mountains the trail goes over, I had just been burning too many calories; all those ten-hour days of constant cardiovascular workouts. It was time to take a deep breath and remember—Balance. Stop pushing the pedal to the metal. Keep tuned to what my body was telling me.

I took a philosophy course back at Penn State in which the title of the textbook was *The Balanced Life*, published in 1959. Our wise old professor, Hans Freund (1905-1994), was its author. I still refer to that book today. On the first page of the Introduction, Freund says:

"Whatever may be the place which providence or chance has assigned him, man knows himself as only a sojourner on the earth."

Achieving balance in life is an endless journey, with the destination always just over the horizon. Balance is the most difficult quality for a person to get right, yet the most important. Every aspect of life is trying to throw you off balance. Quickly we all learn that, in order to get what we want from life, we have to do stuff we don't want to do. Any true definition of freedom reveals how much its achievement necessarily limits us. In other words, "Freedom isn't free." As a basic example: a man loves his wife; he wants to keep her happy because her happiness is essential to his. So he gives up a night out with the boys and tackles that 'honey-do' list she's been nagging him about for weeks.

I have come to find that true balance is Paradox. It is not *a* paradox; it is Paradox itself, with a capital P. A comprehensive life-balance includes the balance between balance and imbalance.

And so, this day, I had to remind myself: time to adjust, time to re-evaluate. Time to re-balance the scale between the thru-hiker's mantra "No pain, no rain, no Maine" and Wellness, Joy, and the Path that goes much farther than Katahdin. Like a foot landing on an uneven place in the trail, the muscles and tendons of the mind need to stay supple and flexible.

There was one more day of side trail hiking to finish this last long leg of the Whites. I came up the 3.6-mile Stony Brook Trail to the gap between Mt. Moriah and North Carter. There I did the 3.2 miles of AT south to Middle Carter and back. I stopped in at the Imp Shelter with its rustic log 'throne' sitting smack dab in the middle of the floor. Rain moved in before I got to the turn-around, and I even sheltered under a thick fir tree for twenty minutes, hoping it would blow on through. But when it became obvious that it was not going to cooperate, I put on a hooded sweatshirt and marched. I got wet but I never got chilled.

To tackle the last leg of this twenty mile segment, I parked at Hogan Road, the Centennial Trail/AT trailhead across the Androscoggin River from US 2. That was at 800 feet elevation, and the high point for the day was Mt. Moriah, just over 4,000 feet, and the last official White Mountain. I noticed the lack of bird song for the first time this year. That was the first sign of fall. It always gives me a pang of sadness. The birds are done nesting and defending their territory, the babies are fledged, and everybody is getting ready to head south.

Day-hiking the AT through the Whites took me twenty days, from that first glorious climb over Moosilauke to today's summit of the 'biblical' Moriah, where God commanded Abraham to sacrifice his only son. I came away learning some lessons. The Whites do indeed demand sacrifice. They will have their pound of flesh. After hiking 15 to 20 miles per day for nearly seven months, I thought I was fit. But I needed to be fitter to get through the Whites. I needed more leg strength, more durability in my knees and ankles, tougher feet. My progress slowed; it took longer than I expected, and I think most thru-hikers find the same. Don't expect to put in the same kind of miles that you had been farther south.

The next day I took an important zero day; not so much to rest but to scout the trail access points ahead through the Mahoosucs. This next 31-mile piece of AT to Grafton Notch had no intermediate road access, so I would have to drive up the private road called Success Pond Road to find several trailheads. The road lived up to its name. The day was a success, as I found all the side trail parking areas I needed.

It would take me five days to cover these 31 miles of trail. The first started back at Hogan Road for the climb up to Mt. Hayes, Cascade Mountain, Wocket Ledge, Bald Cap, and finally the perfectly named Dream Lake. The lake was partly

View of Mt. Madison from Cascade Mountain

shrouded in a dreamy mist on this day. I would be back the next day to find spectacular views of Mt. Madison reflected in its glass-smooth surface. Today's view of Mt. Madison came from the slopes of Cascade Mountain on the way back as the morning fog and rain moved out. Madison was wrapped in a spectacular wreath of cloud with the Androscoggin River gleaming in the valley in the foreground. It was one of the best views the weather gods had yet composed for me. Down on the slopes of Mt. Hayes, the trail was lined with 'clouds' of a very different sort. Reindeer lichen, growing in fields of round puffy gray-green lumps that looked like summer clouds, was soaking up the last of the rain.

Earlier in the day, as I descended from Cascade Mountain on the longest sustained section of really steep trail of the day, with the rain coming down, I passed three guys sitting on a rock having lunch. The nearest one said "Hi" and I instantly slipped and lost my balance, though I didn't actually fall. "I guess I shouldn't have distracted

Trailside lichen clouds on the slopes of Mt. Hayes

170 **P. J. Wetzel**

you," he laughed, to which I grinned and agreed. "Yep, that's all it takes for me—amazing." Somewhere back down south I had met a hiker with the trail name 'Sir Trips-a-lot.' I told him I might just have to steal that name.

The next day, to get more directly up to Dream Lake, I used the 3.1-mile Peabody Brook Trail for access, and hiked the 5½ miles of AT between there and the junction with the Success Trail. I was hiking through the town of Success, NH—fifty-seven square miles, an official township—population zero. Pure wilderness, but this is all second-growth forest. Like almost every other forested tract in the country, the whole township was clear cut in less than a decade, around 1900 when the population soared to 220. By 1930, it was back to zero.

Today's stop at Dream Lake was one of the high points of New Hampshire. The place was church-silent and about as peaceful as a place can be. The reflection of Mt. Madison off the glassy surface was magical, with puffy late-summer clouds drifting across the sky like airborne sailboats. I sat and soaked it up before moving on; something I don't often do.

I got an early start up the Success Trail the next day and was on the AT by 8:00 am. After 1.3 miles, I crossed into Maine and began a 500-foot climb up to Mt. Carlo. That climb was interrupted by a short but very steep drop into Carlo Col. It went through huge boulders with some cave-like spaces big enough to explore, if I'd taken the time (I didn't). At the bottom, I took the side trail about a quarter mile, dropping back 150 feet to visit the Carlo Col Shelter where I found an entry by 'Parkside' dated 6/8, just a week before his tragic accident.

The climb to Goose Eye Mountain's summit was a piece of work. It first involved re-bar ladder rungs embedded in bedrock, then a long wooden ladder that you could see clearly from the shoulder long before you reached it. I made the final, fairly easy hike across from Goose Eye to East Goose Eye, another open bedrock peak. That was my planned turn-around point, but I got there fairly early: 11:45 am. I considered going farther but, after sitting and enjoying the view and drinking a can of Dr. Pepper, I decided against it. Keep the balance. Plus, this would be a great spot to revisit tomorrow.

The 'tomorrow' in question was August 1st, and my first full day in Maine. Even the day's parking area, 1.9 miles down the Notch Trail from the AT, was just across the state line. The Notch Trail is as easy as the Notch is hard. At the junction with the AT, turning left sends you immediately into the Appalachian Trail's toughest mile—the infamous Mahoosuc Notch. But I turned right instead, and began the steep climb up the Fulling Mill Mountain's south peak.

There were some views at the summit and it was above the morning fog. I descended with a few tricky spots of bedrock and reached the Full Goose Shelter. When I had first noticed this shelter's name in the guidebooks, I'd had all kinds of whimsical thoughts about how it got its name. Was there a pet goose here that hikers kept feeding until it was so stuffed it couldn't fly? Was it named after some hiker who became notorious for his ... exploits? Nope. Actually, it is one of the most unimaginative choices for a name possible. The shelter sits between Fulling Mill and Goose Eye Mountains. That's it. So much for my imagination.

F.I.T. Wilderness

From the shelter I made the final climb to the north peak of Goose Eye. The views from the open broad summit were fine on this bright day. I crossed a series of level areas south all the way to the base of East Goose Eye and climbed back up to the summit, my turn-around point.

That climb was steep and over much of the same difficult bedrock as many other mountains, but the local maintainers seemed to have made this climb a testbed or showpiece for how you could stabilize the trail by using board steps and ladders. Most of the way was on man-made structures. On the way back down that section, I was passed by a group of four or five fast-moving, young thru-hikers and later, on North Goose Eye, by a middle-aged man. I talked to all of them briefly, taking little note of them. There was also a group of about six young Boy Scouts with their leader who passed me a little later.

When I got to Full Goose Shelter again, all of these people were there, packs off, eating lunch. I made it to my turn-around point very early, and got back to the junction with Notch Trail at 1:10 pm; way too early to just hike the 45 minutes back to the van. Yet I had planned to devote the next day entirely to Mahoosuc Notch.

I didn't feel like quitting so early, and although the forecast was calling for showers after 2:00 pm, the weather was warm and beautiful. What the heck. On the spur of the moment, I decided to take the plunge and do Mahoosuc Notch today. I figured the rocks would remain wet into tomorrow if the rain came, so why not take this bird-in-hand and hope the rain holds off.

So, in I went.

Mahoosuc Notch's billing as the toughest mile of the entire AT is no hype. Most hikers take well over an hour to get through this gauntlet of house-sized boulders.

The tough trail started around the first bend. There were a few brief breaks, but overall, it was every bit as intensely difficult as I'd heard. At the start, I felt a little overwhelmed by the constant tough footing and all the hand placement decisions and didn't seem able to narrow my focus down to the immediate next 'move' (you can't call it a 'step', as you can for the rest of the trail. Often the 'move' involved arranging at least three limbs and sometimes your butt as you shift your weight up, down, sideways, or forward).

As a result of my poor focus, I trusted all my weight to a particular foothold and slipped because it had been worn smooth by so many other hikers before me. I fell three feet, landing on my butt, bruising it, and scraping my right elbow. My chronically bad left wrist also got re-aggravated. The result was that I felt as though I had been beat up—literally.

I got right back up and went through the place where I had just fallen, no longer trusting that foothold without a good strong hand-hold to help distribute my weight. And that's the way it went the rest of the way. There were four 'tunnels' where you squeeze through openings beneath gargantuan boulders. These were the truly unique highlights of the Notch for me. The rest of it was just making your way over or among behemoth boulders, with a few very difficult ups and downs, but the latter was probably limited to a dozen places.

Near the lower end, there is one completely flat bit of trail, like a serene little meadow. You think it might be over when you get there, but then you plunge right back into the huge boulders again. Still, the lower half of the Notch has slightly smaller boulders and was quite a bit easier. The real gauntlet of continuously huge boulders runs for about a third of a mile at the upper end.

As I was coming down, I was passed by two of the young kids who had passed me coming off East Goose Eye and then stopped for lunch at the shelter. They were doing the Notch like it was a parkour course—lean, nimble, quick. They were joking and taking turns in the lead. The guy, named 'Hawk', had blond hair in a braided Mohawk and wore a braided blond beard. He had put on a gray plastic winged helmet, a cheap fan-prop of the helmets worn by soldiers from Minas Tirith in the "Lord of the Rings" movie. He only wore this through the Notch. The fit young girl was 'Peeper'. They were soon out of sight, but when I got to the east/north end of the notch, they were there eating and apparently waiting for others in their group. I asked if this was the end of the Notch, and they were sure it was. The trail there was leaving the stream and headed up toward Mahoosuc Arm.

We talked briefly and 'Peeper' described her father, who was the middle-aged guy I had talked to on North Goose Eye. I told them I was turning around and heading back through, to do the Notch twice in one continuous session. They didn't seem too impressed. It had been easy for them.

As I headed back up into the Notch, I met 'Peeper's' dad 'Gumpy' and we talked for a few minutes. This father-daughter duo was reporting their thru-hike on Trail Journals (I found their journal that evening). They had hooked up with four others, including 'Hawk', another young couple who I also passed and talked with, and I don't remember the last one, but they weren't in the Notch.

A little later I passed an old guy—truly old, like 80 or more—wearing shin guards and elbow pads, like a kid skateboarding. With him was a younger woman, probably his daughter, but the clear impression I got from their interaction was that she was his 'nurse.' Even with the protection, he already had some cuts, but seemed plenty fit to get through the Notch, and was taking his time. I told them they had nearly made it through the hardest part. There was definitely no quit in him. We were to meet again farther north in a couple days.

I continued on, feeling that the return trip was a little more comfortable. I had gotten into a good zone with my moves and was not wasting as much energy. Then it began to rain; lightly at first, but soon it was gushing down in sheets, and the rock became as totally soaked as I was. Out of necessity, I ignored the rain and clamped down my focus even more intensely. It got to the point where I was rejecting moves that I would have used if the rock was dry, and opting for safer ones; almost always with three good points of contact, all on very secure places (very flat for the feet, very good grip for the hands).

It felt like I had slowed down a whole lot in the rain, but when I checked my watch as I arrived at the start of the Notch Trail, I found that I had taken exactly the same amount of time (an hour and 50 minutes) to do the Notch in each direction.

By then it had stopped raining but so much had fallen that the trees were still

F.I.T. Wilderness

dripping. The hike back down Notch Trail was like a stroll in the woods. It's just such an easy access point to get to such a grueling place. It's amazing that the nature of the landscape can change so abruptly.

For the final assault of the twenty-mile Maine-Mahoosucs segment, I parked at Grafton Notch. I got an early start and it took six hours to get to the turn-around down at the northeast entrance to the Notch. From a bald-rounded, bedrock viewpoint on top of Mahoosuc Arm, I had great views of the gash in the mountains that is the Notch. Steep trail down to the Notch itself was difficult but not out of the range that could be considered 'normal' for New Hampshire and Maine. There were plenty of steep and rocky challenges with bedrock slabs where hikers needed to cling to the edges of the 'dead zone' to get up or down.

Looking south toward Mahoosuc Notch from Mahoosuc Arm

The 'dead zone' is a thing I got to hate about New England hiking. It's the most serious example of failed leave-no-trace ethics caused by the over-use of trail that was poorly located in this landscape. The dead zone is bare exposed bedrock where there used to be a thin layer of soft peat soil built up over the last few thousand years since the glaciers retreated. Long ago hikers had trampled the thin peat to submission and it had washed away. What was left was the underlying steep, smooth bedrock with no good footing that the trail builders did not anticipate and, in most places, have done nothing to fix. Now hikers keep expanding the 'dead zone' wider and wider by hiking on the fringes where their feet can get purchase on remaining soil and tree roots and can use the trees themselves as hand-holds. Eventually the abuse kills the trees they're hanging onto. They die and rot away and the next generation of hikers move laterally and begin to abuse the next generation of trees. So the path of human destruction just gets wider and wider.

One of the peculiar annoyances for me was that the trees you have to grab onto for support often have wounds that are oozing pitch. So, my hands got all sticky and covered in strong-smelling goo that was impossible to wash off.

The only plus to the situation was that the pitch had a nostalgic smell for me.

When I was a kid growing up in Wilmington, Delaware, long before the era of Christmas tree farms with their neatly pruned, perfectly conical Fraser firs, the Christmas trees for sale were all balsam firs cut from the wild way up north somewhere and trucked down. Dad always waited until Christmas Eve to go out and buy a tree, thus always managing to get a serious discount from the sellers. Only the least desirable trees were left, and Dad drove a hard bargain.

Some of the trees we had looked spindly and utterly pathetic compared to the dense, pruned modern trees. But we always filled the sparse branches with ornaments and tinsel. The trees had depth to them, and real character; not like today's pathetic green 'traffic cones.' And Fraser firs have none of that amazing smell. I did love that my hands smelled like Christmas.

Baldpate Mountain, ME

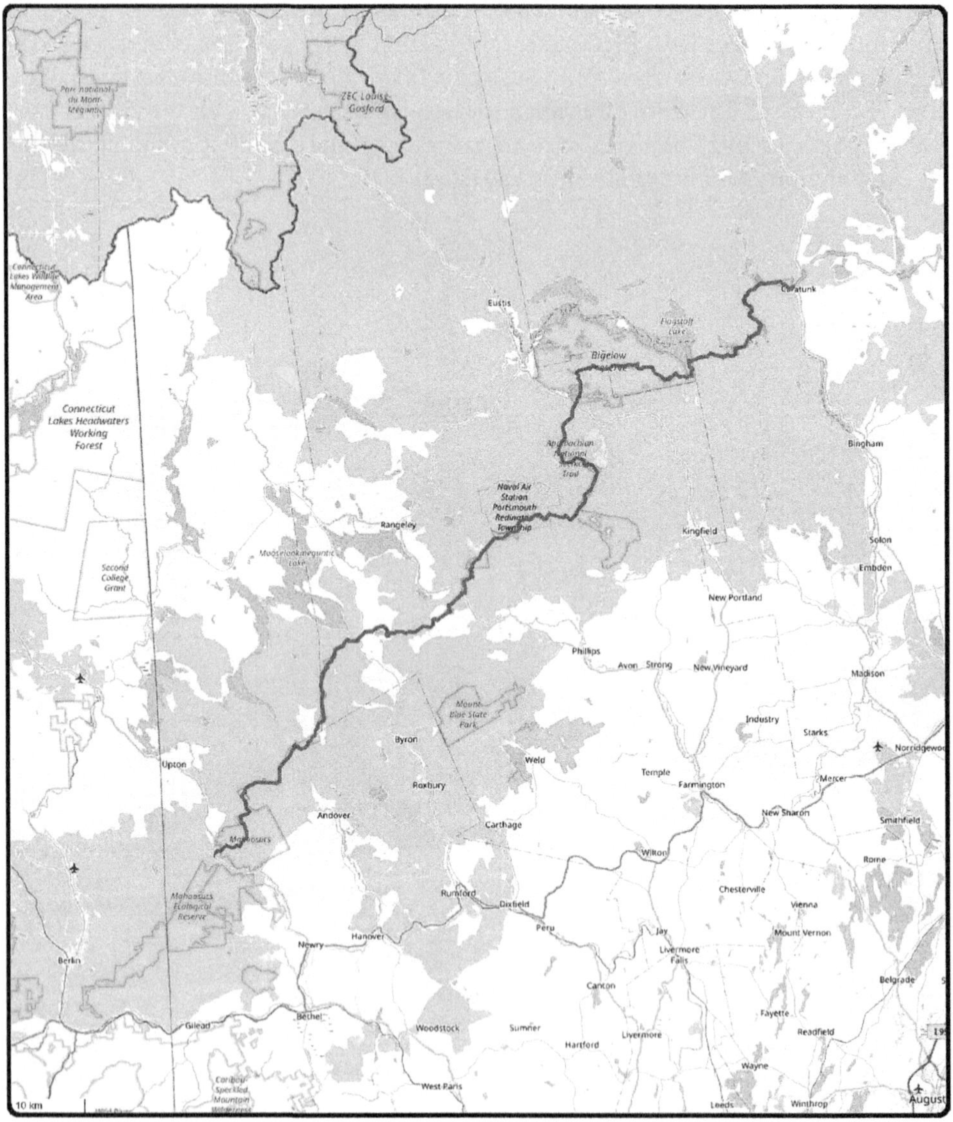
ZEC Louise-Gosford
Eustis
Caratunk
Bigelow
Connecticut Lakes Headwaters Working Forest
Bingham
Rangeley
Kingfield
Solon
Embden
New Portland
Phillips
Avon
Strong
New Vineyard
Madison
Industry
Starks
Byron
Upton
Weld
Temple
Farmington
Mercer
Roxbury
New Sharon
Andover
Carthage
Smithfield
Wilton
Rome
Chesterville
Rumford
Dixfield
Vienna
Peru
Jay
Mount Vernon
Hanover
Newry
Livermore Falls
Berlin
Belgrade
Canton
Bethel
Fayette
Gilead
Woodstock
Sumner
Livermore
Readfield
Hartford
Wayne
West Paris
Leeds
Winthrop
10 km

CHAPTER 14

Grafton Notch, ME to Kennebec River, ME
August 4 - 21; 115.3 trail miles one way

For Day 195, it was back to Grafton Notch to park in their huge paved parking lot. The climb from there up to Baldpate comes in two 1,000-foot sections with a level part in between where the Baldpate Shelter is located. The upper climb is steep, but there was an extensive new trail relocation in place with hundreds of stone steps. The new trail was well built and sustainable—what's called 'durable trail' in leave-no-trace parlance. It meandered up the slope, sort of in switchbacks, staying close to the old, straight-up-the-hill eroded trail.

Once you reach the summit of West Baldpate, you emerge to a view of the much more stunning East peak. Today that view was especially good because of the unlimited visibility and bright sunshine. It was one of those places where I just stood and marveled, uttering "wow" out loud, over and over.

The "wow" was accompanied by a lot of walking on exposed bedrock to the East summit and a lot more up over the summit. The descent on the other side was old-style 'dead zone' bedrock slabs.

But the trail condition there was getting an upgrade. Just before Frye Notch Shelter, I passed a couple of Maine Conservation Corps crews putting in new stone steps and a water bar—beautiful work, built to last. They were funded by the state through a process of competitive proposals, so that the best plans, addressing the places with the most need, are where the work gets done. These were college kids—not highly paid, but

New durable stone steps and the kids who built them, working for the Maine Conservation Corps

F.I.T. Wilderness

very proud of their work. I talked to them a good while and took their pictures on the way back. From the Frye Notch Shelter, I climbed up to my turn-around point at Surplus Mountain. The trail didn't go over the summit and there were no views. As I'd done many times in the past, I marked a waypoint on my GPS and tied a piece of colorful plastic flag tape to a branch at my turn-around point, which I would retrieve when I came back the next day.

My starting point the next day was the trailhead at East B Hill Road—a dirt road, but a very popular exit point for thru-hikers to get to services at Andover, eight miles down the road. I got there at 6:15 am and was getting ready to head out when a familiar vehicle pulled up beside me and two guys got out and put on day packs.

Well, holy flying flamin' happy horse potatoes! Here were Harry and Leo, the day hikers I had last seen down in southern NC near the Nantahala Outdoor Center. I couldn't believe it. They had told me they were just section hiking from Damascus to Springer, no farther. It turned out that when they got to Springer, they liked what they were doing and were getting along so well with each other, that they decided to do the whole trail. They had taken a short break after Springer, then headed up to Katahdin and were now working their way south, again by day hikes using their two vehicles. What a surprise!

They picked my brain about Mahoosuc Notch and I snapped a quick photo. We were all in a hurry, so the meeting was brief. Storms were forecast for the afternoon and we wanted to accomplish our respective hikes early.

AT Day Hikers Harry 'Hairy' Atkins and Leo 'Freedom' Nunnink show up in Maine!

Harry and Leo headed north to South Arm Road. I headed south to Surplus Mountain and back to my van. I did about 3½ miles of the trail north to the south shoulder of Wyman Mountain and back. When I got back, Leo's car was gone. We were now headed in opposite directions so I didn't expect to see them again, but the way I figured it, it defied all odds that we'd actually met at all as we crossed paths. A few minutes either way, and we would have been ships passing in the night.

I hit South Arm Road the next morning. The first clear hint of fall was in the air. Temperatures never got above the low 70's, and there was low humidity all day. An overcast afternoon of lazy flat clouds rolled in on a cool breeze. I sensed a touch of color in some of the forest undergrowth—a few prematurely fallen red and yellow leaves beginning to litter the trail—and the summer birdsong was gone. It was that nostalgic kind of fall feeling from my childhood, anticipating coming into a warm house after a brisk walk in the woods, a fire in the fireplace, a football game on TV, the smell of pot roast slow-cooking in the oven. Ahhhh, the memories.

I hiked south to Hall Mountain, where there was a shelter near the trail's highpoint on the shoulder of the mountain. The log book at the shelter had entries from 'Iceman', 'Viking', and 'Samus', all together on June 9. They wrote "Dear Parkside, you need to catch up with us soon and we'll party all the way to Katahdin." Then 'Spiral' and 'Swivel' had an entry on June 11. That was immediately followed by 'Parkside's' entry, also on June 11 with the time listed as 4:20 pm. Somebody had written 'RIP' next to his signature. It brought a swelling of emotion. There was a SoBo hiker at the shelter who told me he had been at Pierce Pond on July 27 when Paul's family had been there, posting some swimming safety information and setting up (or adding to) a memorial to him. It was good to know there was a memorial there. I had just been in email contact with Paul's mom, Mary. I had sent her my photos of Paul and of all his trail register entries—a couple dozen of them—and she had sent me a copy of the photo Paul took of me back on May 6th. I was really looking forward to visiting Pierce Pond, and bringing a little more closure to my own interactions with Paul.

Heading north from South Arm Road on Day 198, I passed over Old Blue with no view, the flanks of Elephant Mountain where a new bench had been built at a viewpoint, and on to a wonderful view overlooking the deep blue rambling expanses of Upper Randolph and Mooselookmeguntic Lakes from near the summit of Bemis Mountain. The weather was crisp and bright with no haze obstructing even the most distant ranges of hills across Maine's wild interior.

Mooselookmeguntic (right) and Upper Randolph Lakes from Bemis Mountain

F.I.T. Wilderness

Returning to the same spot the next day, the view and the weather were just as great. This time I was parked at the brand-new Height of Land scenic overlook and AT parking area on ME Highway 17, and I found no better view all day than that view from the parking lot.

The trail between ME 17 and ME 4 is an intermezzo before another act full of big gnarly mountains. I did this stretch in two day hikes. Ponds were the features of note on the first, especially Sabbath Day Pond where there's a lean-to, Little Swift River Pond where there was a campsite with a canoe for the campers to use, and Long Pond with its sandy beach.

Coming in from the north, I passed South Pond on Day 201. The whole area was shrouded in fog all day, so everything was wet and dripping. I made it a short day.

Saddleback Mountain, at 4,120 feet, is supposed to have stunning views all the way to Katahdin and back south to Mt. Washington. I wouldn't know. Somebody must have put a hex on me or on the peak. Maybe it was the Killington Hex following me north. Over the next two days, I summited Saddleback three times from three different directions, and never had a view from the summit.

The first time was from the south, up the AT from the road to Rangeley, ME Highway 4. Right from the start, I knew what I was going to face. It was muggy, drizzling, and misty, with dense fog. The trees were intercepting the fog and dripping moisture. My poncho kept me mostly dry as I brushed against all the soaking wet foliage. I used a small bungee cord to pull up the front of the poncho, making it more like a cape that covered my back and arms but allowed unobstructed ventilation of my sweating chest and torso. That's how I hiked the entire day.

As expected, the summit was deep in a gray, dense shroud of fog. I could find no signs identifying the summit, and in the thick mist, I wasn't sure if I was actually there. But then I found a post that had formerly held signs and I saw a well-used side trail that probably went down to the ski area. If so, that was my planned route the following day.

In the fog, I could see no concrete evidence that a ski area even existed here, but I memorized the features around that vandalized signpost and turned around and headed back.

All day I had a touch of an intestinal bug that had been hitting hikers for the past few weeks through the Whites and beyond—stomach queasiness and hints of diarrhea. I didn't let it slow me down. On my return to the van after eight hours in the fog and mist, I realized that I had thoroughly enjoyed having my own little moving cocoon surrounding me all day. It felt protective, soft, and comfortable.

The next day I tackled the summit from the ski area on the north slope of the mountain. The day before, while a bluegrass festival was underway, a friendly girl at the entrance gate had taken the time to give me detailed directions for this unofficial access trail. She said she had just done the summit hike herself. Today, Sunday, the bands were gone and the girl was gone. The festival was over and entrance to the nearly empty Saddleback Ski Area parking lot was free.

Unfortunately, the weather was unchanged: summer humidity, the mountain socked in with fog. I was out hiking past the huge ski lodge at 6:30. There were lots of campers about, remnants of attendees or staff from the two-day Bluegrass Festival. It wasn't too hard to find the foot trail that left the gravel road just uphill from the lodge. I met a girl coming down who had apparently just run to the summit. She confirmed I was on the right track, and gave me more details about getting to the short yellow blazed trail, and the signless post where I turned around yesterday, from the upper end of the chairlift. I was supposed to follow the Grey Ghost Ski trail and then the Tricolor Trail to the top of the chairlift.

It turned out that the vandalized post was not the true summit, but it was the point where the yellow-blazed access trail came out. In dense fog, I got to the familiar post at 7:40 am, breathed a sigh of relief, then headed over the true summit and began to descend. Almost immediately I had to stop and 'graze'. Interspersed among the green-white clouds of reindeer moss, the tundra was packed with tiny blueberries, called bilberries, on 'bushes' no more than six inches high. The berries were ripe and sweet, dew-kissed by the fog, cool and sublime.

An abundance of wild bilberries on Saddleback

The experience transported me to another magical place and time. In the summer of 1970, my college friend 'Perfid Sam' and I were making an epic 12,000-mile circuit of North America in my blue '62 VW Bug with one red front fender and one white one. We usually slept under the stars or in our canvas tent. On the afternoon of Sunday, August 9th, we set up camp in the barrens of La Vérendrye Provincial Park, now called a Wildlife Refuge, in central Quebec, 210 miles NNW of Ottawa.

We were between three small lakes—Lac en Dentelle, Lac Elémi, and Lac Quessy—in an area that must have been some sort of quarry or mine at one time. It was so barren and open that we named the place 'Arizona.' But this was no desert. Sam went fishing in one of the lakes and caught some big walleyes while I explored with my camera. I came upon a vast field of miniature bilberry bushes, and sat down. I imagined myself a ravenous giant seated in an ordinary forest. I ate and ate and ate the succulent fruit until my face was stained a purplish-blue and I was entirely stuffed.

Speaking of Quebec, I was now not far from that French speaking province; and I was reminded of that when I passed a group of French-Canadian Boy Scouts on the way down from the Saddleback summit. They seemed in their mid-teens, and many of them were complaining that they had been hiking in nothing but fog for three days over Sugarloaf, Spaulding, and now Saddleback. I commiserated, saying I wished I had a magic wand. Whoa. Just then the fog began to break—first just briefly, but soon it was clearing quite nicely. They were truly awe-stricken by the sights, as if they had never seen anything like it before, and perhaps they hadn't. The shards and wisps of parting fog added a surreal atmosphere to the unfolding vistas.

I descended the 500 feet to the open saddle and then back up 500 feet to The Horn, where I had some views to the leeward side of the mountain and back to Saddleback. The windward side remained foggy. I passed the Redington Stream Campsite then climbed Saddleback Junior. There was lots of difficult trail, and the wet conditions didn't help. But with six hours of hiking, I still managed to reach the goal I had hoped to reach. That was half a mile past the Poplar Ridge Lean-to where I met and talked to 'Lazagna', a thru-hiker I'd met before who had just bought a pair of the same Brooks Cascadia trail runners I was wearing. They were working well for me and I loved the bright orange shoe laces and trim. 'Lazagna' said he loved them too. He had taken his off and was starting a fire, declaring he was staying there the rest of the afternoon and night in order to dry out.

The following year on July 23rd, Poplar Ridge Lean-to was the last place that thru-hiker Geraldine 'Inchworm' Largay was seen alive. She disappeared into the woods in rugged remote country. Despite massive search efforts, her body wasn't found until 39 months later, at an elevation just above 2,000 feet and roughly 2,500 feet from the nearest point on the trail.

Geraldine's story haunted me for a long time. She was close to my age and hiking alone. She got off the trail in order to take a potty break. When I do that, I make certain to memorize or even mark the way back, because I've had a few brief scares myself. By my estimate, based on where her remains were found, she most likely had forded Orbeton Stream and was climbing up beside Sluice Brook about 3½ miles north of the lean-to. In any case, she got disoriented and never made it back to the trail.

What happened next, we can only speculate, but she did not try to hike out. She tried texting her husband who would regularly meet her at road crossings, but the message didn't go through. She tried to climb to higher elevation in order to find cell service but she did not call 911. From what I understand, a 911 call from any cell phone is picked up by satellites, and would have been much more likely to get through.

The very next day she set up camp in deep woods and no longer moved, apparently believing it was best to stay put, and believing she would be found. Three K-9 search teams came within a few hundred yards of her over the next few days. The story made headlines at the time and again in October 2016, when her body was found and some of the contents of a journal she kept were released.

But for the grace of God, and perhaps my trusty GPS, that could have been me. Leaving a marked trail deep in the wilderness, for any reason, carries grave risk. As a teenager I once got lost in the north woods of Wisconsin. I was hiking alone. I had not told my family where I was going. The 4x4 track I was following dwindled down to nothing, and I decided not to backtrack but to cut through the woods, thinking there was supposed to be another road not far away. It wasn't there. I panicked—completely lost my head. I ran. I cried. Finally, I got hold of myself and climbed the tallest tree. That was the worst moment. I could see no roads, no buildings, nothing but featureless woods in every direction. I was completely lost. After what felt like hours, I stumbled out onto that other road. I was shaking, exhausted, and utterly traumatized. It was a mistake that permanently burned itself into my memory; and Geraldine's journal brought it all flooding back.

As I came back over The Horn, which is a subsidiary summit to the Saddleback, the summit was in the open and offering its fine views. Surely I would finally get to see the views from Saddleback this time, now just a mile and a half away. But no. The hex was on. As I climbed, I watched the fog roll back in. I saw nothing farther than a hundred yards in front of me until I came down the Gray Ghost Trail. Like Killington before it, Saddleback had bested me. The curse of the Ski mountains.

The next day I got a late start because I had to call the local AAA contact in Rangeley and have him come out and give me a jump start. His name was Roger Palmer and he had a little shop on Clay Street with no signs. Everybody in town knew him. He tested the battery and found that it was fine. I had just run it down using my laptop too much overnight without running the engine.

Finally I headed out and inserted myself into this remote area via a Jeep trail called Perham Stream Logging Road. It was closed to traffic a mile and a half from the AT because of a badly rotted bridge that was also partly washed out by Hurricane Irene.

I hiked up the rest of the road and was finally headed south on the AT at 10:00 am. Almost immediately, I ran into 'Kit Fox' and 'Man Cub' sitting along the trail having a snack. This was the third time I had met them in as many days. Micah 'Man Cub' is now a full-time park ranger at Rocky Mountain National Park in charge of a section of wilderness. His specialty was shooting and editing videos at a time when internet bandwidth hadn't yet made vlogging simple and popular. As of this writing, Micah's greatest hit, "ManCub & KitFox thru-hike the Appalachian Trail 2012" had over 118,000 views on YouTube. He was the kid I had first met climbing up Cheoah Bald huffing and puffing, who I had spoken to just long enough to give him a few encouraging words. After our first meeting up north a couple days earlier, I had checked his blog— 'Walk Outside'—and began following it. On this third meeting, I told him how impressed I was with his writing and video production skills. We had a nice long chat and then headed our respective ways.

After working my way down Sluice Creek, which in places really looks like an old log sluice, or a natural water slide, I got to Orbeton Stream. There were stepping stones there, but with all the recent rain, they were underwater. It was a full-on, shoes-and-socks-off ford. I met a man there who had just crossed, a middle-aged man with a German accent who in recent days I had passed several times before but never had an in-depth conversation with.

I should have recognized him. I suppose he should have recognized me too.

As I changed into my Crocs to ford the stream, we talked at length. He said he was from Munich. That rang a bell. Was this the same man I had met at Gingersnap's hanging, bear-proof Trail Magic station near Rock Gap, Franklin, NC on March 22nd (must moments after I met Bomber)? I remembered meeting Johannes from Munich there as he and I arrived at the Trail Magic almost simultaneously. He had told me he was from Munich and had until September 1st to finish his hiking.

My face blindness was in full force; his words rather than his face were the primary triggers to my memory. The man I met today had a goatee and looked lean and fit, quite different from the clean-shaven, slightly frumpy Johannes in a narrow-brimmed rain hat who I remembered from Rock Gap.

But when I mentioned the Trail Magic to him, I could see the 'light bulb coming on.'

Yes. He remembered me because he had taken a picture of me holding the food basket and the register book back then, which I had forgotten until he mentioned it. He had said his pictures were always better with people in them.

Once we established the connection, he was super excited. We took each other's photos and chatted more and he took more photos as I crossed the stream and changed back into my hiking shoes. Then we disappeared up the opposite banks.

I didn't get back to Perham Stream Logging Road until 3:20 pm, but instead of hoofing it down to my van, I started climbing up toward Lone Mountain.

I was determined to hike until dark, if necessary, to cover the miles I had originally intended, despite the late start. I didn't want to have to drive back up this gnarly Jeep trail again tomorrow. I turned around at Spaulding Mountain Lean-To where eight or nine people were already setting up camp. One was 'Banjo,' a gregarious young south-bound thru-hiker who I would meet again climbing the Priest in Virginia. I took the usual photo of the building, with 'Banjo' waving, chatted with everyone about 'Parkside', and signed the register. This one and the previous register at Poplar Ridge had no entries from Paul, but had entries from some of the others who were with or near him.

I headed back down to the road and took just half an hour to walk the road back to where I was parked, arriving there right at sunset. The van, with its freshly recharged battery, started right up.

The next day was a momentous occasion. It was Tuesday the 14th day of August. Deep in the woods between Spaulding Mountain and Sugarloaf Mountain, I walked past a small bronze plaque embedded in a big old moss-covered granite boulder.

I was walking the final piece of trail that had completed the AT exactly 75 years after it was opened. I did not plan this, I swear. In fact, when I started my AT hike that year, I didn't even know it was a particularly special time for the AT. There was a plastic box beside the boulder with a register book in it and cute little AT lapel pins, free for the taking.

Back in my Two Ton Steel Tent that evening, I popped open a can of Spam to celebrate. Embossed on the aluminum lid of the can was a circular emblem with the words:

Bronze plaque commemorating the AT completion, taken 75 years to the day after the event.

Celebrating 75th Anniversary
1937 - 2012

You can't make this stuff up. Spam was and is one of my trail staples. The actual date that Hormel introduced this delicacy to the world was July 5th, 1937.

Day 206 started at the trailhead at the end of Caribou Valley Road. I climbed 2,000 feet up to the wooded summit of North Crocker. As I started down from there, it began to rain. I put on my poncho and continued down, deciding to turn around at the half-way point to the next road crossing, a mile north of North Crocker. I would do the other half later, if the weather improved.

It was a true summer downpour, yet I passed twenty or more hikers. Back at the top of North Crocker, I met a family out for a day hike taking photos. They were bagging this 4,000-footer. They had come up from the same spot where I had parked and were now high-tailing it back there, soaking wet and without rain gear. Much of the way back down, I talked with several of the kids, but mostly the father, as the rain gradually let up and then stopped. By the time we got to the worst rocky stuff halfway down South Crocker, it was a nice day again and the rock had partially dried. I shed my poncho and caught up with the family again. They lived in Maine and had a cabin about ten miles from where we were hiking.

As the dad and I talked some more, I learned that he was a public high-school science teacher. He was a student at Colorado State University during the same time I was, specifically 1977-79. During those years, I was living 'off grid' in an 8' x 16' $75 tar-paper shack on four acres in the foothills eight miles west of town. This was a tiny house before tiny houses were a 'thing'; at a time when 'living off the grid' was anything but cool. Most people who did that back then had no choice. In 1977, after I had lived there for a year, the Rural Electrification Association ran power lines to my property and set up a meter and a basic fuse box without me even asking for it, and completely free of charge.

It rained all day the next day, so I chose to take a break. I headed to a laundromat and did multiple loads. Another of the benefits of hiking with a big mobile steel tent is that I could change clothes whenever I saw the need. Though I wore the same pair of shorts every single day of this adventure (even wearing them under my long pants in cold weather, because of the stuff I carried in the pockets), I carried at least a dozen changes of t-shirt, underpants, and socks.

Besides getting a clean wardrobe, I bought groceries and ate as much as I could—trying to get my weight back up to my target of 153 pounds for the first time in more than a week—and spent abundant amounts of time just resting or napping to the sound of the rain pattering on my roof.

The next day, all bushy-tailed and clean smelling, at 6:30 I headed over to the trailhead at ME Highway 27, arriving to find 'Man Cub' and 'Kit Fox' getting out of a car. I had not expected to see them again. I stopped and talked with them for ten or fifteen minutes. The car belonged to Anna's (Kit Fox's) father, who was from Maine originally and was working there for a while, not really doing close support for them, but helping out occasionally. They had taken the rainy day off too. They went on their way north and I headed south. The entire hike consisted of a climb up the side of North Crocker on trail of easy to moderate slopes and mostly moderate footing. This meant that a good deal of attention would need to be paid to foot placement, particularly in the wet conditions. It only took me 2½ hours to get to my turn-around point and less than that to get back. There was literally nothing to see the entire hike—no vista points and not even a trail crossing or other landmark. It was a beautiful morning and I felt frustrated that I was finished at 11:30am and couldn't do more hiking that day because of the logistics. The next seventeen miles of trail over the Bigelow Range had no intermediate road access.

I hit the first part of that the next day. The climb was 3,000 feet in all, to the high point at West Peak. The weather had finally turned favorable; perfect, in fact.

The day turned out to be one of my top five day hikes of this adventure. The key to a perfect day for me is calm wind under an open sky on top of a mountain. Today I had that. Views were abundant and spectacular. It started with the lush verdant mossy boulder-strewn ascent from the Bigelow Ridge trail junction to The South Horn. The boulders didn't get in the way, just made for interesting views. The high-altitude woods were alive after the heavy rain, its mosses and lichens of a hundred kinds flush and verdant with the new moisture.

Up here in the middle of a rock scramble approaching West Bigelow, I met two hikers hiking in Crocs over the rugged uneven rocks. I told them about 'Corky' and asked them for their opinions of Crocs as hiking footwear. They said they were the best, especially in all the recent wet weather. They pointed out that their dark gray Crocs were a relatively rare version called 'Specialists' that had no vent holes around the toes. That made them perfect for avoiding wet feet in dewy grass, and even crossing streams in shallow water by tiptoeing. I made a mental note. These

Telephoto of Katahdin from Avery Peak. Inset shows the wide view with Flagstaff Lake.

two strong young hikers' confirmation of Corky's testimonial, and the revelation that Crocs came in a version with waterproof toes, was to eventually bring me over to the 'light' side. The standard Croc clogs weigh 205 grams in my size, Specialists weigh 268, and the tough-soled closed-toed Bistro clogs weigh 315 grams. By comparison, the fantastic, comfortable, lightweight Brooks Cascadia's I was hiking in at the time weighed 343 grams. I would eventually settle on the Bistro because of its toughness. Ask any runner. The weight of your shoes has a much greater impact than the weight you carry on your back, because you're literally dead-lifting that weight up off the ground each time you take a step.

I turned around at Avery Peak, named in honor of Myron Avery, the man who made the trail happen and the first one to hike its entire length. Views out over the untamed lands to the north were without compare. I finally got that first glimpse of Katahdin, still 180 trail miles away, though just 85 miles as the crow flies. In the foreground, sprawling Flagstaff Lake glistened a rich cobalt blue beneath the cerulean sky. In the other direction, my nemesis, Saddleback, poked up behind Sugarloaf, taunting me with its infinite views under the open sky.

I hurried back down, keeping a brisk pace. It was Saturday, the day that the Maine Appalachian Trail club was holding its 75th Anniversary party at The Rack restaurant at the base of Sugarloaf, just a couple miles from where I was parked. I was hoping I might catch the tail-end of the festivities.

F.I.T. Wilderness

I got back to where I had parked at 5:40 and drove over there, but there was nothing formal happening. People were just standing and sitting around at the outdoor tables talking, some leaving; the whole shin-dig was seriously winding down. The person at the registration table ignored me entirely when I hovered around there looking at stuff, and at the adjacent table where they were selling memorabilia, I got the same total neglect. The party was over. I just took a couple photos and moved on.

And WOW was I glad I didn't hang around there any longer. On a whim, I drove on up toward the Sugarloaf Base Lodge and hotel. I passed a sign saying 'Watch for baby moose.' Well, right beyond the sign, crossing the road right in front of me was a young moose—not a baby but a nearly full-grown spindly teenager. My first and only moose. I got a couple of good photos of it, which I never would have captured if I hadn't already had my camera out to take photos of the AT gathering.

The return to Avery Peak delivered views every bit as phenomenal as the day before. On the way up, I was particularly impressed by the random arrangement of 'loose' granite blocks the size of warehouses strewn about the south slope of Safford Notch. Another perk of today was meeting three great people and making connections from many months ago. I met the gentleman who took my photo beside the first white blaze and plaque at Mile Zero, the summit of Springer Mountain: 'Night Walker,' packing up his expensive GPS unit with the two-foot antenna and getting ready to go. He told me he had made it north to Erwin, TN, got sick, took some time off, and then flipped up to Katahdin and was now working his way south.

At Little Bigelow Lean-to, where I stopped in to sign the register, 'Terranauta' and 'Mandela' were packing up and getting ready to go. We leap-frogged each other all the way to the summit. The two of them started at Springer on March 1st and hiked north to the Partnership Shelter, Marion, VA. Somehow, I must have missed them. They then took a pre-planned three month break so 'Mandela' could work a good-paying summer job at the Smithsonian in DC. Now they were working their way south from Katahdin. They said they had already met 28 people up north who they knew from their southern leg in the spring, including Johannes, who they met around Damascus, and 'Kit Fox' and

Terranauta (in the shade) with Mandela and Frank 'Nightwalker' Looper at right, taken on the southbound ascent to Avery Peak

188   **P. J. Wetzel**

'Man Cub,' who they met on Blood Mountain. Nice people. I got a group photo of them with 'Nightwalker' at a viewpoint on top of Little Bigelow Ridge.

I gave my Crocs their shot the next day, hiking a full eighteen miles in them. It was an unplanned experiment. I started out in my Brooks Cascadia Trail Runners as usual, but no more than a half mile from my starting point, I came upon a crossing that involved a couple of floating logs spanning six feet to a floating stretch of bog board. None of it would keep me above water, so I switched to my Crocs and made the crossing. Then I figured, what the heck, and just kept them on.

Because I had been hiking in trail runners rather than hiking boots, the change in weight wasn't that noticeable. I got my heels scraped and banged a few times, since Crocs have no heel protection. I got wet in muddy areas more easily and had more annoying trail debris accumulated inside the shoe, both caused by the ventilation holes. But, on the up-side, my socks dried out quickly whenever they got wet, and my feet felt less like they were in a straight-jacket at the end of the day. This outweighed everything else. Crocs keep my feet happy and let them breathe.

The weather remained just about as close to perfect as you can get—true 'chamber of commerce' conditions for 'Vacationland' Maine.

At the crossing of Long Falls Dam Road there has always been a painted notice on the pavement saying "2,000 miles". But this day it was gone. The road had been repaved the day before. Amazingly, on my way back in the afternoon, somebody had already come through with a can of white spray paint and laid down a quick new marker. The actual 2,000-mile point is now between South Horn and Bigelow West Peak, 12½ miles down the trail.

At West Carry Pond Lean-to, I found 'Parkside's' last shelter register entry, written the day he died. He was halfway through his day and stopped in for a break, reading *Moby Dick*. A lot of entries after his referenced the accident. The news had spread like wildfire down the trail grapevine.

It was 1:00 pm the next day when I finally arrived at Pierce Pond Lean-to.

I had been thinking a lot about Paul and his last steps as I approached. It's an ordinary three-sided lean-to tucked under evergreens and facing the pond. Inside there was a picture of Paul in a plastic frame on a high shelf, taken at 'Luce's Lookout',

Pierce Pond, shore-side memorial to Paul

F.I.T. Wilderness

189

the viewing platform atop a private cabin down in Vermont; and there was also a page of swimming safety information. Down by the water in front of the shelter, at the likely place where Paul stepped off dry land for the last time, I found a little memorial carved in a piece of a log with a pile of stones. I added three stones to that, taken from the rocky spot where he probably entered the water.

Back in the shelter, I lit a tea-light candle and set it in front of his photo. A moment later, a breeze came up—really gusty, for just about ten minutes—and blew the candle out. The wind had been light all day and was gentle the rest of the day after that. I left the candle there. It felt as if it had been touched by his spirit. I wrote a long entry in the log book and noticed no entries from Paul nor from any of the others present that day. I had the place to myself. I spent about half an hour sitting on the shore and got pretty misty looking out over the water toward the boat dock on the other side of the dam that he was trying to swim to.

The trail crosses that dam made of wood and loose rocks, and follows the outlet stream down to the Kennebec River. I kept a quick pace because ferry man 'Hillbilly Dave' quits for the day at 4:00 pm. The free ferry provided by the Appalachian Trail Conservancy only runs from 9 to 11am and 2 to 4pm. They started the ferry service back in the mid '80's in order to discourage people from trying to ford the river. Water rises suddenly from unannounced releases from a dam upstream. People have drowned, the most recent being 39-year-old Michael Camiso in May 2018.

I got to the river at 3:35pm. There was an orange flag sitting in a holder by the shore that I waved to get Dave's attention. He waved back and then paddled toward me in his canoe as I put the flag back where it is kept. Dave had no problem fulfilling my request to go across and come right back again. He said he'd been doing this for six years. I just got out and set foot on shore on the north side, noting the exact spot, and then we headed back, arriving at the south shore again at 3:50. I thanked Dave and headed back up the trail, past the forlorn, still empty Pierce Pond Shelter, and back to my rolling home away from home.

Hillbilly Dave ferrying me across the Kennebec River

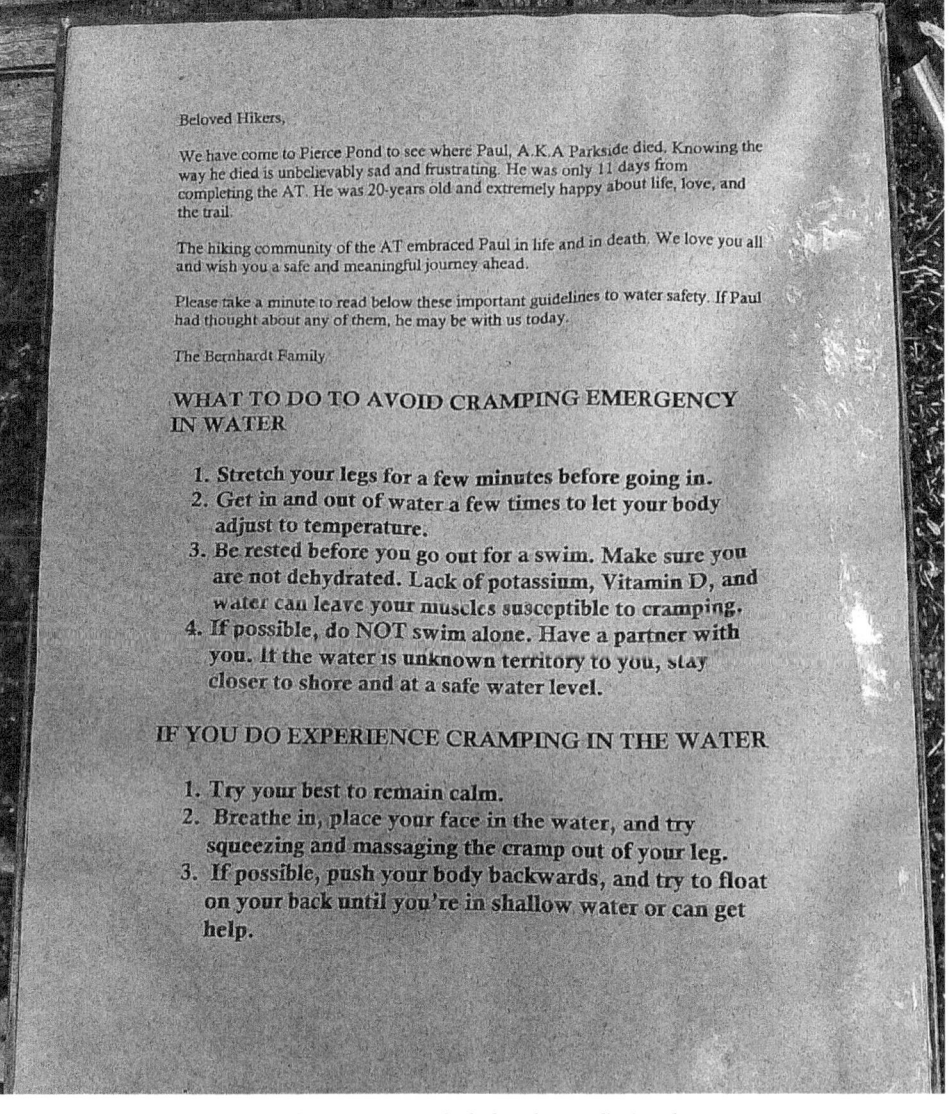

> Beloved Hikers,
>
> We have come to Pierce Pond to see where Paul, A.K.A Parkside died. Knowing the way he died is unbelievably sad and frustrating. He was only 11 days from completing the AT. He was 20-years old and extremely happy about life, love, and the trail.
>
> The hiking community of the AT embraced Paul in life and in death. We love you all and wish you a safe and meaningful journey ahead.
>
> Please take a minute to read below these important guidelines to water safety. If Paul had thought about any of them, he may be with us today.
>
> The Bernhardt Family.
>
> ### WHAT TO DO TO AVOID CRAMPING EMERGENCY IN WATER
>
> 1. Stretch your legs for a few minutes before going in.
> 2. Get in and out of water a few times to let your body adjust to temperature.
> 3. Be rested before you go out for a swim. Make sure you are not dehydrated. Lack of potassium, Vitamin D, and water can leave your muscles susceptible to cramping.
> 4. If possible, do NOT swim alone. Have a partner with you. If the water is unknown territory to you, stay closer to shore and at a safe water level.
>
> ### IF YOU DO EXPERIENCE CRAMPING IN THE WATER
>
> 1. Try your best to remain calm.
> 2. Breathe in, place your face in the water, and try squeezing and massaging the cramp out of your leg.
> 3. If possible, push your body backwards, and try to float on your back until you're in shallow water or can get help.

Swim safety guidelines posted at Pierce Pond Shelter by Paul's family

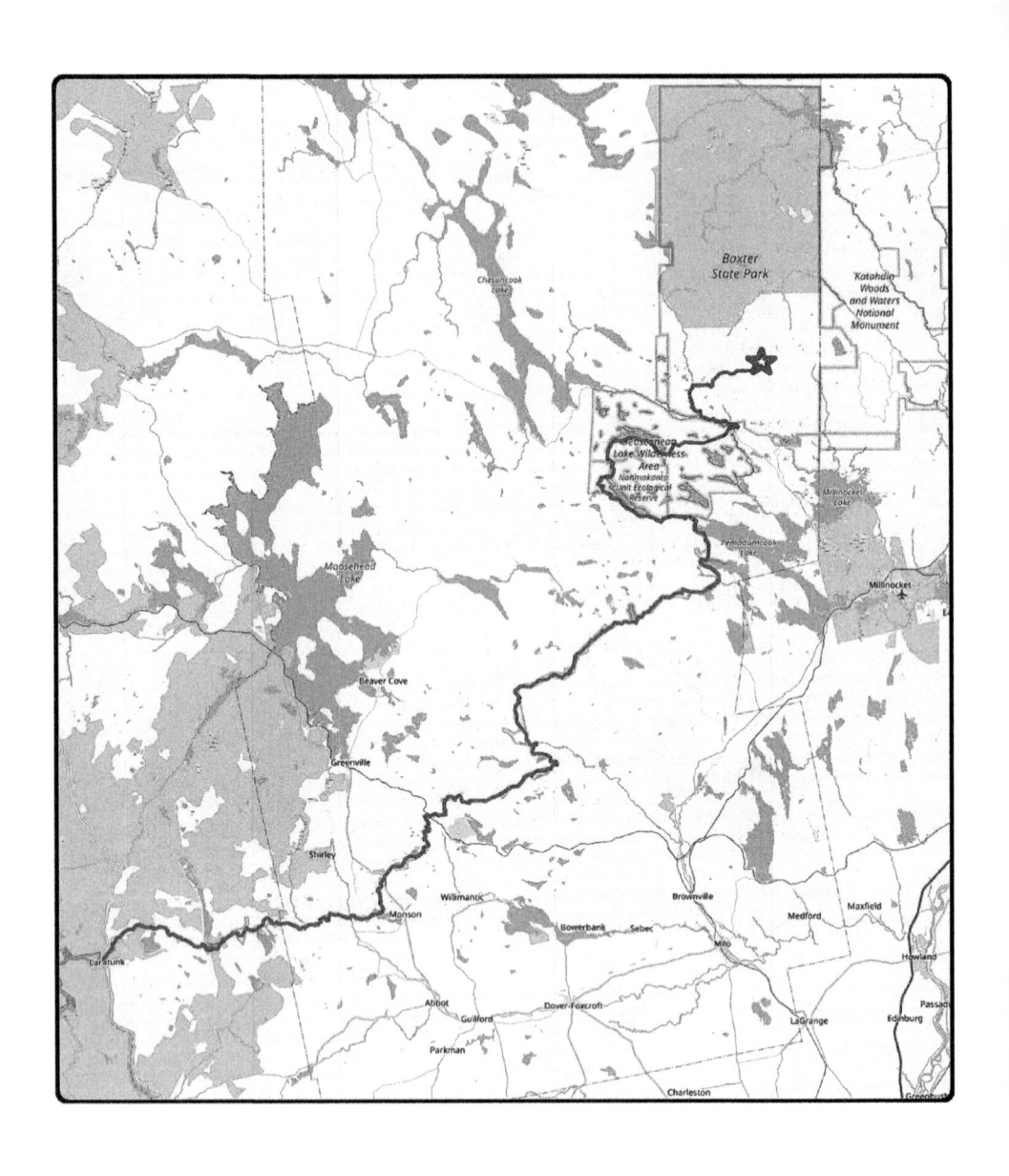

P. J. Wetzel

CHAPTER 15

Kennebec River, ME, to Katahdin, ME
August 22 - September 10; 151.5 trail miles one way

    The crossing of the Kennebec River marked the end of my 'uninterrupted footpath'. This was part of a greater goal I had set for myself, which I called my "Hiking Home Project—a personal continuous footpath." The basic rule was to travel on foot—no boats or bikes, certainly no motorized vehicles—to every address the Post Office had ever delivered mail to me over my life. I was literally going to walk home. I have lived at two dozen different addresses, thankfully all in the 'lower 48' of the continental U.S. I was using the AT as the 'spine' that connected me to all these places. Fortunately, I didn't need this piece of trail north of the Kennebec in Maine to be part of this larger project. I had lived nowhere north of Pennsylvania, except out in Wisconsin. On Friday, November 1st, 2019, at the site of that tar paper shack in the foothills of the Rocky Mountains overlooking Fort Collins, Colorado, I finally achieved that grand goal, having hiked more than 18,000 miles in the process. But because of the required boat ride across the Kennebec, the string of day hikes covered in this chapter is not part of that uninterrupted footpath. 'Hillbilly Dave' pointed out the white blaze on the floor of his canoe as we crossed the Kennebec. If I had not taken the canoe, I would have violated my other rule about 'passing' every white blaze twice. The ferry is the official AT route, period.

    Actually, it is not uncommon for famous long-distance footpaths to be interrupted by ferry rides. Of the trails I've hiked, the Florida National Scenic Trail requires a boat ride across the St. Marks River at the town of St. Marks. The North Country National Scenic Trail requires a crossing of the Mackinac Bridge between the Upper and Lower Peninsulas of Michigan, which can only be walked once a year on Labor Day. I went back there and did that walk, so it didn't break my continuous footpath. The American Discovery Trail requires crossing the Chesapeake Bay Bridge, which can only be crossed on foot during the '10K Across the Bay' run once a year in early November, and also a ferry ride across San Francisco Bay. Wisconsin's Ice Age National Scenic Trail includes a ferry ride across Lake Wisconsin at the town of Merrimac. The Pacific Northwest National Scenic Trail makes use of the public ferry system to cross Puget Sound. North Carolina's 1,175-mile state trail—the Mountains-to-Sea Trail—also uses the local public ferry system to get to and from Ocracoke Island on its hike along the beach strand of the Outer Banks. The Mason-Dixon Trail crosses the Susquehanna River via a bridge that is always closed to pedestrians, so the hiker has to find a ride in a vehicle.

As far as I know, the Pacific Crest and Continental Divide trails do not include any boat rides, but the other trails mentioned above are, by my definition, not continuous footpaths, even though they often call themselves that. Ultimately, it's just a matter of personal judgement. There are no 'hike purity cops' lurking in the woods ... uh ... well, wait. I did spot one back down in Pennsylvania. But seriously, there are no check-points along National Scenic Trails, other than the voluntary trail and shelter registers. You don't have to wear a tracking device (unless you're trying for a Fastest Known Time to be approved by the FKT web site). Earl Shaffer did submit to official questioning in order to convince the world that he had done something that everybody thought was impossible. But normally, out there in the woods, you set your own rules. This is a perfect example of the 'Hike your own Hike' ethos.

You might not notice them, but the trail cops are watching you. Taken in April down in Pennsylvania

Parking at the Carratunk trailhead off US 201, I made my way down to the river bank and placed my foot at the exact point where I had stepped off the canoe the day before, and then I headed northbound. It was pleasant hiking up Holly Brook to Pleasant Pond. Pleasant Pond Shelter has no view of the pond, nor is there a view from the trail. It seems to mostly consist of private land. Finally there was a quick thousand-foot, mile climb to Pleasant Pond Mountain where I turned around. Pleasant weather. Pleasant views. All this 'pleasant' was enough to make me sick.

The next two days I parked beside Moxie Pond at Joe's Hole. Now there are a couple names I could sink my teeth into. On day 213, I did only a half day, hiking south to Pleasant Pond Mountain and back. It turned out that all the 'better-than-pleasant' scenery was on this side. There was a most superb view of Hedgehog Hill, clearly named for its shape, and the north end of Moxie Pond. A red squirrel posed for me on a log. These denizens of the north were feasting on seeds out of the cones of the spruces and firs, fattening up for the long winter and serenading me and each other with their evocative chirps and trills.

The second day it was the rock-hop across Baker Stream below Joe's Hole and then the climb to Moxie Bald, or just Bald Mountain. Near the top I found a fascinating place where the trail goes under a slab of loose rock that forms a roof over the trail and over two adjacent caves. One of the caves is a dead end, but the other is a super-fun 'through' squeeze, that I chose to call The Lobster Claw—about 30 feet of tunnel under that huge slab. I couldn't get through with my daypack on because, like the Lemon Squeezer, it forces you to lean sideways. Then you have to scramble up about three feet onto a projection of the left side wall to complete the traverse. You come out of the upper end just fifteen feet above the route of the AT. I'd love to see the AT go through it. The Lobster Claw would make a great challenge for hikers (they could take their packs around to the upper end and then go through). This mountain, I decided, had the nicest, coolest, and most solid granite of any I'd visited thus far.

On broad smooth open bedrock near the summit, I passed a hiker going south. He was very talkative so we got into a conversation. When I pointed out Pleasant Pond to him, he asked if that was where the thru-hiker had died. Turns out 'Bird Man' started his hike at Springer the same day as Paul, and hiked with him for a couple of days before Paul moved ahead and he got off the trail. 'Bird Man's' way of hiking was to stop to visit friends and acquaintances he had along the trail. He had only made it to Port Clinton before deciding he'd better do a Flip-Flop up to Katahdin and get it done before the cold weather closed the northern parts of the trail. He had also met and hiked with Bomber and asked about his plans to enter the Air Force. I told him Bomber had finished his thru-hike and was doing a week of hiking in the Whites right now before starting basic training (which I knew because I had been following him regularly on Facebook). I wished 'Bird Man' well and we headed our separate ways.

I turned around at the Piscataquis County line. That's the county that Katahdin sits in. I had made it to my last county up north, but it's a huge one, and includes more than 130 miles of the AT. On the return trip, I passed half a dozen hikers, including obvious weekenders and two thru-hiking ladies who had attended the AT's anniversary dinner at Sugarloaf the Saturday before.

Lots of flat trail and river-side walking filled the next day. I crossed three big streams by wading through them. From that point north, I would not find as many footbridges as there had been down south. But the wading weather was perfect—warm air, calm wind, and a sun so bright with a sky so blue that it made the forest greenery look like it was covered in glitter.

Day 216 was a radically different kind of day. I was hiking past Monson. In the afternoon, it got hot and muggy as I hiked a five-mile leg north to Mud Pond, where I turned around. This was the official start of the Hundred Mile Wilderness. The trail starts out moderately difficult and gets full-out difficult as it approaches the Leeman Brook Shelter. The saving grace for all this difficulty was the abundant picturesque ponds. It started with Spectacle Pond right below the highway, then came Bell Pond. A drop down to Lily Pond was followed by a 500-foot climb back up past the shelter to the pick of the litter—beautiful North Pond. The AT follows right along its shoreline for a while with a view of a peninsula with big old leaning trees just dripping with character.

On the way back, they would be dripping with something else. Crossing the outlet of North Pond, I continued on to little Mud Pond, visible through the trees

Beautiful North Pond before the storm developed. Note gray cloud upper left

to the south. A mile from that destination, it began to rain lightly. It was a welcome relief from the heat. I could see lots of blue sky visible to the north, so I didn't bother to dig out any more clothing. I figured it would end quickly. Not. Soon I was in the midst of a tropical downpour—no wind and temperatures still mild, with lots of thunder and lightning crashing above and all around me. This storm hadn't moved in from somewhere. It had formed overhead, and it didn't pass by or end, as most 'airmass showers' do. This one was stuck in place and it just kept regenerating and dumping rain in prodigious torrents.

I was still just in my t-shirt. I hiked back to North Pond and could see clear blue sky to the north of the pond, although sheets and waves of rain were surging across the water, making the pond's surface dance with spray.

Why wasn't this rain stopping? I climbed up onto some exposed bedrock just as several strokes of lightning hit within a tenth of a mile of me.

Suddenly this was deadly serious. Before long, it began to get cold and I felt the rain stinging when it hit my skin: hail—pea-sized at best, but now I was getting seriously chilled. I put on a long-sleeve Patagonia shirt already totally soaked inside my backpack. That's all I'd brought with me on this hot day when the forecast had said "zero percent chance of rain."

After three solid hours of deluge and drenching, I was shivering and near hypothermia when the rain finally ended just as I got back to the shelter—of course it did. It was some sort of sadistic, perverse extension of Murphy's Law.

I needed to continue hiking regardless of the weather in order to make the necessary miles before dark. Several inches of rain had fallen, and, at this point, the trail was more often than not a stream or a lake. The existing streams had quickly swollen, and places where there had been no water were now raging rivers. There was one spot, in particular, that I had noted on my outbound leg as a very poor choice for a trail location because it was essentially a (then dry) stream bed dropping between two boulders that were standing on edge. On the way back, this bed was a raging cascade that I had to struggle right up through—walking upstream in a waterfall.

At the height of the storm, north of Leeman Shelter, the trail was an angry river.

That and the spine-chilling lightning were the low points of the return leg. I was soaked, very cold by then, and fighting upstream against a fast current.

Soon after the rain ended, the sun came out and the air turned warm and tropical, so I started to warm up again. When I got back to the van at 7:00 pm, I found that the three layers of zip-lock bags in which I had stuffed my cell phone had failed. The phone was soaked and never worked again.

I stripped down and got the van's heat on full blast so I could start drying everything out. In my blog, I dubbed this day the Monson Monsoon. Three miles to the north they had no rain. And in Monson? Not a drop. The radar-estimated rain total map showed a little round bulls-eye of nearly five inches centered right where I had hiked.

The next day I began using private road insertion points into the famed Hundred Mile Wilderness. For backpackers, this area is so remote that there is no hope of resupply or anything but an emergency bail-out. But for a normal two-wheel-drive auto, this 'wilderness' is actually full of useful, if rough, access points. The one I parked at that day was past Bodfish Farm on a dead-end trailhead parking area near Otter Pond. From the trailhead, there's a 0.6-mile-long unmarked side trail leading up the lower slopes of Barren Mountain to the AT, a tenth of a mile north of the Long Pond Stream Lean-to.

I visited the lean-to and then headed south through typical Maine trail conditions. There was the usual mix of rough footing in boggy areas and rocky areas. I had three fords to accomplish, each way, which required changing into my Crocs each time, plus a couple of minor ridges to climb and descend from. The fords broke things up and the ridges provided some views. In the mix, were three nice waterfalls—the best by far being Little Wilson Falls, a sixty-foot drop over slate

F.I.T. Wilderness

in perfect angular blocks; so perfect they looked man-made. My guidebook said it was one of the highest falls along the AT.

I came upon two pairs of thru-hikers whom I'd met on previous days. I hadn't known that either of them was actually thru-hiking until today, though. One was a husband-wife team, about fortyish. The husband was too proud to admit he had just fallen while fording Big Wilson Stream. He hemmed and hawed and changed the subject when I asked why he was soaking wet. But in hindsight it wasn't something to be embarrassed about. I almost fell myself, and on the way back in the afternoon, I watched as another guy trying to cross slipped and keeled over and got drenched. Big Wilson Stream was very wide and fairly deep, and full of big rounded slime-covered rocks that were ridiculously slippery. During the Monson Monsoon, I had passed this couple at a time when both of us were drenched to the bone. We didn't spend any time chewing the fat then, but had a little longer conversation today.

The other thru-hiking pair I met were the two women I met on Moxie Bald who told me they'd attended the AT anniversary dinner at Sugarloaf. They were 'Rainbow', age 52, and 'Mamaw B', age 71, from Tennessee. They met on the trail, having left Springer March 15th and March 5th respectively. 'Rainbow' had suffered a serious groin pull from an accident near Sugarloaf and was going very slowly, but given that she was so close, she was determined to finish the rest of the trail. I asked how they fared in Mahoosuc Notch. 'Rainbow' said it took them about 4 hours to get through, but she loved it. I met her straggling behind 'Mamaw B,' right beside Mud Pond, so I had a chance to talk with her twice in quick succession. I learned later that 'Mamaw B' finished her hike on Sept. 6th, but that Katahdin was too much for 'Rainbow' in her condition. She was forced to come back and finish the following year. Considering how much she was hobbling that day, this wasn't surprising.

After seven hours of hiking, I reached my turn-around point at Mud Pond at 2:10 pm. Projecting that forward, it would mean I would return to my van at 9:10 pm, well after dark. I had expected that, and also expected to be finishing in the rain. But the weather held off and I hurried a bit to get back, mostly motivated by the desire to make my final ford of Long Pond Stream before it got dark. I succeeded in that, reaching there at 7:05 pm (sunset was getting earlier each night, and was now at 7:25). It took me exactly an hour from that point until I was finally back to my van. For the sixth time on this adventure, it started raining hard only at the last minute, and I was able to make a dash for my van and get home dry. Of course, that's 'cherry-picking the data'; yesterday's Monsoon had proven that.

After a zero day to let my body recover from four straight 20-plus mile days, I returned to the cute little trailhead at Bodfish Intervale and hiked north over Barren Mountain. At an overlook called Barren Ledges, the fifty-mile vista of the Hundred Mile Wilderness was exquisite. The day had dawned clear and crisp and bright. Looking down on the rounded summit of Boarstone Mountain and across Lake Onawa and Big Benson Pond beyond, I could not identify a single man-made road or structure. The Montreal, Maine, and Atlantic Railroad had track running through that scene, but it was well hidden among the trees.

Hiking over the summit, I paused at the skeleton of a rickety old fire tower that you could climb. I didn't bother. The views were no different than from open ledges, and it was so windy and cold that I had to hold my cap down and put on a long-sleeved shirt. On I

The Hundred Mile Wilderness: View of Boarstone Mountain and Lake Onawa from Barren Ledges

went down the other side, where I took the amazing 0.4-mile side trail to Cloud Pond Lean-To. The shelter does not have a view of the pond but the access trail is basically bog board over the water and runs right next to the shore. The shelter register had an entry from the 'Parkside Fellowship', written by 'Spiral' on June 24th, five days before they finished.

From there I hiked a wide saddle to Fourth Mountain and across Fourth Mountain Bog on a bunch of bog bridges, which were mostly single logs. It was one of the prettiest bogs I'd seen since Harrington Pond, deep in the remote woods below South Kinsman. There were loads of stout pitcher plants that were a deep flaming red-purple, possibly a fall color change. From the summit of Fourth Mountain, I had another glimpse of the hulk of Katahdin looming blue-gray in the distance.

My access point for the next two day hikes was the private but very popular Katahdin Ironworks Road. There is a toll, but the trailhead is situated at a National Natural Landmark called Gulf Hagas, the 'Grand Canyon of Maine'—a deep, rocky gorge that the AT passes through—though the best of the scenery requires taking a five-mile loop trail. The parking area was bustling with day-hikers when I arrived and headed south, climbing 1,000 feet up to Chairback Mountain. There were families on the trail, little five-year-old girls in dresses wearing flip-flops. A little farther up, I met Ridge Runner Audrey, in charge of the southern half of the Hundred Mile Wilderness. She is a Maine native who sought the city life in Chicago and then came back to her roots. She warned me of a tough scramble up the last couple hundred feet to the views at the top of Chairback. They were a challenge, sort of a mix of Mahoosuc Notch followed by the Beaver Brook Trail with its cascades, and then a lot of stone steps on steep ledge, like St. John's Ledges.

While the view from the top was worth the effort, I shared it with a bunch of noisy day hikers. I didn't stay long before I dropped down and passed the forlorn

Chairback Gap Lean-to. The trail literally goes past the front steps. Hikers were hanging out, taking a break, their stuff all spread out, snacking. I continued on up over Columbus Mountain where I promptly met a group of hikers hanging out at the summit sign and chatting.

"Where did you come from?" one piped up, clearly trying to suck me into his clutch of loiterers.

"Uh …"

I always had a hard time with this question. I was hiking southbound at the moment, but I had come from Georgia. 'I came from my mother's womb' seemed far too snitty to say out loud. 'All my ancestors come from Germany. We Westerners are here on a mission to destroy the last vestiges of American Wilderness. Damn nearly got the job done, eh?' Nahhh. 'Came from Jimmy's Grocery Store in Bingham. Just bought 58 pounds of ice in case I can't resupply for a while. Wilderness here, ya know.'

Sometimes I reply with a question. 'Do you mean today, or do you want the bigger picture?'

This gang didn't look like the kind that would have a good story to share in return.

"Up from the parking lot. Gulf Hagas," I finally said, not slowing my pace. The summit had minimal views. I figured I could stop and check them out on the way back.

Yes, I was a little pissed off. Not about these people in particular but about the 'infestation' in general on this busy Maine summer day; or maybe about unmet expectations. I came to the AT seeking that 'footprints in the wilderness' solitude. If there was anywhere on the AT that civilization hadn't yet encroached and turned every significant stopping point (summits in particular) into a yammering people-clogged circus, you'd think it would be the Hundred Mile Wilderness in Maine. Not the case, or at least not on the Thursday before Labor Day, and that left me feeling a little less than sociable. I found myself longing for those chilly January days down in southwestern Virginia where I would hike for days without seeing another person on the trail.

The next day, Friday, would surely be worse, so I got a super-early start. Weekenders don't do early mornings—their jobs make them get up early. Out here they're on vacation. Many of them wouldn't be on the trail until nearly noon.

Anyone going northbound on the AT to the Gulf Hagas loop trails or beyond has to ford the West Branch of the Pleasant River first. It's practically right next to the parking lot. It's a hundred feet across, but was meek and slow moving on this late summer day, no more than knee-deep. The trail then follows Gulf Hagas Stream gradually up 1,000 feet of elevation to the Carl A. Newhall Lean-to. This is well past all the popular day-hiker trails, so it was a peaceful stroll. Beyond the shelter, the trail gets steep but it has all been rebuilt with stone steps—miles of them it seemed. Again, hardly what I expected in this wilderness section. I picked a turn-around point between West Peak and Hay Mountain and came back through the popular areas at a popular time. Things were jumping; people everywhere.

My next insertion point was Logan Brook Road, the first of five road crossings of the AT that fork off of Jo Mary Road. All are toll roads, decent quality gravel roads, and all are popular access points to camping and fishing and hiking in this 170,000-acre private tract. The roads and campgrounds and other facilities are owned by KI Jo-Mary, Inc. and managed by North Maine Woods, Inc. The former is a consortium of landowners who set the rules for the public use of the land. The latter is the management company that man the toll gates and maintain the camps and other facilities. This arrangement has evolved from a haphazard patchwork of gates and private road maintenance and oversight by the individual land owners. In its current consolidated form, it has only been in place since 1986. The roads remain working logging roads and the trucks have the right of way and can come barreling along at any time of day or night, kicking up clouds of choking dust.

I parked at Logan Brook Road and did two out-and-back legs on Day 221. The southward leg took me up over at least 800 excellent, sturdy stone steps, then over White Cap Mountain, the last significant peak before Katahdin. It's a place I'd like to come back to, with grand sweeping views including a great view of the "greatest mountain" itself—that is what Katahdin translates to in the Penobscot/Abenaki tongue. Logan Brook Lean-to had an entry from the Parkside Fellowship, written by 'Drop Out.' They came through on June 26th.

The leg northward featured a dry rock-hop over the North Branch of the Pleasant River. I left a bit of flag tape on a branch about a mile beyond that, near Moun-

Sept. 1st – view of Katahdin from near the summit of Whitecap Mountain

F.I.T. Wilderness

tain View Pond, and scampered back. Fall was in the air today, it never got above 70 degrees F.

The thru-hikers I was meeting now all had 'Katahdin Fever', which comes in two variants. The first sufferers are so focused on finishing that they don't want to talk. The others don't want the experience to end, and want to do nothing but linger and talk. These latter folks were doing shorter and shorter distances each day and savoring the final miles. I had to admit that, after standing on White Cap and beholding the entire remaining path spread out before me, I began to feel a bit of Katahdin fever myself.

Johnston Pond Road, was my next trailhead. It goes right by Crawford Pond, where there's a bit of sandy beach just a short stroll from the road. I did two easy legs—one north, one south. But the highlight of the day was before I hit the trail. I went to McDonald's in Millinocket and had my first hot meal of any sort since the buffet breakfasts at Highland Center Lodge a month and a half ago. Honestly, I don't understand why hikers carry stoves and deal with the fuel and all that gadgetry. Well, maybe I do; they've got nothing better to do while waiting for daylight to return. Fidgeting with the stove is like playing with a kitten. The little hissing flame keeps them company. Using water from a nearby ditch they're hoping to turn a bag of dry mealy powder into something resembling edible food. But there are so many good choices of tasty low-moisture cold food available now that personally, I would just ditch the stove.

Classic 'postcard' view of Katahdin from the shores of Pemadumcook Lake

I spent Labor Day at the beach, like so many other Americans. This beach was the white sandy shoreline of Lower Jo Mary Lake. The water was bathwater-warm, and the sunshine was brilliant. The temperature was in the 70's F. Yet amazingly every other American was at some other beach today. I had the strand all to myself.

Potaywadjo Spring between Lower Jo Mary and Pemadumcook Lakes is a huge outpouring of deep-rock cold water. A fifteen-foot-wide pool bubbles and percolates up through white granite sand. At Pemadumcook Lake, where I turned around, I took in the classic view of Katahdin's looming hulk across the rock-strewn waters of the lake. The mountain was making its own weather. Like the classic Li'l Abner comic strip character, Joe Btfsplk, from the mid-20th century, it seemed to be moping along with a big dark cumulus cloud hovering over its head, keeping the summit in perpetual shade.

I chose this spot as the turn-around, hoping to get a different view the next day. As the crow flies, the summit was just 13.9 miles away, but the trail meanders for 47.7 miles before it gets there. It would take me five more day hikes. The 'Parkside Fellowship' had stopped here for lunch on June 27th and summited two days later.

The cloud over Katahdin was a little puffy white one the next day. Joe, the world's worst jinx, had moved on. This day started at the parking area at Nahmakanta Lake, where the trail offers a shoreline hike for more than a mile to its gravelly sand beach.

The next day I drove the full length of the private KI Jo Mary toll road system, and parked at the Pollywog Stream trailhead, 27 miles from the toll gate. I would stay there overnight. The hike from there south included a climb of Nesuntabunt Mountain, where there is a great viewpoint looking down on Nahmakanta Lake and out to Katahdin. I got there before the morning fog broke up and kept on going. The great views opened up for me on the way back. There's

Gravel beach, Nahmakanta Lake

even some that look back over the much bigger Pemadumcook Lake off to the east-southeast. Over these last two days, the AT had taken me one net mile farther from Katahdin (as the crow flies) than where I had started. When you've got 'Katahdin Fever', suddenly the destination seems more important than the journey. I had to remind myself to take a deep breath and just enjoy the brilliant early fall-like weather and the wild Maine woods.

F.I.T. Wilderness

At sunrise the next morning, I headed north across Pollywog Stream on the newly rebuilt bridge carrying the road. This was going to be a long day—11 trail miles each way. It took me past Rainbow Stream Lean-to early in the day. The trail goes right by the front of the shelter and then crosses the stream on a precarious narrow footbridge, also right in front of the shelter. It wasn't so much a bridge as a skinny wobbly log thrown across the fifty feet of stream. I met a lady there, packing up, who said she was 80 years old, from Ohio. She had hiked a good chunk of the Appalachian Trail starting at age 70 and still hoped to finish it. On this outing she was doing 40 miles and had packed two weeks' worth of food to make that distance. Today she planned to go just four miles to the Rainbow Spring campground. I wished her well and headed on toward that campground myself. I thought I might see her there on the way back but never did.

September 7th in central Maine – a trailside maple was getting an early start on fall

The trail follows the the entire length of the shore of Rainbow Lake. There were plenty of views, but most of the time Katahdin was hiding behind the hills on the far side of the lake. I caught one peek-a-boo view of the very tip of the summit. I ended the day on Rainbow Ledges, but ended up turning around seven minutes short of the iconic viewpoint where the forest had been cut back in a swath pointing straight toward Katahdin.

I would regret that failure, because the next day was socked in with fog and drizzle all day long. I parked at Abol Bridge across from the store and campsite and made my last foray into the Hundred Mile Wilderness. I took a photo of the foggy view that I missed and visited Hurd Brook Lean-to, the last shelter except for the various hiker accommodations at Katahdin Stream Campground. Entries in the register there were very different from those in other shelters. There was a wistful sense of sadness and loss. People were wishing their trail friends who they had pulled ahead of good luck in their new journeys through life. People were congratulating themselves and each other. 'Shenanigans,' who I was to meet climbing Katahdin and at the summit, wrote "Damn. This isn't a loop trail? How am I going to get back to my car in GA? It's been real. It's been fun. Now let's conquer this."

The following day, September 9th, I parked in the day-use parking lot at Katahdin Stream Campground and covered the chunk of trail south of there. I met

Jonathan, the Ridge Runner for that section, sort of loitering around near where the trail enters Baxter State Park. He was wearing a Len Foote Hike Inn visor cap. That's a hiker glamp site/hotel halfway between Amicalola Falls State Park and Springer Mountain, Georgia—the very other end of this long, long trail. We had a fun chat, then I returned to the campground and went to the ranger's cabin, where I spent a long time looking at the ultimate register book, kept in the room where hikers stow their gear while they make the day hike up to the summit.

I went ahead and wrote my entry too, so I wouldn't have to deal with that on the big final day.

And then, at last, it was my turn. Well, they certainly saved the best for last. For the NoBo hiker, this last five miles, with 4,200 feet of climbing, is, by my reckoning at least, the most challenging/difficult part of the whole trail. Coming up to the timberline, there's some serious rock scrambling with steel pins for handholds. That's where 'Shenanigans' passed me like I was standing still, followed by her hiking companion 'Secrets', who I had met briefly the day before at Daicey Pond. The climb up Hunt Spur was exposed, nose-bleed rock scrambling. There was enough wind and cold to make my hands numb. I was also pushing too hard. I was hiking in my head too much, rather than taking the route move by move as it presented itself. I was not pacing myself. In the upper part of Hunt Spur, where the rocks are the gnarliest and the route the steepest, my legs and arms were shaking. It wasn't from fear, though I was scared in places. It was because I was pushing my muscles beyond their capacity.

Then, all of a sudden, I came to 'The Gateway'. It felt to me like the gates of heaven. I half expected to face St. Peter there with his ledger book open, frowning down at it through thick bushy eyebrows as he checked to see if I had been judged worthy for entry or if I was to be banished to the pits of Hades. Beyond the Gateway is a mile of what feels like level ground; a grand promenade, curving along a broad flat table-land of sensitive tundra approaching the gentle hill that holds the actual summit.

Here, exactly 166 years and two days earlier, Henry David Thoreau stood, having left his party behind near timberline and climbed solo onto this table-land. It was a place that, at the time, only a handful of humans were known to have visited. He felt like he had stepped into a new world:

"What is it to be admitted to a museum, to see a myriad of particular things, compared with being shown some star's surface, some hard matter in its home!"

There, alone on the great mountain, 29-year-old Thoreau experienced a sensation of pure unspoiled and untamed wilderness more intense than he ever felt in his life again. His descriptions of that day, published in his travelogue 'Ktaadn,' resonate with pure unbridled wonderment and awe. He was a master at his art—as he put it, "giving expression to Nature ... impress[ing] the winds and streams to his service, to speak for him."

F.I.T. Wilderness

The weather was marginal, very similar to what Thoreau had experienced. The temperature was about 40 degrees F. Fog was flying by on the wind—sometimes clamping down on the mountain, other times lifting just enough to give fabulous views of the lake-strewn lowlands off to the east where every body of water blazed as if studded with luminous jewels, white and shimmering beneath the sun.

As I approached the summit sign, I found a dozen or more hikers hanging around, some having lunch, others taking their turns at the photo-op with the sign. 'Secrets' and 'Shenanigans' came up to me and introduced themselves. They had been following my entries in the registers. They wanted to take a picture of me. Then I had them take my shots with my camera. I tried several poses: I leaned against the sign like it was the only thing holding me up; I stood up straight with a hand around it like it was my buddy; I gave it a loving hug; I tried to look cool and macho, like some mountain man who had just killed a bear; and then I pressed my cheek against the weathered brown sign as if it was my mommy's bosom.

Secrets and Shenanigans' summit celebration—note and pic submitted to and posted at the AT Conservancy in Harper's Ferry, taken Oct 21st.

Most of the photos of me looked stupid. But there I was. Katahdin. I had officially hiked the entire Appalachian Trail over the past three years. To accomplish the double, I had 354.2 more trail miles that I wanted to do both ways that year. I felt complete, satisfied, yet ready for more.

My mug shot with the summit sign—a moment to remember forever

P. J. Wetzel

PART FOUR

Familiar Ground

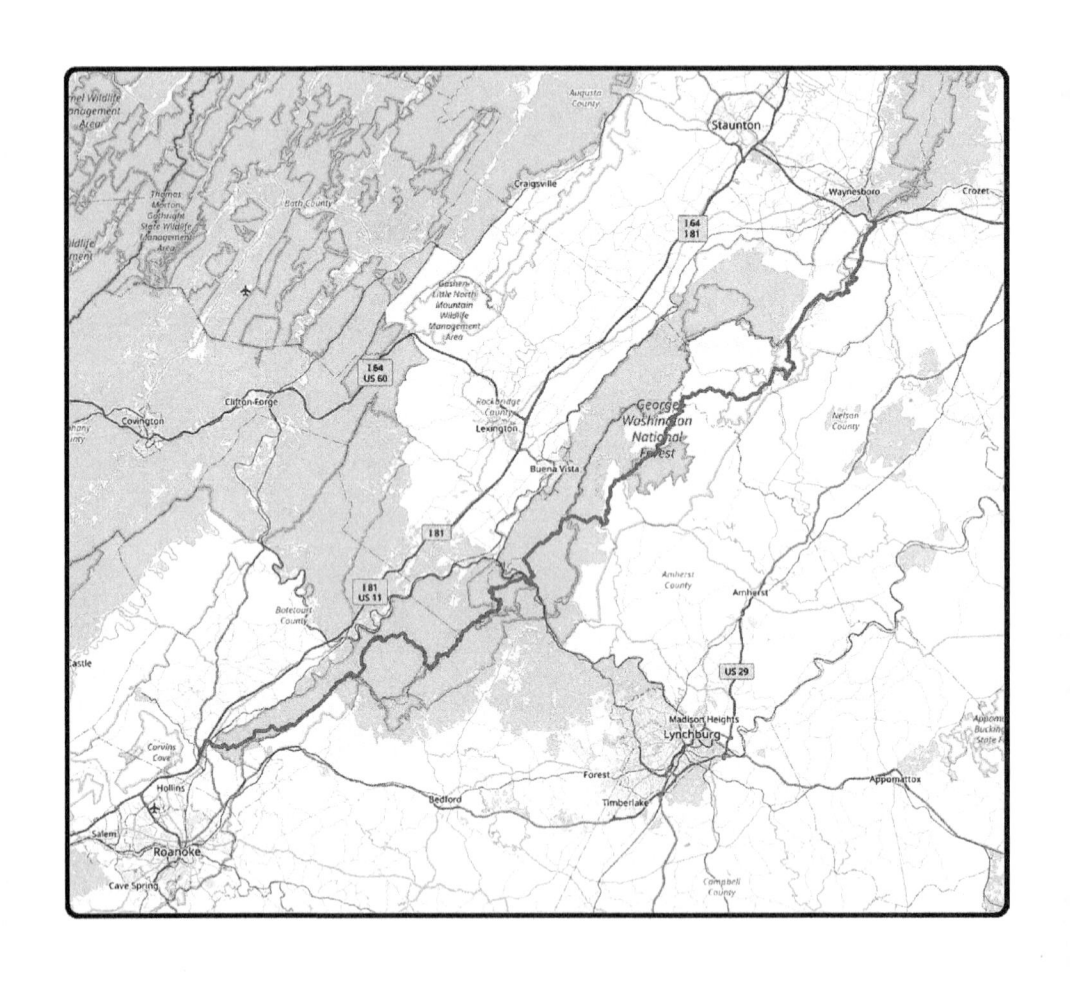

P. J. Wetzel

CHAPTER 16

Daleville, VA to Rockfish Gap, VA
September 15 - 29; 137.4 trail miles one way

I left Millinocket, Maine early the next morning. There were chores to do at home. I lived in a condo on the beach in North Carolina where summer was lingering—bright sun and temperatures in the 80's. The place was tugging at me, imploring me to give up my hiking quest in favor of the daily extended sun-drenched surfside strolls. Soft sand, warm water, a new sunrise to experience every day. And no rocks.

But not just yet ... I would resist. The beach would still be there. I had a mission to complete: 700 miles to hike in the deep-shaded woods. Truth was, the woods were tugging at me too. While away from the trail over that four-day break, I came to realize how much the deep wild woods had become a part of who I am.

I began to wonder what would be next, as so many of those I met at Katahdin were wondering. When I was done on the trail, would it be calling me back as surely as the beach life was beckoning? How would I answer that call? Would I hike the entire AT again someday? It was too soon to answer. I had to let those questions ride. It was time to finish this year's mission.

I got to Daleville, VA bright and early on the morning of September 15th, stuck my toe in the dirt at my own personal 'Mile 0' point, from back on January 1st, and headed north. I had last hiked this bit of trail just ten months earlier, on November 7, 2011, and I was amazed at how much detail I remembered. I remembered the steady climb up to Fullhardt Knob Shelter—1,300 feet of elevation gain from the parking lot—as being a tough climb. But after hiking Maine, this gradual switch-back trail, all on smooth, easy footing and wide and level graded trail with gradual slopes, felt so easy that I could not even walk fast enough to get my breathing and heart rate up to the level I was used to for hill climbing. It didn't feel like an ascent, just a slightly inclined walk. That was a perspective on the difference in trail and in my fitness, which completely caught me by surprise.

From the shelter, I made the gradual descent on the Fullhardt Fire Road (there used to be a fire tower where the shelter is), then the very gradual ascent back up to about 2,500 feet on the ridge, before dropping down to Salt Pond Road where I had parked on November 7th. I remembered quite a bit of detail about the trail all throughout this section. The next bit involved a fairly steep set of switchbacks down to the Curry Creek Trail. But from there, I didn't remember

F.I.T. Wilderness

as much detail or where I turned around in that direction. My records showed that I visited the next shelter, Wilson Creek Shelter, on November 4th, and I did correctly recall the look of this shelter.

I extended my day 25 extra minutes in order to reach that shelter. Then the long hike back, over the several small ups and downs to Curry Creek Trail, went fast, though my feet and legs were beginning to feel the strain of the long day. And after the day ended, I realized that I had taken the downhills way too casually. My knees began to complain and were unhappy with me for several days afterward.

And so, I headed north, destined to be paralleling the Blue Ridge Parkway and Skyline Drive for the next 225 miles. My trailhead for the next day was at Black Horse Gap—the boundary between maintenance responsibility of the Roanoke AT club to the south and the Natural Bridge AT club, based out of Lynchburg, to the north.

Most of this day was ridge walking—right over the hill from the Parkway or just down below it—beside mossy, exquisitely engineered, CCC-built stone buttress walls. There were seven different points of contact with the Parkway. Harvey's Gap overlook is a favorite place for bird watchers to follow the hawk migration. They make counts and keep data, comparing the numbers from year to year. There were at least a dozen devout bird-watchers there, lined up in their lounge chairs, binoculars at the ready.

Just north of Harvey's Gap overlook, and up on a high point above the Parkway near a side trail called Hammond Hollow Trail, I passed a guy who looked like a thru-hiker, sitting on a rock, talking on his phone. He hung up as I approached and then looked at me and said, "I saw you up in Maine."

Uh Oh. Face blindness strikes again. I did not remember him. He was Joshua 'Bobcat' Stacy, and he was doing a Flip-Flop. It turns out that he passed me near Andover, and knew at that time who I was and how I was hiking the trail. All my memory can dredge up is a conversation with a hiker as I was coming to Sawyer Notch, who told me the ford was an easy rock hop. I vaguely remembered the horn-rimmed glasses and I remembered the words, but my mind hadn't registered the face. That was the day after my surprise encounter with Harry and Leo. It must have been them who told 'Bobcat' about me.

Today we had a very nice in-depth conversation. He was from Baltimore and, like me, had hiked a big chunk of this part of the AT in previous years, so he too was covering familiar ground. We both agreed about the luxury of these easy trail conditions after leaping from Maine. He started his hike in Harper's Ferry and hiked north to Katahdin, summiting on Sept 3. Then he took a couple weeks off and returned to Harper's Ferry and was now working south to Springer. 'Bobcat' would finish his hike on October 28th. He mentioned meeting one other hiker, trail name 'Sharkey,' who was trying to do a complete AT double in the more conventional way called a 'yo-yo.' 'Sharkey' had thru-hiked northbound, reaching Katahdin on August 11th, and just turned right around and headed south, apparently on the spur of the moment. He was one of those who just did not want the experience to end.

I wished 'Bobcat' well and headed on, marveling at my new trail connection, and kicking myself for my failure to remember him. But here I was, less than two days on the trail, and I had already made my first connection with a hiker from up north. I continued on, descending to Bobblets Gap and visiting the shelter there—which is a quarter mile down a seriously steep side trail—and then back along the ridge beside the Parkway.

When the Blue Ridge Parkway was in the planning, Benton MacKaye took a hard stand against it. This was the AT's wilderness route. It should be preserved for those who want to walk. After all, the AT was there first. What right did the government have to destroy the pristine nature of the Blue Ridge? Myron Avery, on the other hand, took the position that the AT could make accommodations for the road. It wasn't a commercial road. It remained a wild parkway—a trail in the woods for motorists.

The motorists won out, of course. There are a hundred of them to every pedestrian. On June 30, 1936, Congress formally authorized the project and placed it under the jurisdiction of the National Park Service. This controversy got personal between Avery and MacKaye and led to a permanent fall-out. The dreamer, MacKaye, retreated to his Ivory Tower. Avery stepped on toes, made many more enemies, bullied his way through one problem after another, and got the trail built.

North of Bearwallow Gap, the AT departs from the Parkway, dropping down to cross Jennings Creek before rejoining the Parkway north of the heavily-used Peaks of Otter Recreation Area.

I did this stretch in two day hikes. On the first one, down to the creek and back from Bearwallow, the trail was pretty with all the mosses and lichens showing their various shades of green and gray, flush with the moisture from the fog and morning rain. The fog persisted as I began to drop down beyond the Little Cove Mountain side trail and through a large area that was recently burned. Cove Mountain Shelter is set in a shallow hollow just off the ridge that the AT continues to follow. The fog had parted by the time I returned there, so I got the benefit of the fine view from the nearby rock outcrop, showing the first hints of fall color.

The next day brought an all-day rain so I took a zero, stocked up on calories at the Country Cookin' breakfast buffet in Daleville, and caught up on sleep and on documenting my hike on social media.

Bryant Ridge Shelter, my favorite of them all. This shot was taken 1 Nov 2011

F.I.T. Wilderness

For the next hike, I parked at Jennings Creek and climbed northbound, stopping in at the amazing Bryant Ridge Shelter. This is a memorable place, a shelter designed by architectural students. It was a delight to see and interact with it. The best part about it is the size of the roof, the most important feature for hikers. It covers the picnic table and a large open 'living area'. From there, the trail northbound makes a long steady climb up to 3,500-foot Floyd Mountain. Both that 2,200-foot climb and the climb up Bryant Ridge were so steady and gentle that they didn't feel like climbing. I could 'relax' even as I was moving forward at a decent pace. From Floyd Mountain, I descended a few hundred feet to Cornelius Creek Shelter, visited it on the short side trail, and then headed back the way I came; once again thoroughly enjoying the mid-Atlantic woods, my 'home' ecosystem, and the easy, nearly rock-free and well graded trail.

Day 234 was another day of paralleling the Blue Ridge Parkway. I would cross the road just twice, but it was never far away. This was also a rare piece of trail that I had hiked with a group—part of an organized hike with the Natural Bridge AT Club that made a circuit including the Glenwood Horse Trail and the Hunting Creek Trail. Fall blooming bottle gentians were out in force where most fall flowers were done and gone.

The trail skims through an edge of the Thunder Ridge Wilderness and leads the hiker through the iconic 'Guillotine,' a rock wedged between two boulders high overhead, which the AT dares you to pass under. Then there were some steep rock steps to climb before the trail reached the summit of Apple Orchard Mountain at over 4,200 feet. The summit is open and grassy, but the actual high point is occupied by a big fenced-in radar dome and some other sinister looking towers and buildings. Coming down the south side of the mountain, I encountered one lone apple tree, lending legitimacy to the

Bottle Gentian blooms and the ripe berries of Canadian May-lily, September 20th.

name of the mountain. It was shedding its apples and they were tart yet sweet, crunchy, and free of worms. I ate two, right down to the core, and packed a couple more. What a delightful free snack. The old heirloom varieties you encounter along the trail between here and Harper's Ferry are too small for today's commercial market, but they're much juicier, crunchier, and tastier than the mealy crap you find in grocery stores. Nature's own Trail Magic, or more properly, magic left from a bygone era of rugged pioneer mountain-top homesteaders. Many of these residents were forcibly relocated by the Feds when they pushed the Parkway through.

The next day I was well away from the Parkway again all day, traipsing through the heart of the James River Face Wilderness. I got up at first light and headed to the James River parking area. I was on the trail at 8:15. The first order of the day was to cross the James River Foot Bridge; *not* 'footbridge.' The bridge is named after William T. Foot (1946-2000), longtime trail advocate, president of the Natural Bridge AT Club, and AT thru-hiker, who had worked tirelessly to get this longest pedestrian-only bridge on the AT built on a set of abandoned railroad bridge piles. He and his wife Laurie were also pioneers of the cross-country American Discovery Trail and were the first to thru-hike it in 1997.

Sept 20th harvest from an heirloom tree, the AT at Apple Orchard Mountain

From the river, I headed into the woods and southbound, first along the river, then up Matt's Creek to the shelter by that name. There the trail begins its long climb to Highcock Knob. I turned around at Petite's Gap at 1:25 pm and headed back, enjoying limited views of the James River from the ridge.

The weather was getting hot but the sun felt good. On the way back, I began to meet some hikers, all of whom appeared to be (and two said they were) thru-hikers. There were five in all; a much higher count than any previous day since I got to Virginia.

It was 6:15 when I got back to the parking lot. I was changing clothes in my van when a park ranger pulled up in his SUV. He wanted to talk to me. Was I in some sort of trouble?

Not at all. He was here to inform me that two guys who I knew were looking for me.

Two guys I knew? Yep, he said. They were camped up Hercules Road, a nearby side road that the AT crosses. He said one was named Harry. Was the other Leo, I asked? And the answer was yes.

I could hardly believe it. I dropped everything and drove out to look for them immediately. I eventually found them, with both of their vehicles, in a pull-off at a sharp bend, not at any AT crossing.

What a shock to see these two guys again when I had assumed they were still making their way south from Maine since I'd last seen them on August 5th. But

F.I.T. Wilderness

it turned out that they had been doing many more bits and pieces than I realized, and were going to complete the entire AT the very next day at Lynchburg Reservoir. They had started on February 23rd, and had only spent a handful of nights on the trail. The rest of the time they had done very much what I was doing, usually sleeping in their vehicles and doing day hikes, except they were only hiking one way between their two vehicles.

We had a very long animated conversation, comparing notes, talking about people we had both met, etc. We exchanged contact information and promised to keep in touch. It was dusk before I finally said a reluctant good-bye to these two old friends and headed to town.

Every meeting with those two had seemed an almost magical coincidence. In this case it seemed more than magical; it seemed pre-destined. I was going to be able to hike with them on their last day on the trail.

I returned to the James River parking area well before sunrise the next morning. Just as I was pulling in, Harry and Leo arrived. We discussed hiking where they were going to finish their thru-hike today, about 20 trail miles north, but then they proposed that they'd park a mile up Hercules Road and hike back down, meeting me as I came up instead, so we could get some photos of each other and then get on with the day's business, since we were not actually hiking the same piece of trail today.

That sounded like the best plan, so off they went. I prepared and was on the trail about 7:30 and met them soon after. I'm glad I hadn't chosen to hike with them for long because these guys, though older than me, liked keeping a much faster pace. We took photos of each other as we hiked together back toward their vehicle. My left knee and ankle keep me in a comfort zone of 2½ miles per hour. Leo says he hikes 3 miles per hour and can't keep up with Harry. Harry was chugging along with energy that seemed entirely impossible for a person of any age to sustain. So eventually I gave them my final handshake of congratulations, wished them all the best, and let them go on ahead. They had retrieved their vehicle and were gone well before I got to the road crossing.

From there, the trail follows a dry scrubby ridge to a stream crossing and then begins to climb gradually, passing Johns Hollow Shelter just 0.6 miles from the road crossing. The trail ascends gradually beside Johns Hollow as it took me through one of my favorite types of mid-Atlantic trail settings: an amphitheater-like valley under the high, dense hardwood canopy with little undergrowth that the side-hill trail curves around, providing a balcony view of the broad bowl-shaped drainage. The huge trees stood like the columns in a cathedral, their thick canopies its roof. The sense of a vast yet enclosed space, as grand as any sports stadium and much more peaceful, is what appeals to me.

I turned around at the summit of Bluff Mountain. There are old fire tower foundation blocks there in a small open area with great views, and a nearby plaque marking where a young child was found after having wandered away from his school back in 1890. All day my left knee had been bothering me. It had started with that first fast hike out of Daleville. I took a couple of ibuprofens in the afternoon and was happy to find that most of the downhill walking was gradual enough that the knee wasn't hurting.

The next day I hiked into my fourth season. Fall had officially arrived and it was perfect fall weather, with wall-to-wall sun and light wind, temperatures rising only to the upper 60's and very low humidity. The trail skirted Lynchburg Reservoir—keeping a respectful distance because it is a city water supply—but there were plenty of views through the big hillside trees. Between there and Bluff Mountain, where the views were even better than yesterday, the trail crossed the Parkway. Otherwise, the two go their separate ways and don't get together again until Reed's Gap, nearly fifty trail miles to the north. This portion of the AT is far more generous with its variety of wilderness experience than the Parkway route. Some of my favorite, most memorable settings were coming up.

My case of iliotibial band friction syndrome (downhill-hiker's knee) bothered me again, especially coming down the steep flanks of Bluff Mountain. I took one last dose of ibuprofen and, by noon, the problem had faded and did not come back.

Day 238 was a memorable hike in a memorable place. The last time I hiked this piece of trail over Bald Knob and Cold (or Cole) Mountain was September 16th, a year earlier, and I hiked it with my brother 'Frugal,' who was doing one of his week-long AT backpacking outings. On that first visit I came to believe that somebody long ago had mixed up the names of these two mountains. You see, Bald Knob is all wooded, and it's always cold up on top. Cold Mountain is as bald as a peach, or at least is maintained as a bald, with a long beautiful stretch of mountain ridge AT hiking through fluffy green grass under the infinite sky.

The naming issue gets even more confused when you look into the history of Cold Mountain's name. Quoting from the 2001 Appalachian Trail Guide to Central Virginia, First Edition, revised (pp.79-80): *"Amherst County deed books and will books ... use "Cold Mountain" in the 1850's and 1870's. "Cold Mountain" appears on all maps from 1825 to 1894, when the first USGS map appeared with "Cole Mountain." Still, the Natural Bridge National Forest maps went back to using "Cold Mountain" from 1924 to 1930. Forest Service and Appalachian Trail publications have reverted from "Cole" to the original "Cold Mountain" usage."*

Look. If there's a guy named Cole who is tied into the history of the mountain, then tell me about him. Otherwise, I'd go with the oldest sources. It appears to me that the name Cole is one of many USGS errors that creep into their maps. I have a personal connection with another such error, regarding the name of a small NW Ohio town called "Wetzel" that federal government mappers erroneously re-named "Wetsel" in the 1950's. It took me several letters, with ample proof provided, to get them to change that name back.

I parked at the big Buena Vista trailhead off US 60 and hiked the leg south first. The fall weather had settled in. The morning was cold enough to call for a knit hat and three layers on top, though I still just wore my shorts on my lower half. That was sufficient even though I was hiking downhill. I continued southbound along Brown Mountain Creek, where a number of interpretive signs in-

The open meadow ridge of Cold/Cole Mountain on a brisk fall morning

dicated that a freed slave community had existed during the early 1900's. The trail follows the creek for most of two miles, then climbs a little to the crossing of Pedlar Lake Road, which was my turn-around point. It took two hours to get there, including a long stop at the Brown Mountain Shelter where I perused an old log book with entries from 'Parkside' and several of his long-time hiking companions who I'd met, including 'Samus' and 'Iceman' and 'Viking'. They were all there on the same day, April 7th, though the entries were separate.

Then came the cold climb over Bald Knob and the stretch of million-dollar views at Cold Mountain. I turned around there so that I could come back and bask in their glory one more time.

And so I did. The morning views were even clearer and crisper. Then it was on to stroll through more meadows and rolling mixed open woodlands with drifts of purple and white asters in bloom, and bright red clusters of sumac berries framing the magnificent vista from Wolf Rock. What a perfect early fall day.

The hike from Spy Rock to the Tye River and back includes a brutal, steady, four-mile three-thousand-foot climb over The Priest. This mountain means more to me than any other on the AT. In the 1990's I owned land at its base, straight down the valley from the Priest Shelter and within view of the trail. Up until recently this was the mountain I had climbed and crawled around on more than any other mountain on the AT. On my Day 240 two-way hike, I finally ran into my first rattlesnake, and the only one I was to see on the entire adventure. It was fat and lethargic in the cool high-mountain fall air, slow to give way, but never seemed a threat because I heard it rustling through the dry trailside leaves well before it spotted me.

Down from the south side of The Priest is a side trail to Crabtree Falls, which by some definitions is the highest waterfall east of the Mississippi. It tumbles in seven significant cascades, or steps, through a vertical drop of over 1,000 feet. To all but the most single-minded, myopic, 'eat the miles' thru-hiker, this is well worth the side trip. The side trip to the bottom of the cascades is about two miles, with, of course, plenty of vertical drop. As part of my training for South America, I had once climbed up to The Priest from the Crabtree Falls Parking Lot carrying fifty pounds of water in my backpack. The trail itself is brutal, but straying off it can be deadly. Since the U.S. Forest Service started keeping records in 1982, twenty-nine people have fallen to their death around Crabtree Falls.

The register book at The Priest Shelter has an appropriate theme. You are supposed to make a confession to the Priest. I wrote:

"Okay, my Confession – Priest Shelter ... you were my first. I've now visited every shelter on the AT. Every last one. Guess you could say I've slept around. But I'm back, Priest Shelter. I'm back.

"I'm afraid I'm going to have to stray down the path a bit more before I settle down. But just know, dear Priest Shelter, that you'll always be first in my heart.

"Love,
"Seeks It"

It's true. The Priest Shelter was the very first AT shelter I had ever visited.

On the way back north, descending The Priest in the afternoon, I had my one and only known meeting with a southbound thru-hiker that I had met up north. It was 'Banjo', who I first met and photographed at the Spaulding Mountain Lean-to in central Maine. We talked a while, mostly about rattlesnakes. They, too, ('Banjo' and his hiking companion 'Stilts') had seen one today up on Three Ridges, the equally brutal climb on the north side of the Tye River that awaited me the following day.

So off I went soon after sunrise, across the swinging suspension bridge over the Tye River, and up toward Three Ridges. There's only 25 feet or so difference between the high point on Three Ridges and the summit of The Priest. But the approach to Three Ridges is very different from the no-nonsense, steady climb over four miles to The Priest. Here it takes six miles to get to the summit and there are some ups and downs, some rocky steep scrambles, and many more viewpoints on exposed bedrock. It reminded me of New England in places. The weather added further difficulty. It was calm, hot for the season, and humid. Of course I'd rather be sweaty under a bright sun than rain-soaked in the fog, so I wasn't complaining ... much.

From Three Ridges summit I made it to Maupin Field Shelter, where I turned around and came back via the white blazes. There's a short cut here called the

Mau-Har trail, finished in 1978, that makes for a perfect loop hike. I had hiked it before and preferred it because it followed the loud, rambunctious Campbell Creek past dozens of white-water cascades in deep moist green woods. It was so tempting to abandon my mission and go this way on such a hot day. It is, in places, a gnarly trail, but worth the effort for a waterfall lover. Unfortunately, it has no white blazes, so today there was only one real option for me.

Back I went over the Three Ridges rock-and-roller coaster. The trail seems to want to take the hiker past every possible viewpoint where a rock juts up or a bedrock slab juts out. It somehow seemed much more pointless on the way back. Every view was basically in the same direction, south toward The Priest.

I got it done. Once I got back to the van at 6:00 pm, I drove to nearby Lovingston, tiny county seat of tiny Nelson County, and stayed the night at the Village Inn, a clean, tidy little motel with original hand-painted landscape murals on the walls of the rooms, and every room is different.

Back on the trail through Reed's Gap and past the Wintergreen Resort, I had a damp day, hiking in my poncho. It rained half the time, was foggy half the time, and half the viewpoints were half as good as I would have liked. Dripping Rock under dripping trees was one of three points where the AT and the Blue Ridge Parkway crossed paths on this 8.3 miles of the AT.

The weather improved slowly the next day. I hiked 12.6 miles of fairly easy trail and finished the Blue Ridge Parkway section, reaching Rockfish Gap and the south entrance to Shenandoah National Park. I passed a number of signs of the old homesteaders here—a sturdy rock hog-fence and an old stone chimney built to withstand the direct hit of a nuke. It was after 8:00pm when I finished in the dark.

It was a Saturday, and on the way past Paul Wolfe Shelter in the twilight, I was bombarded by the shouts of kids and the clamor of people chopping wood and pounding tent stakes. A bunch of boy scouts and a collection of adults who I had met on the trail, and who had arrived as three or four separate parties, had all chosen this place in the wilderness to spend the night. I counted at least a dozen tents, and the shelter was throbbing, buzzing like a beehive; it was a small city. I couldn't get out of earshot and back to the peace of the evening fast enough.

What kind of hiker would willingly hike miles to spend a night in such a noisy, crowded place? It was why I chose to stick to day hikes. It was why, in my darker moods, I wondered if that ideal trail, built for those who seek fellowship with the wilderness, was nothing but a cruel joke. It was why the AT Conservancy started its 'Flip-Flop' festival and asked thru-hikers to voluntarily register in order to distribute trail usage more evenly. Perhaps it was why seasoned hikers like me began to think about seeking wilderness elsewhere. There are thousands of miles of wild trails out there that get little use. The AT even has a new parallel path called the Great Eastern Trail that runs 1,600 miles from Flagg Mountain, Alabama to the Finger Lakes Trail in western New York. This is such a new trail that the first pair of thru-hikers didn't complete it until the following year (2013). I knew this because I was following their progress. One of them, Joanna 'Someday' Swanson, was a hiker I had met on the AT in northern Virginia in 2010.

It's a trend, folks. To paraphrase Yogi Berra: "Nobody hikes the AT anymore. It's too crowded."

View of the open expanses on Cold/Cole Mountain

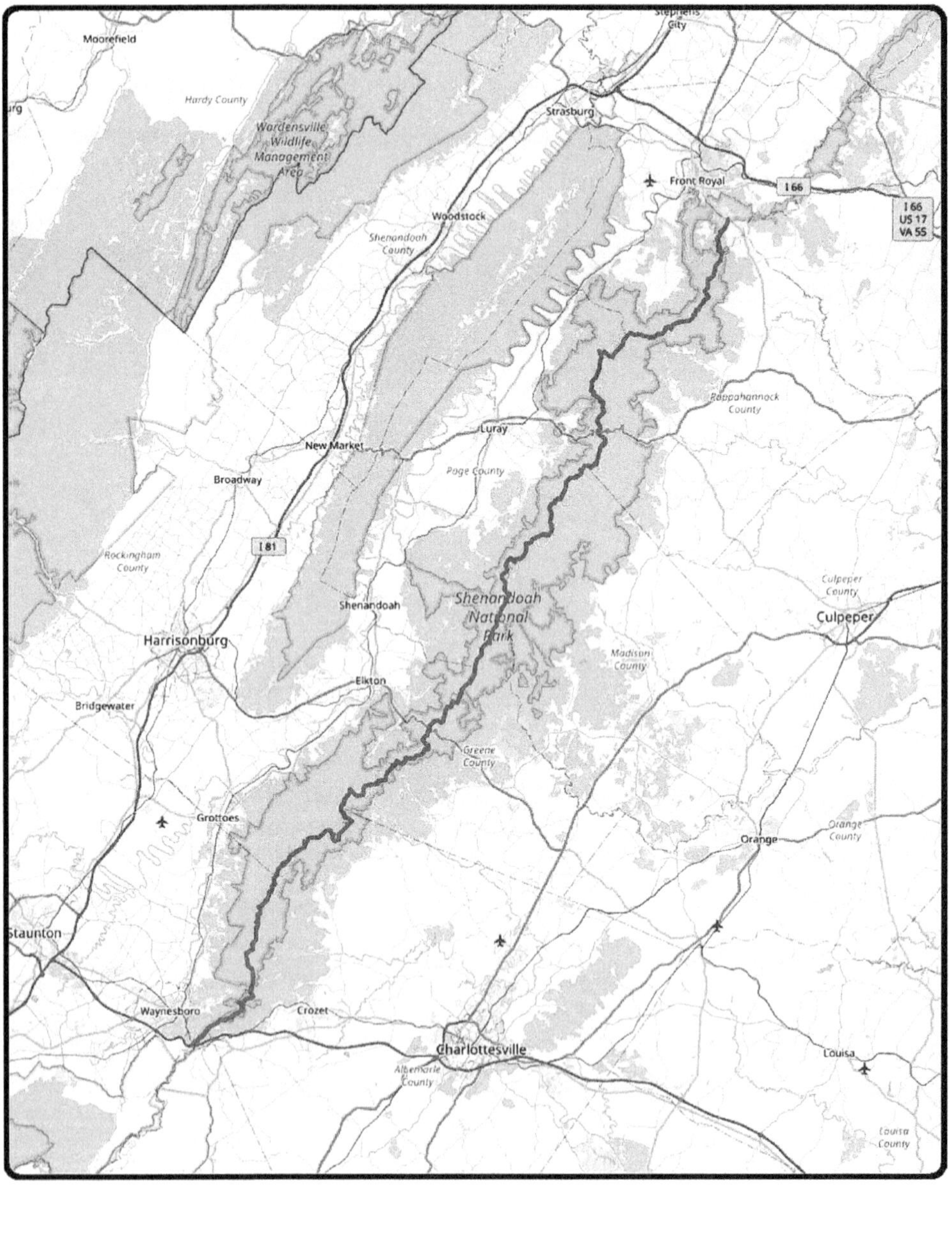
Moorefield
Hardy County
Wardensville Wildlife Management Area
Strasburg
Front Royal
I 66
I 66
US 17
VA 55
Woodstock
Shenandoah County
Rappahannock County
Luray
New Market
Page County
Broadway
I 81
Rockingham County
Culpeper County
Culpeper
Shenandoah
Shenandoah National Park
Harrisonburg
Madison County
Elkton
Bridgewater
Greene County
Grottoes
Orange
Orange County
Staunton
Waynesboro
Crozet
Charlottesville
Albemarle County
Louisa
Louisa County

CHAPTER 17

Rockfish Gap, VA to US 522, Front Royal, VA
September 30 - October 14; 107.1 trail miles one way

The Blue Ridge Parkway and Skyline Drive and I have a long history. In July, 1955, on the way home from a vacation in Wisconsin, my dad proposed we drive the entire length of this fancy new road system in our fancy new 1954 Studebaker Champion V-8. Parts of the Parkway weren't even built yet, so there were detours and delays. My mother remembered the drive as a pure nightmare.

The adventure began on Thursday, July 28th after we passed through Great Smoky Mountains National Park and got on the southern end of the Parkway near the Cherokee reservation, heading north. That night we got as far as Asheville, staying at the Ever Green Court Motel, 612 Merrimon Ave., a mile north of downtown. The room, complete with air conditioning and all-tile showers, cost $12.

The next day it took us all day to drive to Roanoke, VA. We had intended to make it to Buena Vista, VA, but the going was just too slow. I remember stopping for a picnic by a stream that day. It was mid-summer but the water was ice cold.

I remember my poor mom enduring the restless antics of my brother and me hour after hour. I was just six, my brother was four. You see, Dad wanted to drive the road because it was a linear motor-park, the wilderness equivalent of a drive-in theater. No need to ever get out of the car. We didn't stop except to look out the windows at overlooks. We certainly never just got out and walked, except to go to the bathroom; even though the AT was right there. For gosh sakes, the legendary AT hiker Emma Gatewood, had just walked through there three weeks earlier.

Yes, as a six-year-old, I came very, very close to meeting Emma Gatewood during her epic thru-hike. But the closest encounter wasn't here on the Blue Ridge Parkway. We had left our home in Wilmington, DE at the start of this vacation on the afternoon of Friday, July 15th, 1955. We were headed for Niagara Falls first, but our motel for this night was in Duncannon, PA. As far as I can reconstruct it, Emma Gatewood walked into Duncannon at 11:00 am on July 14th, walked up High Street, crossed the Susquehanna River on the same bridge we would cross the next day, had lunch at a restaurant within sight of our motel, and then hiked up Peters Mountain. If only I knew then what I know now. If only …

But back to the Blue Ridge Parkway. From Roanoke, we completed the Parkway and drove Skyline Drive through Shenandoah National Park on Saturday, July 30th, arriving back in Wilmington, DE in the late afternoon, road weary and exhausted. For the next couple years, our vacations to Wisconsin involved no such meandering. It was straight through on the PA and Ohio turnpikes.

F.I.T. Wilderness

Back on the AT, the fall season was upon me. It was the last day of September, and it was a Sunday. I was completing nine months on the trail. Yes, babies were being born that had not yet been conceived when I started my hike.

Every fall, especially on weekends, Skyline Drive becomes a mecca for 'leaf-peepers.' Motorists, most of them from the Washington DC and Richmond VA metropolitan areas, travel there seeking this once-a-year natural spectacle of the hardwood forest. The woodland's green tunnel suddenly transforms into a kaleidoscope of yellow, orange, red, purple, and even pink. In recent years, the result has been hopeless congestion—a bumper-to-bumper traffic jam that rivals the worst of DC's beltway at rush hour. What the harried urban working masses have come to escape, they brought with them. It's a blight.

Although the AT pretty closely parallels the highway through Shenandoah National Park, it still provides some respite. Most of these motorists aren't interested in, or aren't even capable of, walking more than fifty feet from their cars, and such epic treks are usually undertaken at the overlook parking areas, or the developed waysides, snack bars, restaurants, and visitor centers.

But there were some real trail folk out too. As I hiked north into the park from Rockfish Gap, I passed two women headed south. They said they'd seen me starting out that morning walking the short road walk on the bridge over I-64 and US 250. They had driven into McCormick Gap, the first place the northbound AT crosses Skyline Drive, and were doing the 3.7 miles in the downhill direction.

For this first leg of the bright morning, I turned around at McCormick Gap. On my way back, I found a dropped pair of sunglasses. Later I came upon the two women resting on some rocks. Yes, the glasses belonged to one of them, and she was most grateful to have them back. She hadn't yet even realized she had dropped them. The other hiker was 'Three Day', who had been hiking the AT via long weekend day hikes (i.e., three-day chunks) for 7 years, since she turned 50. Her friend was a relative who lived locally. 'Three Day' tries to recruit someone she knows as support, and in this case, to hike with. She had done about 1,000 miles of trail from 20 miles into NH down to this area.

My next base of operation was the wide-open grassy meadows of Beagle Gap, one of my favorite spots. I hiked south over the long summit of Bear Den Mountain. The meadow walking is what appeals to me here. On the ridge, beside a cluster of communication towers, there is a semi-circle of old metal tractor seats planted in the ground beside the trail, where hikers can have a convocation.

On the leg north from Beagle Gap, the meadow features a bunch of old apple trees near the edge of the forest, and they were full of red ripe apples. I had last hiked here almost exactly two years earlier (Sept. 17, 2010), and had sampled the apples then. Near these trees, at the upper end of the field, I found that the AT had been rerouted since my last hike. In fact, the reroute looked to have just been opened sometime that summer. It curves around to the NW side of Little Calf Mountain and climbs gradually up to that summit, which is a very scenic open meadow that was only formerly reached by an unmarked side trail.

I turned around at Calf Mountain Shelter, and on the way back, the tide of weekenders was swelling. I passed many families with young kids and slow-moving folk considerably older than me. It's clearly a well-known area for short easy hikes.

Jarman Gap is where Shenandoah Park really begins. South of there, Skyline Drive runs through a very narrow corridor of park-owned land (and the AT is often outside of that corridor). North of there—actually north of the power line that crosses the ridge a quarter mile south of Jarman Gap—the park-owned land becomes very wide and extensive and continues in that fashion all the way up to the doorstep of Front Royal.

Jarman Gap is where I began day 245. Here along Skyline Drive, I was taking advantage of the many trail access points and short hiking legs; today six legs in all. Early in the day, I came across two medium-sized black bears in quick succession, possibly juvenile siblings. The first one spotted me before I saw it, so I could take no photo. But, perhaps because that encounter ramped up my alertness, I caught sight of the second fellow before he saw or heard me and got a half-decent shot.

It was Monday, and the thru-hikers had re-established dominance. I counted seven Southbounders over the seven miles of trail I covered going northbound, and one befuddled northbound section hiker who I passed three times. At the last of these encounters, I finally explained my 'leap frog' hiking strategy to 'Mailman.' It turned into a long visit and as we talked, a SoBo thru-hiker named 'Chuck-e-Fish' arrived and stopped to join the conversation. He said he was doing a flip-flop from Harper's Ferry and had summited Katahdin on September 12th. When I told him he just missed me by two days, he asked if I was 'Seeks It'. He had been reading my entries in the shelter log books and was hoping to catch me before the end. He got his wish.

Rain was beginning to fall, so we cut our chat short and headed on our respective ways.

Rain. The next day my good friend rain took another step toward changing my hiking habits. It was the day I wore my Crocs all day. They were meant to just get me through some wet trail at the beginning of the day, but I kept them on for the duration.

I got a late start, parked at the Riprap trailhead, packed my poncho in my belt pack, put Crocs on over two pairs of socks, plus nylon liner socks, left my day pack and trekking pole and cell phone in the van, and headed out into the foggy tropical mist.

At first there was only a little drizzle as I began the hike south to my turn-around point—halfway to the Wildcat Ridge Trail junction but it soon got heavier, so I put on my poncho and hiked with it on the rest of the way. I varied how I wore it, either fully draped over me, or tied up in a bunch and dangling behind my head like a huge ponytail when I was too hot and it wasn't precipitating. The latter mode turned out to be the case the majority of the day. The trail was easy with gentle grades, and few enough rocks that they weren't a problem. I noted how comfortable my feet felt.

F.I.T. Wilderness

Late in the day as the weather was clearing but while everything was still lusciously damp, I revisited a quarter mile of trail with my good camera to photograph the lichen colonies on a particularly fascinating flat boulder. I took some 'macro' close-ups of the amazing 'drama' of competition for surface space between closely related clones of the same variety and between several different types of lichen. The all-out war that is depicted there, hundreds of millions of years in the evolutionary stew-pot, could fill volumes. At the same moment, this exact sort of life-and-death battle was taking place over my head in the forest canopy, with each tree battling with its neighbors for the sunlight. We humans live our self-involved lives so hopelessly unaware of what's going on around us in the natural world. Life, the profoundly interconnected web of it, is the cradle that sustains us. Yet most of the time our response is to ram through, bulldoze it down, and call it progress.

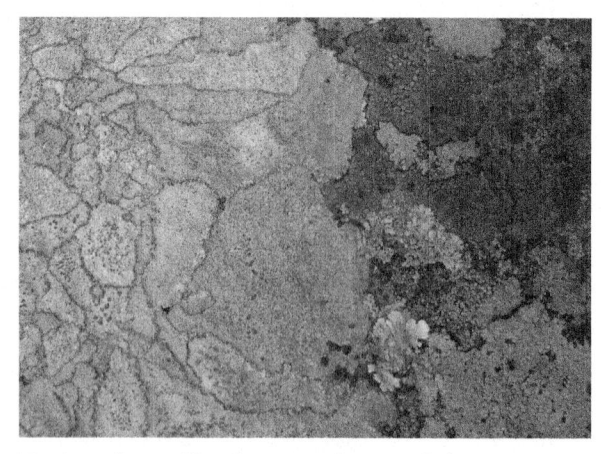

The front lines of battle on a rock, near Skyline Drive

The next day I did half a dozen more individual out-and-back legs. It was pretty walking, with cool morning weather followed by a mild humid afternoon with a slight east wind pushing fog against the east slopes of the highest ridges. The views to the west were open. Fall color was sweeping the forest now, and a lot of the birches and white ash trees—both of which produce a scattering of yellow amid green and brown—were already dropping leaves. Around the Loft Mountain campground, I confronted half a dozen or more deer. Deer in Shenandoah National Park have lost all fear of humans. I got within ten feet of a four-point buck and got a good photo of it. Near the junction with Frazier Discovery Trail, which makes a quarter-mile bee-line to the comforts of Loft Mountain Wayside and not much of anywhere else, I passed two day hikers without packs. Otherwise I didn't see many people today; just two or three who could have been southbound thru-hikers.

Late the next day I passed the invisible but majestic 4,000-mile marker. That left only 368.4 miles to go. The weather and trail were bland. There was no sunshine, no fog, no heat, no chill in the air. The scenery was more of the same: some views, lots of trees, hardly any fall color. Where I hiked on high dry ridges, the oaks mostly just turn brown. For some reason, I found my mind starting to drift, thinking about being somewhere else. I turned around for the day at an apple-less apple tree on top of a summit with no name.

The most notable thing that happened today happened near Simmons Gap when I went well off the trail to answer nature's call. I came around a tree and there was a bear skull, neat as you please, sitting on the moss. I saw no other bones around, just the skull. There were gnaw marks on it. Squirrels and other rodents use bones like this to sharpen their teeth. No way a squirrel could drag something as big as that around, but it seemed recently moved. Maybe a mountain lion? Or maybe just a bobcat. I'd caught a glimpse of the backside of a mountain lion up in Baxter State Park a few weeks ago. There are unsubstantiated rumors that they live here in Shenandoah too. At least the idea gave me something to think about on the way back down the trail.

On Day 249, the weather doldrums were over. The sun rose clear and bright. I climbed Hightop Mountain twice on two separate legs, turning around at the summit with an excellent vista to the southwest across the Shenandoah Valley and Massanutten Mountain. Hightop was later to become a point of significance for my family. It is where my daughter Ellen's boyfriend got down on one knee, pulled out a ring, and proposed marriage.

Another summit of significance came the next day. Hazeltop has the distinction of being the only place on the AT that I have camped. It was June 2009 and I was on one of my first AT excursions with my brother and his son. We spent an idyllic night at the overlook, a few yards off the AT, watching the sunset and then sleeping under the stars.

This was a Saturday, and the popular spots along the trail were packed, especially Bearfence Mountain, which is full of great rock scrambles for kids and is barely a quarter mile from a parking area. The AT wisely avoids all the heavy traffic spots there—the viewpoint, the rock scrambles, and the various rock spires along the 'Fence'. It passes beside the base of the ridge and bypasses the summit altogether, letting a loop trail and a direct trail up from the parking area take most of the traffic.

The season changed in a hurry. After a day off for a family party, my hike into Big Meadows featured snow grains and sleet. It was 35 degrees but I still hiked in shorts. The well-worn Columbia polyester tan-khaki cargo shorts were the one piece of equipment I carried every single mile of this adventure. They had developed a tear where my GPS unit rubbed them, so I had repaired them with a gaudy strip of blaze-orange polyester fabric. It was my fashion statement.

People carry funny stuff with them on their thru-hikes. 'Bomber' carried a rubber chicken the whole way from Springer to Katahdin. 'Terranauta' carried a mandolin. I had originally intended to use my 1971 REI day-pack the entire way, but had set it aside in favor of the much more convenient belt-pack bought at Eastern Mountain Sports in Manchester Center, VT. On these short yo-yo legs, I was doing through Shenandoah Park, I barely even needed that. Some days I did as many as seven separate little hikes.

Big Meadows Wayside is indeed located at the edge of a very big meadow—several hundred acres of high rolling grassland. The name seems both obvious and appropriate. So, it was a shock to learn that the place is actually named after the family who once owned this land, surnamed Meadows. To prove this point, the AT plunges the hiker through the Meadows family cemetery not far from the

Fog near Franklin Cliffs, Shenandoah National Park

lodge and visitor buildings. I spotted at least half a dozen headstones with the name Meadows. The family retains the right to bury relatives there, so Big Meadows continues to acquire more and more Meadows all the time.

Franklin Cliffs, just north of Big Meadows Campground, is a steep rock escarpment facing west with a panoramic view of the Great Valley and the Allegheny Front. Skyline Drive hogs all the vistas from the top of the cliffs. The Appalachian Trail meanders through the woods along the ragged base of the rampart, and that's where all the fun was. The next day the morning fog had transformed the place as I hiked through. There was magic there. A spell had been cast. A bank of fog, pushed by a persistent gentle east wind, spilled over the ridge and down the cliffs like a slow-motion waterfall. As the morning sun climbed through the crystal blue sky above, its ever-changing shafts and rays streamed down into the mist and brought it to life. The shafts of silver light radiated through dew-drenched, mossy, fern-draped undergrowth and mingled with the thousand-colored leaves of the autumn forest. Maples in red, orange, yellow and regal pink. There were drifts of hickory leaves of such pure yellow that they seemed to outshine the sun. The setting so enchanted me that I forgot all about hiking. I lingered, meandered, took dozens of photos. Here was the realm of angels and fairies and creatures of renown from myth and legend. Here I was granted an audience with the gods.

As the sun rose ever higher, the fog finally yielded and I moved on. I made it to Little Stony Man that day, an ultra-popular hike from the nearby Skyland parking lot. There's no doubt that the concentration of high peaks here in the heart of Shenandoah National Park is the main reason for the park, yet the AT doesn't go over any of the 'Big Three.' Hawksbill and Stony Man proper, which, respectively, are the highest point in the park and the northernmost 4,000-foot summit in the Blue Ridge, are short blue-blazed side trail walks, heavily trampled. Old Rag, at only 3,284 feet, is popular for its rocky prominence and its 360-degree panoramic views. It may be the single most often-climbed mountain in the mid-Atlantic. Thru-hikers can make the side trips if they want to bag these peaks. The last time I came through, I fought the crowds for a look at Stony Man. I've never made it to Hawksbill or Old Rag.

At Pinnacles Picnic Area between Little Stony Man and Mary's Rock, the AT passes a water fountain and a rest room, both literally right on the trail. There's a sign there that's always been my favorite, gently promoting the AT. It says:

> *Appalachian Trail. Elevation here 3400'*
> *Enjoy a short hike along this famous trail,*
> *a 2,000 mile footpath from Maine to Georgia.*

The morning started out cool and crisp and calm, with a spidery cloak of fog nestled deep in the hollows of the Shenandoah Valley and a single lonely cap of cloud covering Stony Man. Mary's Rock is a wonderful rock outcrop with unobstructed views to the east and to the west and down onto Thornton Gap just to its north. It's one of a handful of places that I've visited on three separate hikes. When I came through that afternoon, the fog had lifted and the only clouds were the puffy white kind. Drifting steadily west to east, they painted random moving patches of shadow across the land, giving an extra dimension to the riot of fall color.

Late in the day, I had time to do a short leg north of Thornton Gap to Pass Mountain Hut, where I found five guys setting up to spend the night. Four of them were people I had passed multiple times throughout the day and even the day before. So we had some nice conversation, though quick, as I signed the register and needed to head back before dark.

The next day I parked at Beahm's Gap, the next trail crossing north of Pass Mountain Hut, and was on the trail at first light. It was a frosty morning, clear, calm, and nippy. When I got to the side trail to Pass Mountain Hut, no one had yet emerged onto the AT. I had no reason to visit the hut a second time, so I turned around. Soon the fastest of the bunch passed me.

Besides meeting this particular hiker at the hut yesterday evening, I had passed him twice earlier in the day. Our conversations each time were friendly but superficial. I didn't learn his trail name. He was a fit man, 40-ish, a fast hiker, and he said he had a deadline to meet. His section hike would end at Front Royal where he was to meet his pick-up by 1:00 pm tomorrow. Still, we had a conversation before he pushed ahead, though I still didn't ask his trail name.

Somehow the conversation picked up again before he was out of ear-shot, and he slowed down again. I learned that he had started at Montebello last Wednesday, just out hiking for a week and a half. On that rainy frigid day when sleet and snow fell, he had the unexpected luxury of staying at the hiker cabin at Loft Mountain Campground, something neither he nor I knew existed. And when he asked, I told him the basics of my adventure, explaining that I had just a bit over 250 miles left to hike. Then I apologized for slowing him down and bid him good luck getting to US 522 by 1:00 pm tomorrow. He wished me well on my final 250 miles.

Nice guy, really glad to have met him. I still hadn't learned his trail name.

Well, the guy was still in sight when he got to the crossing of Skyline Drive at

Beahms Gap where I had parked. He started to turn right to follow the road toward the overlook, not seeing that the trail went into the woods a bit to the left. I called out to him to correct him, and pointed out my vehicle, which was parked as close to the AT crossing as I could park in the south end of the overlook. I asked if he needed anything—snacks, water, etc.

"Thanks, I'm fine," he said, "Where are you from?"

I answered that I had just moved to NC, to a condo at the beach.

"I live in North Carolina too, at the other end of the state, in Boone."

"Oh?" I said. "You know, I've met a few hikers from Boone during this adventure. One who stands out in particular is 'Huckleberry.' Met him way down south in Smoky Mountain ..."

"That's my son!"

Whoa. Talk about a small world. After a bit more discussion, the amazing connection was confirmed. 'Huckleberry' was one of the special foursome who I took the time to talk with at Tricorner Knob Shelter on a day when I had no time to talk, a day I needed to cover 30 miles before midnight. But this bunch impressed me with their chemistry and friendliness, so I just had to take the time to get to know them better.

The father's trail name was 'Mag-Lev,' as in 'magnetic levitation'. 'Mag-Lev' had met the other three in that group as well—'Green Bean', 'Moses', and 'Spoon.' They had spent a night at his home as 'Huckleberry' was getting off the trail. He was as impressed as I was with that gang of kids.

I snapped his photo by the road and off he went. As we parted ways, the other three guys from the shelter came by. I asked them if they needed anything from my van. They were low on water, they said, but expected to get some at a spring less than half a mile ahead, so they turned down my offer. We passed again at the spring and again later after I turned around at the Neighbor Mountain side trail. One of the three had decided not to take water from the sketchy-looking spring, so he was now pretty thirsty and accepted an unopened water bottle that I was carrying, but insisted on paying me a buck for it. It only cost me ten cents. I tried to explain about Trail Magic, he just felt better paying for it. He guzzled the bottle in two seconds and I took the empty back to return for recycling. I expected to meet these guys again later in the day, but never did.

My final turn-around for the day was at the seventh meeting of the AT and Skyline Drive at Milepost 20.8, just north of Hogback overlook. The AT has a unique 'overlook over the overlook' there. The trail is perched on a rock outcrop well above the vehicle overlook, with a grand view of the Shenandoah Valley. It was a chilly day with very low humidity, so the view was great—almost no haze to obscure it—and I would get to visit it again the following day.

It was a nippy windy day when I returned, and too early for good photography. The best views of the day were farther north, from the twin peaks of North Marshall and South Marshall and from a hang-glider launch on Hogback. I had the photographic option of pairing the hundred-mile views with deep red sumac berries or with yellow twisting witch-hazel blooms.

My final day in Shenandoah National Park came on a warm sunny Sunday with the leaf color at its peak. The place was a certifiable madhouse. A circus. A zoo. Every overlook and every trailhead parking area was packed to overflowing. As I drove out of the park for the last time in early afternoon to relocate at the US 522 trailhead, the lines waiting to get into the park stretched for two miles. It boggles the mind. Yet once I got more than a mile into the back country on any trail, the sudden silence almost hit me like a bludgeon. The contrast was astounding. Few if any of the 'leaf-peepers' had any designs to explore the forest, although a nasty rumor was circulating that the forest was actually the source of the leaf color.

Sumac berries with view, South Marshall summit

Witch Hazel with view, North Marshall summit

The peaceful walk south from Rt. 522 was also ... a zoo. But I saw no human crowds and no animals either. Huh? It's like this: I was hiking along a fence beside the grounds of a 3,100-acre National Zoo property called the "Smithsonian Conservation Biology Institute." It's not open to the public. This place is all business, and their business is captive breeding of seriously endangered species, such as the scimitar-horned oryx from North Africa, which had gone extinct in the wild by 2000. They breed some of the rarest cats, including cheetahs and clouded leopards, as well as red pandas, nearly extinct birds; I could go on and on. That place is doing some seriously important work.

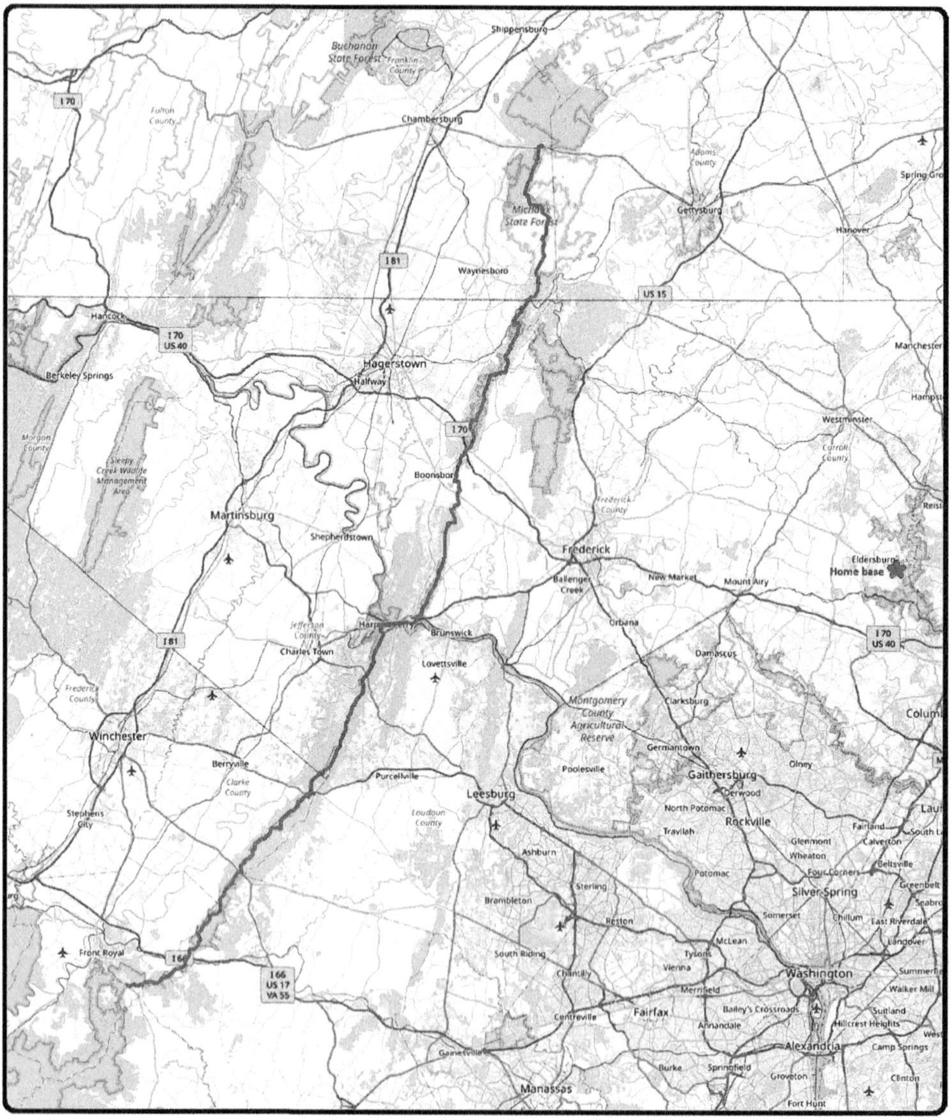
Shippensburg
Buchanan State Forest
Chambersburg
Gettysburg
Hanover
Waynesboro
Hancock
Berkeley Springs
Hagerstown
Halfway
Boonsboro
Martinsburg
Shepherdstown
Frederick
New Market
Mount Airy
Eldersburg
Home base
Westminster
Manchester
Charles Town
Brunswick
Lovettsville
Urbana
Damascus
Clarksburg
Germantown
Gaithersburg
Olney
Winchester
Berryville
Purcellville
Leesburg
Poolesville
North Potomac
Rockville
Ashburn
Sterling
Reston
Silver Spring
Front Royal
Chantilly
Centreville
Fairfax
Washington
Alexandria
Manassas
Gainesville
Springfield
Burke

CHAPTER 18

US 522, Front Royal, VA to Caledonia State Park, PA
October 15 - November 3; 112.7 trail miles one way

This was home ground. When I finished my day's hiking at US 522 on the evening of October 14th, I got in my van and drove home, two hours and twenty minutes, to a condo on Liberty Reservoir in the bedroom community of Eldersburg, west of Baltimore, Maryland. It was a place I was getting ready to sell. I had moved to the beach but had held onto the old place to ease the transition. For the last two weeks of hiking, I would commute to the trail from there.

The drive back the next morning took just two hours. I parked closer to home, at the VA 638 trailhead and hiked a long leg south to 522. The sky opened up just as I got to US 522, so it was a soggy hike back. While drying stuff and changing into other dry stuff, I moved the van to the trailhead near the I-66 overpass and did the rest of the day's hiking from there. The rain had stopped. I hiked the short leg south past one of my favorite spots on the trail. It's on top of an open grassy hill with no name that I've heard. There at the top of the hill stands a lonely old heirloom apple tree with a bench under it, with seating for two, facing the pastoral view to the west. It was past apple season, and most of the leaves had already fallen off the tree, but I took time to sit for a bit and just soak in the input from all my senses. The feel of the damp bench, the distant hum of traffic on I-66, the smell of raindrops on autumn grass, the taste of Goldfish crackers, and the view of the rural farms and homes around the little hamlet of Linden, VA.

The most memorable moments the next day didn't quite happen on the trail, but at Manassas Gap Shelter nearby. Two years earlier, on Sept. 7, 2010, I had first visited that shelter and found no log book there, just a single sheet of paper from the art pad left by photographer-artist 'Mark', who was hiking with Joanna 'Someday' Swanson, both headed south just a day ahead of me. I had been crossing paths with them for a number of days back then. I signed Mark's sheet of paper, lamenting the lack of a register book, and had then gone home for the night.

I had dug out a huge old one-inch-thick hard-bound record book, a book I had no particular use for, and brought it with me the next day when I returned to the shelter and left it there to be the new shelter register book. In the months that followed, I had always wanted to visit again to see if the book was still there, but never did. After more than two years, I had no expectation that it would still be there. If I were to put a probability number on it, I would have said about 1%. But yes, lo and behold, the book was still there, all frayed and a bit tattered after two

F.I.T. Wilderness

years of wear and use. A third of the pages had been torn out in the back, probably used for personal notes and personal hygiene. The entries I had made on the first two pages were missing, and the binding was disconnected from the cover, but otherwise the old book was in good shape and had been signed by many of this year's hikers that I knew, including Paul/'Parkside'. As I paged through and saw familiar names, I just kept saying 'Oh My God' over and over. I ended up staying there for half an hour looking through the book and writing an entry.

What happens to old trail registers when they're filled up? As far as I can tell, there is no formal archive. I know the huts in the White Mountains keep all their old registers in their library right there in the hut, and I suspect some maintainers and some local clubs might have informally saved register books. But most clubs don't really have formal office space. The Appalachian Trail Museum in Pine Grove Furnace has digitized a handful. There's so much history in those books, it is a shame to see them just disappear.

The next day I started my ride through 'The Roller Coaster,' an infamous stretch of trail with about seven short but steep hill climbs and descents in quick succession on sometimes rocky trail, taking you near the West Virginia border. Of course, the way I do my daily hikes, I got to stop the ride in the middle this day, put the roller coaster in reverse, and ride back to the beginning.

The Roller Coaster is necessitated by the fact that the main ridge, where the all the deep little ravines smooth out, is occupied by Blue Ridge Mountain Road, VA 601, and by the Mt. Weather Emergency Operations Center. At this center, there's a super-secure government base with an underground bomb shelter where the president and congress would be based in time of a nuclear war.

At Ashby Gap the next morning, before I even hit the trail, two hikers came by going northbound, both of whom I'd met separately on previous days. We struck up a conversation that ended up lasting at least 15 minutes. 'Shaky' was 55 and hiking a section to Harpers Ferry, and 'L.A.', was hiking to New York City. Where else would 'L.A.' go? Actually, he was doing a section from Rockfish Gap to Bear Mountain Park. They both stayed at Bears Den Hostel last night.

We headed our separate ways around 8:30. I climbed up to Bears Den rocks and absorbed the only view of the day, with some intense fall color under the bright sunlight. I visited Bears Den Hostel, but it seemed all dark, and, as usual, the backpacker hostel was locked up; day hikers not welcome. This place gave me the impression of an unfriendly fortress both two years ago when I visited in the middle of the day, and again this morning.

After the hike was over, I visited Blackburn Trail Center, an official trail shelter that was much easier for me to visit by car than by trail. Two years ago, I had hiked the steep trail to it down from the ridge and back up, and saw no reason to repeat that this time. I talked to the caretaker for a few minutes about the terrible condition of the road. He said the guy who volunteered to grade it had quit and they couldn't afford to pay somebody. I suggested they look into a cheap road grading implement, much like a heavy rake, towed behind an ordinary pickup truck. I had seen this used very successfully on those KI Jo Mary private roads up in Maine.

Then I bumped and rattled my way back down and headed home as it got dark.

Day 261 was foggy; a very dense, calm, mild fog that was soothing and magical. As I've mentioned, fall color in the fog is a special sight. I crossed the state line into West Virginia and turned around at the side trail to Buzzard Rocks, passing a bunch of good viewpoints with no views. But on the way back it cleared up, and got bright and sunny. I saw everything I missed, and the trail seemed a new and different place.

On Saturday, October 20th, I hiked the 'technicolor tunnel' into Harper's Ferry and made my official turn-around point at the ATC headquarters office. Peak of fall color lasts only about a week, and it was here, or

The technicolor tunnel near Bears Den

maybe even a day or two past prime. It was still spectacular, still one very special woods-walking experience. It wasn't until Sunday, on my return from the north, that I finally 'officially' hiked through and got my mug shot taken by the ATC staff in front of the Headquarters building. Both days I had extended chats with trail information guru Laurie Potteiger (who just retired in 2021), along with other staff. Laurie confirmed that they would take two separate mug shots of me, since I was doing a double. They took the photo of me going southbound as I arrived.

I chose a full body shot, head to toe. Just before I left to head back northbound, they took the second one, a head and torso close-up. Flip-Flop hikers number 89 and 90, sitting side by side in their log book. *Same guy twice? 'Splain that'n to me, guv'nuh.* It's going to perplex AT researchers for the rest of time.

On the way back out of town, I again crossed

Crossing into West Virginia on a foggy day

F.I.T. Wilderness

the Potomac River and was officially in Maryland. I climbed up to Weverton Cliffs and got the benefit of the spectacular view back down over the hillsides dabbed with multicolored trees and the glistening waters of the Potomac.

A cool morning gave way to a mild afternoon the next day. My two end points were shelters and there was one in the middle too. Maryland is good to its hikers. The Ed Garvey Shelter is named after an icon of the trail. Ed thru-hiked in 1970 at the age of 55, one of just ten people to complete the trail that year. His hike memoir, *Appalachian Hiker: Adventure of a Lifetime,* helped to popularize the trail, even just with its title. He was a president of the Potomac Appalachian Trail Club and served on the Appalachian Trail Conservancy board. I love 'his' shelter because it has a big 'AT' logo built into the railing of the loft.

But the big news that day was the footwear. It was the dawn of a new era. I felt like keeping my feet aired out, so I wore the Crocs for the whole day. I had done all-day hikes in them twice before during this adventure, but today I liked how they felt so much that I decided to wear them the rest of the way. I've never gone back to 'foot packers.' I wear Crocs exclusively, at home and away, and for all my hiking. Since that day, as of this writing, I have logged more than 12,500 trail miles, all but a few of them in Crocs.

The original Washington Monument, built in 1827 on top of South Mountain overlooking Boonsboro, MD, has a much better view than the more famous one in downtown DC. The obelisk on the mall is just 555 feet 5 inches high and stands in a former swamp. The original one is shaped like one of the old iron works furnaces, and towers 900 feet above the Great Valley to the west. It's not precisely on the AT, but a hundred-yard side trip up the road gets you there. Best of all, you don't need a ticket and there are no lines.

It was Day 265. I tromped up the spiral stairs to the observation perch of the monument and back down to the trail, and on north to Black Rock. Included on today's route was another place where Maryland pampers its hikers. It is the Dahlgren backpacker's campground, just minutes walking time from the Old South Mountain Inn restaurant on Old National Pike at Turner's Gap. The hike-in facility includes picnic tables and grounds for a dozen or so tents, and a heated washroom with hot showers and flush toilets.

Black Rock Cliffs had several great viewpoints. It's sort of the McAfee Knob of Maryland. So I was glad to come back the next day and spend more time there. The visibility was great, but the mostly cloudy sky muted the show of fall color. At the nearby site of the old Black Rock Hotel, some industrious folks had spent hours constructing a fire circle with stone lounge chairs—six of them, each with good sturdy backrests. I pushed north all the way to Raven Rock Hollow. There was a pretty but tense meadow walk among some seriously nasty looking longhorn cattle, with horns spanning four or five feet between their spear-sharp tips. Fortunately, they didn't seem particularly interesting in impaling hikers that day.

Trees on the adjacent hills were mostly brown and bare already. Fall's brief extravaganza was winding down, and the leaves were adopting their new role as pleasant crunchy padding under foot. They can, in this season, make navigating a poorly marked trail difficult. But here the white blazes were doing their job where needed, and elsewhere, the narrow rocky ridge of South Mountain, with its sides dropping steeply off in both directions, kept the hiker literally on the straight and narrow.

Now I was really on the home stretch. On day 267, I crossed the Mason Dixon Line into Pennsylvania. It was a dreary foggy day with an east wind keeping the fog pushed up against the ridge and causing the trees to drip. I was hiking in Crocs for the third day. At this point, I only had the standard clog style, and the side vent holes let moisture get into my socks, but I was never uncomfortable, and the vents also let the moisture evaporate quickly.

I headed south past the normally great views at High Rock. I was delighted to find that the new shelter that replaced the Devils Racecourse Shelter was not at all in the same location, as I had expected. The last time I came through, the old site was a tough downhill 0.3-mile side trail to a seriously leaning, rotting old shelter with a tarp over one end of the roof. The new Raven Rock Shelter was just a hundred yards west of the trail and at the same elevation. There were a couple of SoBo thru-hikers still at the shelter, getting a late start. One of them wore a bright hunter orange knit cap. This was 'Carry On' whose excellent blog I began to follow. She completed her flip on December 9th. All the talk that day was about Hurricane Sandy. It was drawing a bead on the mid-Atlantic and hikers were being urged to find a safe haven to hunker down. The timing for me was not a problem. I had two more day hikes to do before the ceremonial last mile into Caledonia State Park, which I had scheduled for a week later, after Sandy had passed.

On my leg back north, as I was coming toward Pen-Mar, I began passing some military types who seemed to be racing. There were three middle-aged men at Pen Mar Park standing beside the trail with stop watches and a clipboard. The runners stopped there, seemed to check in, and then wandered up to the parking lot. As I reloaded supplies at my van and headed north into PA, I kept passing more of these people, including women. Then I began to pass slower ones, some of whom didn't look to be in as great physical shape as the military types up front (short cropped hair, greeting me with that formal 'hello, sir').

I got so curious about what was obviously a group event that I talked with one pair, a man and a woman, who were stopped, resting on the steep climb up from Falls Creek. Immediately I got the vibe that they were being evasive, as if they were part of some secret military group. Really? Running some sort of mission on the AT? Come on. All I was asking was where they'd started, but the answer wasn't forthcoming until I rephrased it to ask how far they'd come. The answer was 13 miles today, 15 yesterday; just a two day affair.

As I moved on, I passed two more guys and asked what the group was, and got the totally evasive answer: 'Just a fun club'. Finally, I passed two women hiking with clown-style rainbow-colored tutus around their waists. These were the obvious stragglers, forced to wear the outfits as a badge of faux-shame. They were just as evasive, not admitting the size of the group they were with, and that alone told me that they were with that big group. And they gave the same evasive an-

F.I.T. Wilderness 235

swer about the group: Just a bunch of hikers out having fun. Okay, fine. I wasn't going to get anything more out of them. Clearly it was a fun event rather than some sort of serious military exercise, although the guys with the stop watch and clipboard seemed to indicate that there may have been some serious purpose for the faster ones at least.

The thing is ... Fort Richie is right near there. It's a military base that was supposedly closed in 1998. Was there some sort of ultra-super-secret, completely under-cover military unit still based there? Maybe they were so super-secret, so completely isolated in order to avoid 'compromising' their mission, that nobody could get the news to them that the base had been closed for a quarter century. Something to think about.

But seriously, I do not just let a mystery like this drop; I get obsessed. Back home I dug deeper. I found that there is a big active military complex with the mysterious name 'Site R' that is located just east of the town of Blue Ridge Summit, PA and just five miles east of the AT. Its more approachable name is the Raven Rock Mountain Complex, and it is also known as the "underground Pentagon." Like Mount Weather in Virginia, which houses the civilian government in time of nuclear attack, Site R is where the military brass take cover.

The knee-jerk paranoia of those people drew attention to themselves. Surely that is exactly the opposite of what their superiors would want. It could even be considered a security threat. If they had simply called themselves the 'Raven Rock running club', I would have had zero suspicion, and wouldn't have given them a second thought.

Hurricane Sandy was a growing threat. For my Day 268 hike, there was that looming cloudy stillness in the air—a muggy humid day, as if the world was holding its breath. The calm before the storm. I was out hiking from the Old Forge parking area at first light. Today's hiking included five shelters. The twin Deer Lick shelters were first, then the Antietam Shelter next to the Old Forge Park grounds. There's a water spigot next to the baseball field that the trail goes right past, and then north of the park, I stopped in at the twin Tumbling Run Shelters, home of the "no-snoring" and "snoring" lean-tos with a picnic table under a roof between them. This is the shelter I officially dubbed the place with the best water on the trail. It tumbles out of the deep rock under Briar Mountain. They would probably tell you to treat it or filter it, but it is as pure and cold as any well water—perfect mineral balance, perfect taste.

I turned around at PA 233 near where the AT splits from its pre-1986 route, now called the Raccoon Run Trail, before it reconnects in Caledonia State Park. I had less than five miles of the AT left to do.

I was on the trail the next day at 8:00 am. No rain, no sun, still that deep looming overcast. Somehow it seemed like just another day out on the trail, not the last real hike. Along the ridge of Rocky Mountain, it had its ups and downs (literally), its little annoyances, and its little pleasures. The place is aptly named. The trail bounced you up on the rocky spine of the ridge for a mile and change, 'showing' you some interesting rock formations, the best of which I call 'hole-in-the-rock.' The real reason for the trail to leave rock-free ground to take the hiker into a rock scramble seems to be the corridor of public land that runs through it. The easy route had property markers and painted trees indicating private land.

I visited the very last shelter and was delighted to find entries in the log book from some trail acquaintances among the early NoBo crowd, including 'Parkside'.

Somehow their messages felt personal to me, as if they were offering their congratulations.

As I began to descend toward Caledonia State Park, I was looking for a nice turn-around point for the ceremonial finishing hike that would take place with family in eight days. I settled on a spot at a dead pine tree where I could carve a "4368.4" into the wood. It was in the middle of a lush growth of 3-4-inch-high teaberries (American Wintergreen). It took 20 minutes or so to do that carving, then I rolled back down the hill, finishing at 1:15 pm.

I drove up to Caledonia State Park to scout it out for the family celebration. I had already reserved the Oak Picnic Pavilion, a big roofed space with a dozen or more picnic tables that the AT literally goes right past. There was a guy there blowing leaves out from under the picnic tables, and I approached him to ask a few questions. Lo and behold, it was none other than Jim Stauch, the 'Innkeeper' at the country-cottage-like Quarry Gap Shelter, which I had visited on my first day starting north toward Katahdin, back on Easter Sunday, April 8th.

Jim is one of those people with a big heart—down-to-earth, humble, and truly happy doing what he does. We had a long, wide-ranging conversation. He had been caretaker at Quarry Gap for 35 years, and his work here in Caledonia Park was also freely given volunteer work. What a great guy, and what an honor to meet him.

Well, I would meet him again in eight days. But before that, Hurricane Sandy rolled through, dumping half a foot of rain. It was nowhere near as bad along the AT in southern PA as it was right along the east coast, where some communities felt historic impacts. The storm surge of nearly 14 feet inundated most of Manhattan. At the time, the storm's 65 billion dollar damage toll was the second largest in history, with only Katrina being worse.

At Caledonia State Park, the only impact along the AT was some minor washouts and some puddles. Shortly after noon on November 3rd, my im-

Innkeeper Jim Stauch with his leaf blower, Caledonia State Park

F.I.T. Wilderness

mediate family gathered at the Oak Pavilion for the celebration. It was cloudy and in the mid-40's—not the best day, but what can you expect for early November?

I had prepared a cake with 'AT 4368.4' in red frosting on it. I was wearing an orange t-shirt with '4368.4' in big bold numbers across the chest. I had prepared a casserole of sorts out of trail food—canned spam, boxed mac and cheese, and canned peas and some extra cheese. It had to include Spam, given that the famous meat product was also celebrating its 75th anniversary. It was all a hit. At my daughter Ellen's urging, I had contacted professional photographer Adriane Hornung of Wraven Design to document the day.

Everything was going smoothly. We were getting ready to sit down for a picnic lunch before heading out to hike the ceremonial last mile when a commotion off to the right caught my attention. A SoBo hiker came rushing up and asked for 'Seeks It.'

Of all the astounding coincidences and small-world stories this hike had produced, this had to be the most stunning.

The hiker was none other than 'Sharkey,' the only other hiker who was doing a yo-yo that year. He had met Quarry Gap Shelter 'innkeeper' Jim Stauch up the trail about a mile. Jim knew we were here because he had been working in the park when I arrived at 9:00 am to set up.

Well, as you can imagine, 'Sharkey' and I were both excited by the coincidence. I told him I had heard about his double attempt from 'Bobcat' down near Daleville on Sept. 16th. 'Sharkey' had done a NoBo thru-hike back in '92 and half the trail (GA - PA) in '08. This year he decided to celebrate the 20th anniversary of his thru-hike by doubling it. He planned to reach Springer before Dec. 31st, though it would be a close call.

To have him there helping me celebrate made me feel truly blessed. I recounted to 'Sharkey' all my other chance encounters—things that you couldn't dream up if you tried. Like the day in June when I decided to drop in at Harper's Ferry before returning to the trail in New York, and ran into thru-hiking friends 'X and N Trovert', who just happened to have arrived at the ATC office minutes before I did. Then there were the three times I met fellow day hikers Harry and Leo on the trail, including the evening before they finished their adventure. There was the coincidence that I was able to pass the plaque celebrating the anniversary of the AT's completion on the very day of the 75th anniversary of that completion. And finally, there were all the amazing weather breaks I had along the way—not a trace of snow on Mt. Rogers or Clingman's Dome in March, not a breath of wind on Mt. Washington on the day of my double presidential traverse.

What a ride it had been. And today's gathering was the icing on the cake.

Of course we invited 'Sharkey' to sit down and have lunch with us. My daughter Ellen asked 'Sharkey' a question she had also asked me. "What profound and deep new wisdom has your hike given you?" and 'Sharkey's' answer was one that echoed my own. The hike actually helps you get *away* from profound and deep thinking and lets your mind sync with your body in just accomplishing and appreciating the simple things. Some might go to the woods seeking such profound insights and answers, but what we find is that we have been seeking the wrong thing. What we find is not what we want, but what we need, to paraphrase the famous 1969 Rolling Stones song.

After we ate, we headed out, with photographer Adriane hiking along. She had told me her father had hiked a big chunk of the AT back in 1974. We clowned around as we hiked through the bit of washed-out trail and then over Conococheague Creek, where Ellen risked falling in by trying to cross on a fat mossy fallen log. Fortunately, she has much better balance than me. Before we got out of the park, Jim Stauch came up in a golf cart and we had a nice chat and I introduced my family to him.

We crossed US 30 and headed up into the woods, stopping at the thick growth of wintergreen berries to sample them. Then we turned around when we reached my '4368.4' carved in the dead pine tree.

'Sharkey' took a video with his phone, which he later shared. Adriane was busy covering every angle with her camera and creative eye. When we got to the carving in the tree, I gave 'Sharkey' a big hug and wished him well and off he went.

We returned to the park where we had set up a long paper banner across the trail saying, what else? '4368.4 AT Double 2012' and I did the ceremonial breakthrough, triumphantly bursting through the paper like a finish-line ribbon, with family marching along right behind and cheering. At my two-ton steel tent, I affixed a custom-made white oval sticker that read '4368.4'. In small lettering around the rim, it read 'Appalachian Trail' on top and '2012 Double' on the bottom.

It was a joyful wrap-up to this ten-month adventure. We adjourned as darkness approached, and we headed to the nearby hiker friendly Flamingo Restaurant for dinner.

On the way home, my stomach comfortably stuffed, I could not have felt more contented.

Crossing the ceremonial finish line with family, Caledonia State Park, November 3rd.

F.I.T. Wilderness

Trail scene on Brushy Mountain between Kimberling Creek and Lickskillet Hollow

EPILOGUE

4368.4 Miles in 270 Day Hikes

My chosen trail name was 'Seeks It.' Foremost among those things that I sought during my ten months on the Appalachian Trail was that special sense of joy and awe that comes when everything just feels right—that magical feeling of connectedness and oneness with the universe. Those moments of perfect fulfillment that you can get from things as tiny as a patch of green moss after a cleansing rain, or a spider spinning its web in the morning sun, to gazing at the infinite sky on a clear starry night far from the interference of city lights.

All my life I'd been escaping into the woods whenever possible. But I'd never been able to draw so abundantly from this tap as I did that year.

Was it a sacrifice? Hardly. Any sacrifice I made had been repaid a hundred-fold. No wealth of kings can compare. No words can adequately describe …

The most important physical lesson from this 4,000-mile hiking adventure was that walking provides a *huge* benefit to the human body. Despite the daily little aches and pains, I felt younger and healthier at the end than I had in years. A decade-long battle with chronic back pain, which I had thought was an inevitable result of aging, was entirely gone. Not improved, gone. Cured. Ten years later (with ongoing regular hiking) my back remains entirely free of pain.

Yes, I knew I would not stop walking. I had that greater hiking goal: my 'Personal Continuous Footpath' connecting every place I had ever lived. That gave me the impetus to hike North Carolina's State Trail, the Mountains-to-Sea Trail, in 2013 and 2014, including helping the 'Friends of the MST' scout and establish a new 270-mile reroute called the Coastal Crescent. It sent me back to the southern end of the AT in August 2015 where I headed south via the Benton MacKaye Trail, then end-to-end on the Pinhoti Trail. Late in 2015, I continued south across Alabama and hiked the Florida Trail and the Florida beaches and the Everglades all the way to Key West. Then in Spring 2016, I began a meandering route westward to Penn State, western New York, then via the North Country Trail to northern Wisconsin and on to Fort Collins, Colorado where, in the fall of 2019, I crossed the threshold of the house I built there between 1976 and 1980, the last of the two dozen addresses where I had lived.

And that will not be the end of my hiking. I had imagined a greater goal of connecting my unbroken footsteps to every state (except Hawaii, where I have also done extensive hiking). I designed a continuous footpath that I call the 'Fifty

Trail,' at least 30,000 miles in length, connecting all 49 continental states and the District of Columbia in one continuous walk, starting at a rocky Pacific Ocean beach south of Seward, Alaska called South Beach—the site of a World War II military barracks in Caines Head State Recreation Area—and ending at West Quoddy Head lighthouse on the very easternmost tip of Maine. I'll be scouting and improving that route and possibly extending it to reach the Arctic Ocean in NW Canada, and the coast of Labrador. The dreamer in me wants to walk ever on.

So, what's it take to do what I did? I don't feel extraordinary, yet I had just become only the 6th person in history to report hiking the AT both ways in a single calendar year and the first to provide full documentation—GPS tracks of every step. And I was the oldest to report this accomplishment. According to Laurie Potteiger, previous yo-yo thru-hikers ranged in age from 20 to the mid 50's.

No, I didn't feel extraordinary, and upon completion my overall reaction to my adventure was, and remains, "it wasn't all that hard."

So what gives? What makes it hard is the commitment it requires. Focus, patience, persistence, and perseverance. It was a feat that required a willingness to sacrifice every other aspect of my normal existence for nearly a full year. And a year is no small part of a human life.

And no small part of that sacrifice is the social aspect. Few people maintain the types of social bonds that are flexible enough to be put on hold for a year, to flourish for that long without much 'face time.'

I think it helped that I had a running start. I had hiked 350 miles of the AT the previous two years, had summited three 6,000-meter peaks in South America the previous year, and had done a lot of other hiking as well. I also think that my body structure worked to my advantage. I am long and lean, not too dissimilar from Jennifer Pharr Davis, who held the unofficial AT speed record for both men and women at the time I hiked (she did the entire AT in 46 days). Long legs mean fewer steps. Light weight—I averaged about 150 pounds on my 6'2" frame—meant less wear and tear on feet, joints, muscles, tendons, and ligaments. Maybe there's a genetic predisposition involved—the part of the equation we can do nothing about.

Everyone says an AT thru-hike is more mental than physical. I wholeheartedly agree. First of all, you spend a lot of time alone. It helps immeasurably if you 'like yourself' and know how to entertain yourself 'in a vacuum.' I imagine that a successful thru-hiker would also be a person who would come out of a solitary confinement prison sentence smiling, or at least feeling no worse for the experience. It helps to have a healthy measure of plain old damn stubbornness; that jaw-clenching determination that nothing is going to keep you from achieving your goal. And finally, it helps if you have some sort of over-arching motivation—some reason to see your effort through to the finish even when the going gets tough.

So, let's talk about motivation a bit more. Many successful hikers draw on positive support of family and friends. A steady flow of encouragement is often motivation enough. A good hiking partner is a huge help. Some hikers are hiking for a cause—to raise money or to raise awareness for something close to their heart. These days my cause is to raise awareness for the National Trails System and to advocate for a fully connected Interstate Trail System as robust as the Interstate Highway System. But in 2012, my motivation was a little more internal. I simply wanted to do something hard and see it through from start to finish—something that takes a lot of work, and something that nobody else had done (hike the AT both ways by day hikes in a calendar year), and maybe something that I could call my 'fifteen minutes of fame' accomplishment, the feat that I might be remembered for if I was remembered at all.

My dad always said he didn't believe in 'luck.' I'm tempted to say that, in order to succeed, a thru-hiker has to have some amount of good luck not to trip over a rock and twist an ankle, not to get sick, etc. But in the end, I think my dad was right. You make your own luck. David 'AWOL' Miller seriously sprained his ankle in Maryland, less than halfway through his NoBo hike, and hiked the rest of the way to Katahdin in an air cast. He used the injury to strengthen his motivation rather than as an excuse to fail. This is a key item on the list of essential winning qualities: A successful thru-hiker needs to be willing to take responsibility when something goes wrong, not to look around for someone or something external to blame. Placing blame weakens your character and resolve; taking responsibility builds them.

So when we sum up the list of qualities needed for thru-hiking success, does it describe a person of extraordinary character? I think not. Ordinary people can do extraordinary things. You just have to set your mind to it.

APPENDIX

Listing of day hikes

Each entry includes the Day number followed by the **Searchable Title** on the Heart and Sole blog [pjwetzel.com] and the new Hiking Hermit Blog [hikinghermit.com]; Start point (only given if different from previous day's end point) and end point of the portion of the AT hiked both ways on this day, and total distance hiked, as measured by my GPS (which includes side trails).

1. **Appalachian National Scenic Trail**; Park and Ride, Troutville, VA to Lambert's Meadow Shelter—Today's Miles: 17.46
2. **You just have to keep going**; to Brickey's Gap—Today's Miles: 11.05
3. **On Drugs**; to VA 311 parking area, Catawba VA—Today's Miles: 14.67
4. **Small Pleasures**; to VA 624 Crossing—Today's Miles: 10.96
5. **Bit by the Dragon**; to Trout Creek (VA 620)—Today's Miles: 14.68
6. **Beautiful day in the wilderness**; to Craig Creek Valley (VA 621)—Today's Miles: 14.48
7. **Bringing the Trail to life**; to Sarver Hollow Shelter—Today's Miles: 14.03
8. **The day in pictures**; to Kelly Knob—Today's Miles: 15.10
9. **Baptized**; to Lone Pine Peak—Today's Miles: 13.98
10. **Real Wilderness and faux wilderness**; to VA 734 crossing near Bailey's Gap Shelter—Today's Miles: 12.16
11. **Playing in the rain**; to Pine Swamp Branch Shelter—Today's Miles: 6.32
12. **Big Miles, Lonely Miles**; to Spring, 1.6 miles north of Rice Field Shelter—Today's Miles: 20.03
13. **A walk in the Rice Fields**; to Morris Avenue, Pearisburg—Today's Miles: 16.72
14. **Where Angels Rest**; to Doc's Knob Shelter—Today's Miles: 15.63
15. **You hike eighteen miles and what do you get?**; to Wapiti Shelter—Today's Miles: 17.82
16. **A day in the valley (for a change)**; to Kimberling Creek footbridge—Today's Miles: 14.92
17. **A Tree**; to VA 611—Today's Miles: 17.19
18. **Remarkably Nondescript**; to Helvey's Mill Shelter—Today's Miles: 13.17
19. **Day 19: A Day to Savor**; to VA 612 parking east of I-77 overpass—Today's Miles: 2.96
20. **Day 20: Side-hill walking**; to Primitive campsite off FS 282—Today's Miles: 11.40

21. **Rain Delay**; to Jenkins Shelter—Today's Miles: 11.02
22. **With apologies to Carl Sandburg**; to Walker Gap—Today's Miles: 15.99
23. **Beautiful Chestnut Ridge**; to Lick Creek—Today's Miles: 13.50
24. **Just about the perfectest day**; to Tilson Gap, Walker Mountain—Today's Miles: 17.13
25. **Are Trekking Poles just a fad?**; to I-81 Groseclose/Adkins VA—Today's Miles: 16.27
26. **Vaught Branch paradise**; to Locust Mountain—Today's Miles: 14.56
27. **A final brush with Brushy Mountain**; to Teas Road (VA 670)—Today's Miles: 20.80
28. **A full course dinner**; to Power Line clearing north of Hurricane Shelter—Today's Miles: 19.00
29. **The rolling stone gathers abundant moss**; to Pine Mountain Trail junction—Today's Miles: 16.10
30. **Sensory Overload**; to Wilburn Ridge—Today's Miles: 17.20
31. **Farewell to Mount Rogers**; to Saddle between Buzzard Rock and Beech Mtn—Today's Miles: 18.20
32. **Woulda … Coulda … Shoulda? … Naahhh!**; to Summit Cut, US 58—Today's Miles: 7.25
33. **Oh, the Temptation!**, to Rock ledge near Bridge 26 of VA Creeper Trail—Today's Miles: 19.94
34. **Trail Town, USA**; to Water Street, Damascus—Today's Miles: 14.93
35. **The 'Damascus Freeway'**; to Abingdon Gap Shelter—Today's Miles: 21.13
36. **A new touch of winter, but a sure sign of spring**; to spring 0.8 mi S of Double Springs Shelter—Today's Miles: 19.01
37. **What fog hath wrought …**; to spring and camp south of Turkey Pen Gap—Today's Miles: 20.80
38. **Marathon day before the bad weather**; to Fisherman's camp, Watauga Lake nr Griffith Branch—Today's Miles: 23.23
39. **Let's talk gear for a minute**; to Pond Flats—Today's Miles: 8.92
40. **Spotlight on the trail builders**; to Dennis Cove Road—Today's Miles: 12.35
41. **Just sayin' …**; to USFS 293, Bitter End—Today's Miles: 18.90
42. **From Bitter End to sweet beginning**; to Elk River—Today's Miles: 13.69
43. **Vitamin I**; to US 19E, Mountain Harbour Hostel—Today's Miles: 12.91
44. **In and out like a bandit**; to Hump Mountain—Today's Miles: 10.10
45. **The Roan High Balds**; to Carver's Gap—Today's Miles: 20.17
46. **Clinging to winter on Roan High Knob**; to Little Rock Knob—Today's Miles: 14.10
47. **Ridge Ramblin'**; to Iron Mountain Gap—Today's Miles: 14.34
48. **Summer!**; to Indian Grave Gap—Today's Miles: 23.12
49. **Five Bridges and a log**; to Temple Ridge summit—Today's Miles: 19.86
50. **No Business**; to Spivey Gap—Today's Miles: 16.60
51. **Repeal the Earth's Curvature Now!**; to Low Gap—Today's Miles: 19.85
52. **Following the fence**; to Hogback Ridge Shelter—Today's Miles: 12.10
53. **Opposite Day**; to Devil Fork Gap—Today's Miles: 13.20
54. **Big Butt**; to N jct, bad wx trail, Firescald Knob—Today's Miles: 20.35
55. **Trail guide, my version**; to Allen Gap—Today's Miles: 19.17
56. **The Magic begins**; to USFS 113, Mill Ridge—Today's Miles: 20.95

57. **Hot Springs, NC**; to Deer Park Shelter—Today's Miles: 16.64
58. **Gettin' up**; to Bluff Mountain—Today's Miles: 15.00
59. **Max Patch, Mini Patch**; to Max Patch Rd, SR 1182—Today's Miles: 19.61
60. **A neatly wrapped package**; to Snowbird Mountain—Today's Miles: 18.04
61. **On the brink of the deep Smokies**; to Davenport Gap—Today's Miles: 14.03
62. **Thumbs up**; to Tricorner Knob Shelter—Today's Miles: 31.42
63. **Hike *this***; to Newfound Gap—Today's Miles: 32.83
64. **... and to top it all off**; to Clingmans Dome—Today's Miles: 15.93
65. **Gardens and grass**; to Spence Field Shelter—Today's Miles: 34.34
66. **Smoky Mtn Park - the easy end**; to Fontana Dam Trailhead—Today's Miles: 32.49
67. **Fontana, end to end**; to Fontana Marina, NC 28—Today's Miles: 6.12
68. **Familiar surroundings**; to 0.5 mi S of Yellow Creek Gap—Today's Miles: 13.37
69. **A spot of magic**; to Stecoah Gap—Today's Miles: 13.84
70. **Quick summary of a short hike**; to Sassafras Gap Shelter—Today's Miles: 13.21
71. **Swim Bald ...**; to NOC, Wesser, NC—Today's Miles: 13.55
72. **Another 'hairy' bald**; to Tellico Gap—Today's Miles: 15.64
73. **600 miles**; to Wayah Bald—Today's Miles: 19.15
74. **Toes in the grass**; to Rocky Cove Knob—Today's Miles: 25.24
75. **Many miles**; to Little Ridgepole Mountain vista—Today's Miles: 25.34
76. **Friends and connections**; to Deep Gap—Today's Miles: 20.17
77. **From Standing Indian to Seated Squaw**; to Bly Gap—Today's Miles: 13.06
78. **Bunny Trail**; to Dicks Creek Gap, US 76—Today's Miles: 17.73
79. **In too Deep**; to Deep Gap Shelter—Today's Miles: 7.90
80. **Three Mountains**; to Unicoi Gap—Today's Miles: 26.19
81. **A Jekyll and Hyde kinda hike**; to Low Gap Shelter—Today's Miles: 19.32
82. **Amazing news**; to Cowrock Mountain—Today's Miles: 14.71
83. **Walasi-Yi**; to Jarrard Gap—Today's Miles: 21.65
84. **Short hike, long drive**; to Woody Gap—Today's Miles: 10.92
85. **The Home Stretch**; to Summit 0.8 mi N Hightower Gap—Today's Miles: 22.78
86. **Springer!**; to Springer Mountain—Today's Miles: 19.53
87. **The Approach Trail**; to Amicalola Falls SP Visitor Center—Today's Miles: 16.50
88. **North to Katahdin**; from Caledonia State Park, PA to Birch Run Shelter—Today's Miles: 18.89
89. **hiked ...**; to Toms Run Shelters—Today's Miles: 12.74
90. **Half way**; to Mtn Creek Campgd side trail—Today's Miles: 20.59
91. **Rocky Ridge**; to Whiskey Spring Road—Today's Miles: 15.73
92. **Boiling Springs**; to Old Stonehouse Road—Today's Miles: 26.08
93. **Friday the Thirteenth**; to PA 850—Today's Miles: 23.35
94. **Duncannon, town of contrasts**; to W end Clarks Ferry Br, Duncannon PA—Today's Miles: 21.56
95. **No Theme**; to Table Rock—Today's Miles: 18.67
96. **The Dragon of Shikellimy Rocks**; to PA 325—Today's Miles: 16.12
97. **Fast lane**; to Sand Spring Trail junction—Today's Miles: 17.13
98. **What I like**; to vista N of I-81, Swatara Gap—Today's Miles: 22.00

99. **Bob's story**; to Rt 501 Shelter—Today's Miles: 21.64
100. **100 day hikes**; to Game Comm Svc Rd N of PA 183—Today's Miles: 19.59
101. **Hats off to the maintainers**; to Sand Spring Trail junction—Today's Miles: 9.61
102. **Port Clinton in the rain**; to Port Clinton, PA—Today's Miles: 20.18
103. **Memories of spring**; to Windsor Furnace Shelter—Today's Miles: 11.90
104. **Pinnacle and Pulpit**; to Hawk Mountain Road—Today's Miles: 19.75
105. **Pennsylvania Rocks!**; to Allentown Shelter—Today's Miles: 15.27
106. **On the Knife Edge**; to Bake Oven Knob Road—Today's Miles: 18.69
107. **First thru-hiker sighting**; to Lehigh Gap—Today's Miles: 18.11
108. **Beauty from destruction**; to Little Gap—Today's Miles: 11.46
109. **Flatsylvania**; to 1 mile S of Leroy Smith Shelter—Today's Miles: 19.59
110. **The two faces of Wind Gap**; to campsite 1/2 way between Wind and Fox Gaps—Today's Miles: 4.20
111. **Gettin' better by the minute**; to Mt. Minzi—Today's Miles: 17.88
112. **On reaching New Jersey**; to Turquoise Trail, Sunfish Pond—Today's Miles: 16.84
113. **Found it ... in abundance**; to Millbrook-Blairstown Rd—Today's Miles: 18.31
114. **Friday May 4th**; to 1 mi S Brink Road Shelter—Today's Miles: 20.12
115. **More morning fog**; to Tinsley Trail junction—Today's Miles: 19.15
116. **Connections**; to valley 1 mi N of Rutherford Shelter—Today's Miles: 17.60
117. **High and Low**; to Uniontown Road—Today's Miles: 19.80
118. **The Drowned Lands**; to Lake Wallkill Road—Today's Miles: 12.22
119. **2000 miles**; to small summit 0.3 mi N of Barrett Rd—Today's Miles: 20.85
120. **On leaving New Jersey**; to cairn 1.2 mi S of Village Vista Trail—Today's Miles: 16.54
121. **Creatures of all sorts**; to Mombasha High Point—Today's Miles: 18.68
122. **Agony and Ecstasy**; to Elk Pen, Arden Valley Rd—Today's Miles: 12.15
123. **Lemon Squeezed** (and a second post entitled '**Now here's the rest of the story'**); to William Brien Shelter—Today's Miles: 19.19
124. **Watershed**; to Perkins Drive—Today's Miles: 12.03
125. **How it should always be**; to US 9, NY 403—Today's Miles: 21.19
126. **Crossroads**; to Dennytown Rd—Today's Miles: 18.48
127. **Sunk Mine musings**; to Long Hill Rd—Today's Miles: 16.77
128. **Fishkill Plains**; to I-84 overpass, Stormville Mtn Rd—Today's Miles: 17.88
129. **Three people-stories**; to Nuclear Lake—Today's Miles: 16.53
130. **Man-made trail sights**; to NY 22—Today's Miles: 11.77
131. **Half Way** (with a capital 'W' – [see day 90]); to Ten Mile Hill—Today's Miles: 17.84
132. **Connecticut**; to NY-CT State Line—Today's Miles: 11.51
133. **CLOBBERED by summer**; to Skiff Mtn Road—Today's Miles: 13.71
134. **A stroll along the Housatonic**; to Old Sharon Road—Today's Miles: 17.78
135. **What was cool today**; to Sharon Mountain Campsite—Today's Miles: 16.16
136. **Taking the heat in stride**; to Limestone Spring Shelter—Today's Miles: 17.46
137. **Rand is Grand, Billy's just silly**; to CT 41, Undermountain Rd—Today's Miles: 9.22
138. **Splendor**; to Laurel Ridge Campsite—Today's Miles: 15.41
139. **Some real mountains again**; to Jug End Road—Today's Miles: 15.98

F.I.T. Wilderness

140. **Four relaxed strolls**; to Housatonic River, Kellogg Rd—Today's Miles: 11.19
141. **A is for Apathy**; to MA 23—Today's Miles: 15.01
142. **B is for Brittle**; to Mt Wilcox Shelter North—Today's Miles: 10.44
143. **C is for Connections**; to Webster Road—Today's Miles: 15.85
144. **D is for Damp**; to US 20, Lee—Today's Miles: 15.31
145. **E is for Escargot**; to West Branch Rd—Today's Miles: 15.63
146. **F is for Flat**; to Day Mountain—Today's Miles: 19.06
147. **G is for the Gray Grumblies**; to The Cheshire Cobbles—Today's Miles: 17.68
148. **H is for Highpoint**; to Mt. Greylock—Today's Miles: 19.19
149. **I is for I**; to Pine Cobble Trail—Today's Miles: 18.27
150. **J is for Just about**; to Consultation Peak—Today's Miles: 16.32
151. **K is for Knocks**; to VT 9, Bennington—Today's Miles: 14.13
152. **L is for Leptocosmosis**; to 2 mi. N of Glastenbury Mtn—Today's Miles: 24.03
153. **M is for Mission Statement**; to Stratton-Arlington Rd.—Today's Miles: 18.16
154. **N is for Nagging**; to Stream 1.3N Winhall R. Bridge—Today's Miles: 19.75
155. **O is for Overlook**; to VT 11 and 30—Today's Miles: 15.22
156. **P is for Peak-bagging**; to Peru Peak Shelter—Today's Miles: 19.21
157. **Q is for Quiddity** (Note: '**R is for R.I.P.**' was a zero-day post memorializing Paul "Parkside" Bernhardt); to Danby-Landgrove Rd—Today's Miles: 17.29
158. **S is for Simple Abundance**; to VT 140, Wallingford—Today's Miles: 17.60
159. **T is for Terse**; to Keiffer Road—Today's Miles: 19.80
160. **U is for Up**; to Cooper Lodge—Today's Miles: 16.71
161. **V is for Victory … or Vanquished**; to US 4, Rutland—Today's Miles: 13.00
162. **W is for Which Way?**; to summit 1.9mi S of Stony Brook Shelter—Today's Miles: 18.79
163. **X is for X-factor**; to 0.5 mi N Lakota Lake Lookout—Today's Miles: 13.88
164. **Y is for Yonder**; to Woodstock Stage Road—Today's Miles: 18.94
165. **Z is for Zapped**; to Joe Ranger Road—Today's Miles: 16.98
166. **New Hampshire - the Prelude and Overture**; to Power Line above Elm St, Norwich—Today's Miles: 21.89
167. **New Hampshire - the opening Aria**; to 1 mi. N of Etna-Hanover Ctr Rd—Today's Miles: 21.21
168. **Fun with Trail Signs**; to Holt's Ledge—Today's Miles: 18.84
169. **Scenes around Lyme-Dorchester Rd**; to Lyme-Dorchester Rd—Today's Miles: 7.24
170. **Smarts Mountain, the ups and downs**; to Hexacube Shelter—Today's Miles: 17.84
171. **Mount Cube and the trials**; to NH 25C—Today's Miles: 19.67
172. **On the threshold of the White Mountains**; to High St., Glencliff—Today's Miles: 13.65
173. **Mt. Moosilauke!!!**; to NH 112, Kinsman Notch—Today's Miles: 14.49
174. **Reality Check**; to Harrington Pond—Today's Miles: 15.91
175. **Fishin' Jimmy and the South Face of Kinsman**; to US 3, Franconia Notch—Today's Miles: 14.78
176. **Into the Tundra**; to Mt. Lafayette—Today's Miles: 13.62
177. **Mt. Lafayette, takes 2 and 3**; to Mt. Garfield—Today's Miles: 13.84
178. **Into the Gale**; to South Twin Mountain—Today's Miles: 14.91
179. **Catching some Zeas**; to Zealand Trail junction—Today's Miles: 18.68

180.	**Made it to Crawford Notch**; to Crawford Notch—Today's Miles: 15.45
181.	**Webster Cliff Trail, end to end**; to Mt. Pierce—Today's Miles: 12.42
182.	**The Big Summit**; to Mt. Washington—Today's Miles: 12.14
183.	**Mount Washington on a perfect day**; to Mt. Madison—Today's Miles: 13.52
184.	**Wrapping up the Presidentials**; to Pinkham Notch Visitor Center—Today's Miles: 13.09
185.	**Four Shelters and a pond**; to Wildcat Ridge Trail junction—Today's Miles: 10.63
186.	**One tough day**; to Carter Notch—Today's Miles: 8.27
187.	**Another bite out of the Whites**; to Middle Carter Mtn—Today's Miles: 15.50
188.	**Out in the clear, back in the rain**; to Stony Brook Trail jct—Today's Miles: 13.08
189.	**White Mountains - A Fork in the trail**; to Hogan Rd., Centennial Trail—Today's Miles: 14.61
190.	**One Empyrean Moment**; to Dream Lake—Today's Miles: 16.12
191.	**Success!**; to Success Trail junction—Today's Miles: 13.68
192.	**New Hampshire - The Fat Lady Sings**; to E. Goose Eye Mtn.—Today's Miles: 11.43
193.	**The Notch**; to Mahoosuc Notch, East end—Today's Miles: 11.90
194.	**Parkour mixed with Yoga**; to ME 26, Grafton Notch—Today's Miles: 12.26
195.	**Baldpate Mountain splendor**; to Surplus Mountain—Today's Miles: 12.26
196.	**Some Old Friends**, to S. shoulder, Wyman Mtn—Today's Miles: 14.45
197.	**First taste of fall?**; to South Arm Road—Today's Miles: 11.17
198.	**Perfect Weather**; to view 0.6 mi N Bemis Mtn summit—Today's Miles: 13.11
199.	**Mooselookmeguntic**; to ME 17—Today's Miles: 11.37
200.	**Day 200**; to Chandler Mill Stream—Today's Miles: 18.31
201.	**A bog in the fog ...**; to ME 4 – Rangeley—Today's Miles: 7.07
202.	**ME 4 to Saddleback**; to Saddleback Mountain—Today's Miles: 10.32
203.	**Saddleback - the curse of the ski summits**; to 0.5 mi. N of Poplar Ridge Lean-To—Today's Miles: 14.33
204.	**Equipment Malfunction, and a surprise**; to Spaulding Mountain Lean-To—Today's Miles: 16.80
205.	**Happy 75th, Appalachian Trail**; to Caribou Pond Road—Today's Miles: 10.72
206.	**Crocker in the Rain**; to 1 mi. N of N Crocker Mtn—Today's Miles: 8.53
207.	**Nothing to see here, folks ...**; to Stratton Brook Pond Road—Today's Miles: 9.13
208.	**Big Beautiful Bigelow**; to Avery Peak—Today's Miles: 13.30
209.	**First look at Katahdin**; to E. Flagstaff Road—Today's Miles: 15.41
210.	**Hiked in Crocs**; to Sandy Stream—Today's Miles: 17.97
211.	**Pierce Pond and the Kennebec**; to Kennebec River, Carratunk ME—Today's Miles: 21.73
212.	**Under 1000 miles to go!**; to Pleasant Pond Mountain—Today's Miles: 14.03
213.	**The better part of valor**; to Moxie Pond Road—Today's Miles: 9.74
214.	**The Lobster Claw**; to 1 mi, N Bald Mtn Stream—Today's Miles: 19.50
215.	**River walking**; to Logging Haul Road near Monson—Today's Miles: 20.55
216.	**Monso(o)n**; to Mud Pond—Today's Miles: 19.99
217.	**A finish in the rain in the dark**; to 0.1 mi N Long Pond Stream Lean-To—To-

F.I.T. Wilderness

day's Miles: 21.21
218. **Promise fulfilled**; to Third Mountain Trail jct—Today's Miles: 15.88
219. **Wilderness?**; to W. Br. Pleasant River—Today's Miles: 14.34
220. **A walk in the woods**; to Saddle between West Peak and Hay Mtn—Today's Miles: 17.36
221. **The Greatest Mountain**; to 0.3 mi S Mountain View Pond—Today's Miles: 17.85
222. **Easy Walker**; to 1.3 m N Cooper Brk Falls Lean-To—Today's Miles: 15.64
223. **Labor Day at the beach**; to Pemadumcook Lake—Today's Miles: 21.78
224. **Trail Angel**; to Gravel Beach, Nahmakanta Lake—Today's Miles: 16.03
225. **Another look at the Great One**; to Pollywog Stream—Today's Miles: 12.76
226. **Rainbow**; to Rainbow Ledges—Today's Miles: 21.46
227. **Abol Bridge**; to Ford, lower fk Nesowadnehunk Strm—Today's Miles: 21.14
228. **On the threshold**; to Katahdin Stream Campground—Today's Miles: 11.85
229. **Katahdin**; to Katahdin—Today's Miles: 9.47
230. **Back to the trail**; Park and Ride, Troutville, VA to Wilson Creek Shelter—Today's Miles: 25.00
231. **Blue Ridge Parkway**; to Bearwallow Gap—Today's Miles: 21.82
232. **Trail companions**; to Jennings Creek—Today's Miles: 14.00
233. **A Palace in the Woods**; to Cornelius Creek Shelter—Today's Miles: 17.41
234. **Small pleasures**; to Petite's Gap—Today's Miles: 19.83
235. **Great hike, then a huge surprise afterward**; to James River Foot Bridge parking lot—Today's Miles: 20.33
236. **James River to Bluff Mountain**; to Bluff Mountain—Today's Miles: 18.25
237. **Four seasons of hiking**; to FS 38, Pedlar Lake Rd—Today's Miles: 19.23
238. **Bald Knob is Cold. Cold Mountain is Bald**; to 0.4 mi N Cold Mountain summit—Today's Miles: 19.74
239. **Going from A to B ...**; to Spy Rock (Fish Hatchery) Rd—Today's Miles: 22.65
240. **My first Rattler**; to VA 56, Tye River—Today's Miles: 18.80
241. **Another major climb**; to Maupin Field Shelter—Today's Miles: 17.80
242. **Back along the Blue Ridge Parkway**; to Battery Cliff, S end Humpback Mtn—Today's Miles: 16.73
243. **A few rare trees are not trees at all ...**; to Rockfish Gap, US 250—Today's Miles: 25.30
244. **Nine Months on the trail**; to Jarman Gap—Today's Miles: 18.87
245. **If it weren't for the Bear ...**; to High point 1.2 m N Wildcat Ridge Trail—Today's Miles: 14.87
246. **Can't do it**; to Skyline Dr MP 87.2 crossing—Today's Miles: 10.12
247. **Blackrock and Loft Mountain**; to Viewpoint E, Loft Mountain—Today's Miles: 20.22
248. **4000 miles!**; to Summit 1.5 mi N of Simmons Gap—Today's Miles: 16.41
249. **Hightop Mountain on a gorgeous day**; to South River Picnic Grounds—Today's Miles: 23.77
250. **Seven Little Yo-yo's**; to Hazeltop Mountain—Today's Miles: 21.13
251. **Snow!**; to Big Meadows Lodge—Today's Miles: 9.45
252. **So much to see**; to Little Stonyman summit—Today's Miles: 19.89
253. **Views galore**; to Pass Mountain Hut—Today's Miles: 21.21
254. **Trail people - a connection that boggles the mind**; to Hogback, MP 20.8,

	Skyline Dr—Today's Miles: 21.84
255.	**Viewing Variety - and some commentary**; to Compton Peak—Today's Miles: 21.75
256.	**Finished with Shenandoah Park**; to US 522, Front Royal—Today's Miles: 13.37
257.	**A rainy 20-mile day**; to Manassas Gap Shelter—Today's Miles: 21.27
258.	**Ghosts from the past**; to Ashby Gap, US 50—Today's Miles: 20.85
259.	**The Roller Coaster**; to VA 605, Morgans Mill Rd—Today's Miles: 14.50
260.	**Fall color**; to Snickers Gap, VA 7—Today's Miles: 14.14
261.	**West Virginia!**; to Buzzard Rocks—Today's Miles: 20.78
262.	**The technicolor tunnel**; to ATC side trail, Harper's Ferry—Today's Miles: 20.91
263.	**Harpers Ferry check-in day**; to Ed Garvey Shelter—Today's Miles: 15.87
264.	**Why so sad?**; to Rocky Run Shelters—Today's Miles: 18.98
265.	**Washington's original Monument**; to Black Rock Cliffs—Today's Miles: 22.14
266.	**Maryland's Best Viewpoint**; to MD 491, Raven Rock Hollow—Today's Miles: 20.22
267.	**Into Pennsylvania**; to Bailey Spring—Today's Miles: 18.64
268.	**Day 268 - the last long hike**; to PA 233—Today's Miles: 19.39
269.	**4366.4 / 4368.4**; to Waypoint 0.7 mi S of US 30—Today's Miles: 8.68
270.	**There should have been confetti**; to Caledonia State Park, PA—Today's Miles: 2.67

ACKNOWLEDGMENTS

The compilation of a book of this type involves an assemblage of people and influences that is too long and too complicated to recount. Family, trail friends, social media followers, and the many authors of other books in this genre all played important roles. Instead of naming them individually, which would surely lead to omissions and stepped-on toes, this acknowledgment section is limited to those things that are obligatory.

The cover photograph and the very last photo of Chapter 18 are the work of Adriane Hornung of Wraven Design. All other photos and graphics are the original work of the author. Amanda Ayers Barnett and Sandra Friend read and offered comments on near-final versions of the text. Kim Emerson provided all graphic design work, including help with the back cover and spine. Maps were created using Open Street Map (© OpenStreetMap contributors: openstreetmap.org/copyright).

FASTEST KNOWN TIME RECOGNITION

In early 2023, PJ Wetzel submitted a full set of GPS tracks, photos, and web documentation (his blog, AllTrails, Trail Journals) to the web site fastestknowntime.com, which is the informal arbiter of speed records of selected, curated hiking routes around the world. His submission was evaluated, approved, and published on 10 March 2023, which was, co-incidentally, the same day that PJ's total documented miles hiked surpassed the 22,000-mile mark.

Although the purpose of PJ's Appalachian Trail hike was not speed, there had been no Fastest Known Time (FKT) speed record established for an AT double (called a yo-yo), so by default PJ's hike now holds the record in the categories of Supported and Self-Supported AT double thru-hikes.

Speed records are made to be broken. PJ looks forward to encouraging others to attempt the double in either style. The Supported style allows any sort of help along the trail, the only rule being that the participant must always propel him/herself. The Self-Supported style requires the hiker to accept no help from anyone, though s/he may make use of equipment and facilities that are available to the public, such as spending a night in a hotel. Matt Kirk, who PJ met on the Florida Trail in Dec. 2015, and who held the AT self-supported (one-way) record from 2013 to 2017, established a precedent of not getting in a vehicle for any reason during his Self-Supported AT attempt, although this is not one of the FKT website's guidelines/'rules'. For his double, PJ has established the precedent that his own personal vehicle was part of his equipment. He did not accept rides in any other vehicle, or any other form of help from anyone. PJ's hike was obviously not traditional 'backpacker-style' as Matt's was, but emphasizes a new and innovative way to achieve a double—via a string of individual out-and-back day hikes. Discussion and opinions are inevitable, and PJ welcomes it, but stands firmly on the side of inclusiveness. He hopes that there will be attempts at his record that follow both the backpacker style and the day-hiker style.

ABOUT THE AUTHOR

"He was unheeded, happy and near to the wild heart of life." –James Joyce.

P.J. Wetzel's fascination for the natural world goes back as far as he can remember. He grew up hiking the countryside around White Clay Creek, now a National Wild and Scenic River at the fringes of the megalopolis in SE Pennsylvania. He studied Atmospheric Science at Penn State and Colorado State University then worked at NASA, developing models of the interaction of the landscape with the lower atmosphere, which helped improve weather and climate models. In retirement he set about getting back in shape, climbed a 20,000-foot mountain in South America, and then took up hiking in order to stay fit. His first hiking adventures were close to home in central Maryland, where he helped the Maryland Dept. of Natural Resources with early efforts at documenting the spread of the invasive Wavyleaf Basket Grass. As part of that work, he acquired his first hiker's GPS in 2010. He began exploring the Appalachian Trail, and soon realized that what he loved best about hiking was exploring a new facet of Nature's wild playbook every day.

Also since his earliest days, P.J. has enjoyed writing about his discoveries, real and imagined, so as to better remember them and especially to share them with others. This physical book, which can be touched and explored, is his 'souvenir' from his 2012 Appalachian Trail adventure. He hopes you enjoy.

Hiking Tinker Cliffs, Virginia, on a cold day in January

F.I.T. Wilderness

P. J. Wetzel

Printed in Dunstable, United Kingdom